British Children's Literature
in Japanese Culture

Bloomsbury Perspectives on Children's Literature

Bloomsbury Perspectives on Children's Literature seeks to expand the range and quality of research in children's literature through publishing innovative monographs by leading and rising scholars in the field. With an emphasis on cross and interdisciplinary studies, this series takes literary approaches as a starting point, drawing on the particular capacity for children's literature to open out into other disciplines.

Series Editor:

Dr Lisa Sainsbury, Director of the National Centre for Research in Children's Literature, Roehampton University, UK

Editorial Board:

Professor M. O. Grenby (Newcastle University, UK), Dr Marah Gubar (University of Pittsburgh, USA), Dr Vanessa Joosen (Tilburg University, the Netherlands)

Titles in the Series:

Adulthood in Children's Literature, Vanessa Joosen
The Courage to Imagine: The Child Hero in Children's Literature, Roni Natov
Ethics in British Children's Literature: Unexamined Life,
Lisa Sainsbury
Fashioning Alice: The Career of Lewis Carroll's Icon, 1860–1901, Kiera Vaclavik
From Tongue to Text: A New Reading of Children's Poetry, Debbie Pullinger
Literature's Children: The Critical Child and the Art of Idealisation, Louise Joy
Rereading Childhood Books: A Poetics, Alison Waller
Irish Children's Literature and the Poetics of Memory, Rebecca Long
Metaphysics of Children's Literature, Lisa Sainsbury
British Children's Literature and Material Culture, Jane Suzanne Carroll
Space, Place and Children's Reading Development, Margaret Mackey
British Activist Authors Addressing Children of Colour, Karen Sands-O'Connor
The Dark Matter of Children's "Fantastika" Literature, Chloé Germaine Buckley

Forthcoming Titles:

Marketing Chinese Children's Books, Frances Weightman
Children's Publishing in Cold War France: Hachette in the Age of Surveillance and Control, Sophie Heywood

British Children's Literature in Japanese Culture

Wonderlands and Looking-Glasses

Catherine Butler

BLOOMSBURY ACADEMIC
LONDON • NEW YORK • OXFORD • NEW DELHI • SYDNEY

BLOOMSBURY ACADEMIC
Bloomsbury Publishing Plc
50 Bedford Square, London, WC1B 3DP, UK
1385 Broadway, New York, NY 10018, USA
29 Earlsfort Terrace, Dublin 2, Ireland

BLOOMSBURY, BLOOMSBURY ACADEMIC and the Diana logo are trademarks
of Bloomsbury Publishing Plc

First published in Great Britain 2023
Paperback edition published 2025

A catalogue record for this book is available from the British Library.

A catalog record for this book is available from the Library of Congress.

ISBN: HB: 978-1-3501-9547-9
PB: 978-1-3505-1190-3
ePDF: 978-1-3501-9548-6
oBook: 978-1-3501-9549-3

Series: Bloomsbury Perspectives on Children's Literature

Typeset by Deanta Global Publishing Services, Chennai, India
Printed and bound in Great Britain

To find out more about our authors and books visit www.bloomsbury.com and
sign up for our newsletters.

For Martin and Corinne

Contents

Figures

Acknowledgements

The research for this book might be said to date from 2013, when I began – not quite on a whim – to learn Japanese. My first, brief visit two years later cemented my interest in the country and made me a devoted (if ignorant) student of its culture and history. However, the current book's outline began to take a more definite shape only in 2017, when I was invited to give two talks on the representation of Britain in anime, at Tōkyō Woman's Christian University (TWCU) and the National Diet Library in Ueno. The research for those talks, combined with my long-standing interest in the cultural geography of children's literature, perhaps made it inevitable that this book would eventually be written, but acquiring the knowledge, skills, contacts and experience necessary to write it was neither a quick nor a simple undertaking.

In that task, I have been guided and encouraged by dozens of people, and to describe my various debts in the detail they warrant would be to turn this Acknowledgements section into a chapter. My Japanese teachers, Yūko Hasegawa, Rihae Yū, Midori Addison and Kei Yamauchi Forsythe, all played indispensable roles in leading me to such competence in the language as I now possess. Kei patiently heard me read and translate Kaho Nashiki's *The Witch of the West Is Dead* over the course of many lessons, while Midori was one of several people who kindly helped with spoken, handwritten, idiomatic and otherwise tricky passages in Japanese, others including my friends and sometime lodgers, Ayako Katsube and Rei Koga. My Italki conversation partners, Yuki Hitomi, Chiho Ikeda, Mamie Kanō, Haruka and Yūko Kodaka, Tomoko Nozawa, Mitsuko Onishi, Yōko Spiess and Yuka Yorifuji, not only helped my conversational Japanese but also became real-life friends in Japan, with several accompanying me on research trips for this book: Chiho to Yufuin Floral Village in Ōita, Mamie to Lockheart Castle in Gunma and to Sapporo and Kushiro in Hokkaidō, Yuka to Kōbe's Kitano Ijinkan and Haruka and Yūko to Shuzenji Niji no Sato in Shizuoka. Haruka was also my companion on some British expeditions, notably my very first visit to Fosse Farmhouse in 2017 and by bus from King's Lynn to Burnham Overy Staithe in 2021. Eriko Kawanishi shared a Dreamton B&B with me in Kyōto Prefecture, as well as giving me the anthropological inside track on Glastonbury's goddesses, while Naoko Selland kindly drove me to Daitō Bunka University's Beatrix Potter Reference Library in Saitama Prefecture.

I have been the eager recipient of countless tips, recommendations and casual remarks that blossomed into fruitful research enquiries over the course of several years and fear that many will necessarily go undocumented here. I am grateful to Akira Suwa for tipping me off about Lockheart Castle, to Tomomi Tanaka for telling me of the existence of *Onegai! Samia-don*, to Yūko Kamei for her local knowledge of Kushiro and to Elaine Massung for mentioning the botanist Marianne North and being an online anime-watching companion over the months of lockdown. The helpful assistant at the Tourist Information Office in Broadway who identified the missing half of Chise and Angelica's pub as the Mermaid in Burford has my eternal gratitude but must, like numerous other donors of useful information, remain nameless. Gili Bar-Hillel, Dann Chinn, Lesley Downer, Janet Eastwood, the late Jerry Griswold, Vanessa Joosen, Meredith MacArdle, Gill Othen, Lucy Pearson, John and Christine Roe, Laurence Williams and Henrietta Wilson are among those who have offered helpful suggestions or welcome encouragement. I am especially grateful to Micky Burrow and Noriko Kawabata, Diana Wynne Jones's son and daughter-in-law, and to Laura Cecil, her agent, for their generosity in racking brains and looking up notes. Jessica Yates has, as ever, been an indefatigable collector and generous disseminator of many kinds of material.

The library staff at Cardiff University, TWCU, the National Diet Library, the Tōkyō Children's Library and the Ōsaka Prefectural Central Library have all been gracious and accommodating; I would also like to thank Rosalind Bos and the staff at Seven Stories for locating and scanning a letter from the Diana Wynne Jones archive without my having to travel to Gateshead in the middle of a pandemic. Rei Uemura of Tokuma Shoten, Shigeru Tateishi of MAG Garden Corporation, Takuya Sekoguchi of Hōbunsha, Jack Baker and Harriet Wilson of HarperCollins and Chihiro Tsukue of Studio Ghibli have been very patient with my various enquiries.

I have been encouraged by numerous academic colleagues, notably the ever-inspiring Ann Heilmann, Perry Hinton, Susan Napier, Clémentine Beauvais, fellow pro-*gaijin* Sarah Olive and Christopher Hood, who not only inducted me into the world of Japanese contents tourism studies but also (Shropshire lad as he is) helped pin down the setting of Studio Ponoc's *Mary and the Witch's Flower*. Children's literature scholars in Japan have been a source of wisdom, knowledge and encouragement. My acquaintance began with a chance encounter with Satomi Isobe and Mikako Sugaya at the IRSCL conference in Worcester in 2015. Through them, I met Mihoko Tanaka of TWCU, who, as well as becoming a close friend, has been signally supportive ever since, sponsoring Visiting Scholarships, issuing invitations and introducing me to a wide range of Japanese academics. Her own work, particularly in the field of translation studies, has been hugely important to this study. Hiroko Sasada and Yoshiko Itō, whom I first met in 2016 at ChLA in Columbus, Ohio, have been valued scholars and *nakama*, and our sashimi-and-sake evenings in Sugamo are among my treasured memories of Tōkyō. I am also grateful to Hiroko for catching various errors in my Japanese translations. Philip Seaton and Takayoshi Yamamura were hospitable hosts at the 2018 conference on contents tourism at the Tōkyō University of Foreign Studies in Fuchū and subsequently very understanding editors. Yasuko Doi of the International Institute for Children's Literature in Ōsaka was kind enough to comment on the historical account of Japanese children's literature in Chapter 2. I am also in the debt of Nozomu Hayashi, Yoshihide Kawano, Nobuhiko Hishida, Naoko Nakamura, Junko Nishimura, Yuri Shimizu, Sanae Yamagami, Keiko Yoshida and the members of the Japan Society for Children's Literature in English.

I am grateful to the proprietors and staff of various destinations that I visited during my field research, who kindly agreed to be interviewed for the project. Caron Cooper of Fosse Farmhouse, Carolyn and Henry Chesshire of Lower Buckton House, Mayumi 'Marie' Haruyama of Dreamton and the staff at British Hills in Fukushima were all most generous with their time, as were David Strachan of Totteoki Cotswolds Tours and the Cotswolds Tourism Officer, Chris Jackson. The memories of Caron's cream teas and of Henry Chesshire's triumphant expression as he emerged from his study carrying a bound 1885 volume of *Punch* are especially warm ones.

I would like to offer particular thanks to Kore Yamazaki and her editor for making the time to talk to me and Mamie in Sapporo and to Karey Kirkpatrick for agreeing to be interviewed about the American dub script of *The Secret World of Arrietty.*

My family was, as ever, a source of strength and purpose – both my immediate family and the deeper stratum of nineteenth-century Butlers who cropped up with unexpected regularity during my research into the Meiji era. These include my great-grandaunt, Annie R. Butler, whose *Stories about Japan* features regularly in the book's early chapters; her sister Fanny, who founded a hospital in India with the Japan-exploring Isabella Bird; and their father's first cousin Louisa, who turned out to be Marianne North's closest friend. I was happy to encounter them on this journey.

The research for this book was carried out with financial and logistical help from several sources. My employer, Cardiff University, gave me a semester's research leave and a grant towards translation costs, while TWCU's Institute for Comparative Studies of Culture awarded me Visiting Scholarships in 2017 and 2022. I also received an award from the Japan Foundation Endowment Committee, which covered much of my field research in 2018, and from the Daiwa Foundation, which helped finance my final visit to Japan (for this project, at least) in the summer of 2022. I am grateful to all of them and to the administrators who guided me through their various regulatory mazes.

Note on the text

Japanese in this book is generally silently translated into English, with a parenthetical phonetic transcription where this seems helpful. Japanese characters (*kana* and *kanji*) have been included only where they are directly relevant to the discussion. Words with no direct English translation are written in italics, unless they are common enough to have passed into general English usage: hence, '*sakoku*' and '*furoshiki*' but 'manga' and 'haiku'. This can be a fine judgement, and in some cases I have used Google Ngram Viewer to double-check my own impression of a word's currency. Long vowels are indicated by a macron.

When first introduced, Japanese personal names are written with the family name following the given name. For clarity and consistency, I thereafter use the family name, even in cases where the given name is often preferred in Japanese: for example, Kenji Miyazawa is 'Miyazawa' rather than 'Kenji'. I refer to Japanese emperors using their era names rather than their personal names: for example, 'Shōwa' rather than 'Hirohito'.

When referring to English translations of Japanese texts, I use the published English title followed by a parenthetical phonetic transcription of the Japanese but do not provide a literal translation of the latter unless there is a specific reason to do so. Thus, Studio Ghibli's 1989 film is referred to as *Kiki's Delivery Service* (*majo no takkyūbin*) rather than as *Witch's Delivery Service*.

On the other hand, when referring to Japanese translations or adaptations of English texts, I use direct English translations of the Japanese titles, where these differ from the original English. For example, Joan G. Robinson's novel *When Marnie Was There* (1967) was translated by Masako Matsuno as *Memories of Marnie* (*omoide no mānī*) and subsequently adapted by Studio Ghibli under that title. The English-language release of the film reverted to the original title of the novel. Thus, I use *When Marnie Was There* to refer to Robinson's novel and the English-language release of Ghibli's film but *Memories of Marnie* to refer to the Japanese translation of the novel and the Japanese-language version of the Ghibli film.

Earlier versions of some passages in this book appeared in previous publications. Specifically, a small section of Chapter 4 (pages 122–7) draws on

'Arrietty Comes Home: Studio Ghibli's *The Borrower Arrietty* and Its English-Language Dubs', published in the *Annals of The Institute for Comparative Studies of Culture* 80 (2019: 57–71); while in Chapter 5, pages 147–50 and 153–77 draw on 'Japan Reads the Cotswolds: Tourism, Children's Literature and the Japanese Imagination', published in *Children's Literature* 48 (2020: 198–233).

The Covid-19 pandemic and its attendant restrictions on travel were inevitably a disruptive influence on the research for this book. Much of the fieldwork, especially for the chapter on tourism, was undertaken before the pandemic began, but while this was lucky for the project, it means that the chapter describes a state of affairs, including mass travel from Japan to the UK, that at the time of writing is resuming only gradually. Whether it will return to something resembling its previous form or whether that chapter is destined to be yet one more portrait of 'vanished Japan' remains to be seen.

Introduction

Writing from the outside in

This book is an exploration of the relationship between Britain and Japan in one of its more striking domains, that of children's literature. Specifically, my subject is the history and reception of British children's literature in Japan,[1] and in discussing it I will make two key arguments. The first is that British children's literature has contributed in significant ways to the development of modern Japanese children's culture, including not only books but films, television and toys, and to more general ideas about children and childhood. The second is that British children's books have provided a set of tropes, narratives, settings and characters that have significantly shaped Japanese people's understanding of Britain itself.

In a previous book, *Four British Fantasists* (2006), I developed a critical approach that combined literary and historical analysis with cultural geography, with the aim of placing British children's fantasy literature in a more multifaceted context than had previously been achieved. Here, I extend that approach to incorporate a different culture, language, literature and history. This is a significantly more complex undertaking, and it has been made possible only by building on the work of previous scholars, both Anglophone and Japanese, in translation and reception studies, Japanese studies, comparative literature and children's literature itself. However, the larger story that emerges, of the complex and surprisingly central position of children's literature in the cultural relationship of Britain and Japan, is substantially new.

In writing this book, I am very conscious of the extent to which my perspective is coloured by my own cultural, linguistic and personal history. Having lived in Britain for six decades means that I can discuss British culture on the basis of some knowledge and experience, although that experience comes with its own

---

1 The place of Japanese children's literature and culture in Britain also merits discussion, as does the representation of Japan and the Japanese in British children's books (a subject recently covered in relation to American children's literature by Sybille A. Jagusch (2021)); however, while these topics are touched on in this book, they are not its primary focus.

legacy of partiality and normative assumptions. Japan, by contrast, I inevitably approach as an outsider. The relationships I have with the two countries at the heart of this study are strikingly asymmetrical, and this is bound to inflect my discussion. This is not, of course, a new problem. Western commentators, for whom Japan has sometimes functioned as a particularly acute instance of cultural incommensurability, have long dwelt on the futility of attempts at comprehension. Mary Crawford Fraser, novelist and wife of the British attaché to the Meiji government, wrote in May 1890:

> As for explanations, ask them not of a Japanese! The springs of action for him and you are separated by an almost impassable gulf. After years of intercourse, he might understand the real drift of your question; more years would have to elapse before you could understand his answer. (Fraser 1904: 357)

Almost 130 years later, the British-born writer Pico Iyer began his *A Beginner's Guide to Japan* with the confession: 'I've been living in western Japan for more than thirty-two years, and, to my delight, I know far less than when I arrived' (2019: 3). It is easy to trace a rhetorical lineage running from one of these statements to the other, though harder to determine in either the respective parts played by modesty, honest incomprehension, love of a paradoxical flourish, philosophical scepticism and complicity in the Orientalist trope of Eastern inscrutability. We can at least note the longevity of the sentiment and the fact that both Fraser and Iyer did, in the event, manage to write books about Japan.

I do not underestimate the difficulties involved in that endeavour. Any British person's understanding of Japan and the Japanese will draw to some degree on their existing cultural repertoire, a reliance that cannot be circumvented because that repertoire determines the very tools of perception and judgement available. This point can be illustrated by comparing the cover of Annie R. Butler's children's introduction to the country, *Stories about Japan* (first published by the Religious Tract Society in 1888), and the engraving by Edward Whymper on which it is based (Figures 0.1 and 0.2). Whymper's engraving was in turn taken from a photograph and had originally appeared in Isabella Bird's travel memoir, *Unbeaten Tracks in Japan*, in 1880. It depicts what is clearly to be taken as a typical Japanese scene: the interior of a tea house, where an attendant holds two cups of tea while wearing a kimono and *tabi* (socks with a separate space for the toe). She is standing on a *tatami* floor, next to a box of tea-making equipment. In the background is a terrace with a natural view, as is common in traditional tea houses. A hanging scroll is just visible on the far wall.

Figures 0.1–0.2 (*Left*) 'Tea-house attendant'. Engraving by Edward Whymper, from Isabella Bird, *Unbeaten Tracks in Japan* (1880). (*Right*) Annie R. Butler, *Stories about Japan* (1888), cover detail.

The version on the cover of Butler's book has introduced many changes. The *tatami* mats have turned into a rug, the outside view has been replaced with wallpaper and a skirting board and the box of tea things on the floor has become a British-style teapot on a side table. All these alterations are in the direction of Anglicization. However, the artist has also added some 'Japanese' touches. The woman is now wearing wooden *geta* (a form of footwear never worn indoors), she sports prominent *kanzashi* hair ornaments and a bonsai tree has materialized on the side table. Both British 'norms' and Japanese stereotypes have found their way into the revised picture.

We cannot be sure how far these changes were motivated by a wish to render Whymper's illustration more culturally legible to a readership of British children or indeed the extent to which they were deliberate at all. Nor, for that matter, can we easily compare Whymper's engraving with the original photograph or know how far that photograph was itself posed in accordance with Western principles of composition, as was the case with some of the other illustrations in Bird's book (Spiker 2018). As Ernst Gombrich showed long ago, in copying objects taken from an unfamiliar cultural context, even artists attempting a faithful representation are liable to create what he called an 'adapted stereotype', melding the object represented with types taken from a mental lexicon of known forms (Gombrich 1960: 61). The cover of *Stories about Japan* offers a relatively extreme

– and therefore conveniently visible – example of this phenomenon, and it is not only possible but inevitable that I will perform the same kind of manoeuvre in my own account. You can't run away from your own feet.

To address the issue, I have utilized a fourfold strategy, the components of which may be labelled contextualisation, mitigation, transparency and provisionality. First, I have tried to contextualize the present study by cultivating, both in myself and in my readers, an awareness of it as one in a long series of Western analyses of Japanese culture, a series that has from the beginning accumulated various distinctive tropes. This book's primary concern is with the ways that Japanese people have understood, responded to and adapted British children's literature (and Britain through that literature), but my account also forms part of the history of the British reception of Japan. In the first chapter, especially, I seek to provide a context for my own reactions by considering the uses made of children's books by some of my predecessors in describing Japan and their experiences of it.

Second, like many previous Western writers, I have endeavoured to mitigate the dangers of ignorance. I have studied Japanese for ten years and done all I can to learn about the country's culture and history and to experience its places, sounds and tastes. I am lucky enough to have travelled in many parts of Japan, from Kagoshima to Hokkaidō, and to have enjoyed personal and professional relationships with numerous Japanese people. Nevertheless, no visibly non-Japanese person can fail to be aware that, in a country orientated so strongly around notions of in- and out-groups, they will always be for many purposes positioned on the outside of Japanese cultural experience. Nor have I shared in the complex and multitudinous processes of acculturation undergone by someone raised in the country, which – however diverse Japanese childhoods may be – will involve some commonalities to which I must remain a stranger. Mitigation, then, can take me only so far. I have thus also tried to cultivate transparency about my own interests and biases, in so far as these are visible to me. This book deals with what is potentially a very wide range of topics, and my choices of text, critical methodology and the general scope of my argument may say as much about me as about my ostensible subject matter, reflecting my prior interests in, for example, history, cultural geography and fantasy literature. I have tried to give a balanced account, but by being open about the process I can place my reader in a better position to compensate for any idiosyncrasy of approach. Finally, I have deliberately framed my observations and conclusions as exploratory excavations in a field where there is still much to discover and where I hope that others will extend and correct my findings.

British reactions to Japan can be said to fall on a spectrum running between two contrasting ways of perceiving the country, for which the titles of Lewis Carroll's *Alice* books – *Alice's Adventures in Wonderland* (1865) and *Through the Looking-Glass, and What Alice Found There* (1871) – provide convenient labels. The first way, exemplified by Fraser and Iyer, is to view Japan as a Wonderland, a place alien to Western experience and impenetrable to Western understanding. To enter a Wonderland is to undergo a process of culture shock, of disorientation, of constant surprise; it is to realize that the familiar landmarks by which one usually navigates social situations have been replaced by others that defy interpretation.

The alternative approach is to see Japan as a Looking-Glass – that is, as a place in which one's own society is uncannily reflected. In the case of Britain and Japan, this is a seductive possibility. Despite their obvious differences, it is a commonplace that the two countries share many striking features. Both are island nations, situated near continents that have had a profound influence on them in terms of language, culture and religion but from which they have traditionally positioned themselves as distinct. They have common obsessions with tea, politeness, the weather, gardens, queuing and so on, as well as much darker histories of colonial expansion and exploitation. When I began my study of Japanese culture I found these kinds of connections reassuring, although I suspected that many might turn out to be superficial or to have disappointingly mundane explanations. (I have since been assured by a Japanese friend that the custom of queuing, now brought to such a fine art in Japan, was – like *katsu* sauce and driving on the left – actually a British import.) Even so, these points of similarity seemed to offer a key that might be used to unlock Japanese culture by reference back to my own. Such doubtful footholds should not be asked to bear much weight, but as an initial hermeneutic strategy, explaining the unknown in terms of the known, however provisionally, is not unreasonable.

Success in interpretation is of course to be celebrated, but failure is not without value. It is, in any case, inevitable. The reference points available from one's own culture can offer only approximate metrics for analysing other people's, and, as I have noted, attempts by the British and Japanese to understand each other are unavoidably inflected by their prior experience. In practice, however, misinterpretation can be more revealing than perfect communication, particularly in exposing the habits of thought, the pervasive metaphors, the expectations, fantasies and desires of those doing the interpreting. The relationship I am discussing is moreover iterative, dynamic and bidirectional; while the British look in fascination at Japan, Japanese people are in their turn constructing a fantasy Britain (in which endeavour children's literature is one of their most potent tools). Each party is aware of the other's gaze and continually adjusts its self-presentation to accommodate, or perhaps frustrate, expectations. The result is rather complex.

The structure of this book

My first chapter, 'Wonderland or Looking-Glass?', will explore in more detail some of the issues raised in this Introduction, using a historical perspective. Many of the tropes still applied to Japan by Westerners have their roots in the Meiji period (1868–1912), when contact between Japan and the Western world increased rapidly and British visitors first began to arrive in numbers. While the accounts of those visitors often drew on the Orientalist ideas and language widely applied to non-Europeans at the time, some reactions were more specific to Japan and to its unique position as it ended its long period of national isolation. I will show that children's literature was from the beginning an explicit component of those observers' experience and hence of their ways of understanding Japan and the Japanese. Books such as Carroll's offered templates for navigating a puzzling and unfamiliar country and affected the ways in which Japan was understood, both as a place fascinating for its very strangeness and as a looking-glass in which the British could perceive a version of themselves. The Alice books also provided a space to consider what it might mean, not only to see an unfamiliar culture but to be seen *by* it, much as Alice is observed and judged by the characters she meets. Over the course of the Meiji period, British visitors' assumptions that their points of view took priority over those of the Japanese they encountered began to be unsettled, if not deconstructed entirely.

The second and third chapters consider the role of British books in the development of Japan's own children's literature, paying attention to the work of writers, translators, editors, publishers and critics and to the many cross-germinations between these various roles. Initially as one among several foreign models of what a children's literature might be and do, then as a conduit for more specific ideas about style and genre, British children's books were always influential in Japan, both on individual authors and more generally. 'Britain and the origins of Japanese children's literature' gives a historical account of Japanese children's literature's development in the Meiji, Taishō (1912–26) and Shōwa (1926–89) eras and the role of British children's books in that story, especially the ways that Japanese priorities and values affected the reception of British texts. In 'Canons to the West, canons to the East: British children's books in Japan' I expand the discussion to provide a broader account of the processes that have given rise to a Japanese canon of British children's books significantly divergent from that in Britain itself and trace the influence of British books, both on Japanese children's writers and in other areas of cultural production.

'Hayao Miyazaki and British children's literature' is a case study of a figure with a reasonable claim to have done more to shape Japanese perceptions of British children's books than any other individual in the last forty years. Through his advocacy for individual authors and for children's books in general, through his early anime work, and above all through his Studio Ghibli adaptation of Diana Wynne Jones's *Howl's Moving Castle* (2004) and his screenplay for *The Borrower Arrietty* (2010), Hayao Miyazaki has introduced millions of Japanese to key British children's books and shaped their understanding of them. He has also inspired younger directors, such as his protégé Hiromasa Yonebayashi and son Gorō, to direct their own adaptations of British children's books, both within and beyond Ghibli, a legacy that continues even as Miyazaki himself has gradually withdrawn from an active role. The chapter discusses the ways in which Miyazaki and those he has influenced have accommodated changes not only of medium, from book to film, but also of implied viewership, from English-speaking to Japanese-speaking, and the cultural constraints and opportunities involved.

The final substantive chapter bookends the first. Rather than focus on British visitors to Japan, 'Children's literature, tourism and the Japanese imagination' considers Japanese visitors to Britain and to the various Britain-themed attractions to be found in Japan itself. I will show that children's literature plays an important part in shaping and filtering Japanese tourists' experience, even of places with little or no direct connection to children's books. I will discuss the Cotswolds region in southern England as a prime example of such a place and argue for a method of analysis that looks beyond locations with conventional claims as destinations for literary tourism.

1

Wonderland or Looking-Glass? Meiji Japan through the lens of children's literature

The history of Japan's relationship with Britain,[1] though complex, has not been of long duration. The inhabitants of the two archipelagos were unaware of each other's existence until news of Japan was brought to Europe through the reports of the Venetian merchant, Marco Polo, who had heard accounts of it while at the court of Kublai Khan in the 1270s. The first European visitors were Portuguese merchants, who arrived in 1543 and began to trade from Nagasaki. The Spanish missionary Francis Xavier landed at Kagoshima a few years later and started to propagate Christianity, particularly in the southern island of Kyūshū. A handful of Japanese converts later visited Catholic Europe, beginning with Bernard of Kagoshima in 1553 and culminating in the so-called Tenshō embassy of 1582, but travel in that direction was generally sparser.

From this tentative early history of Japanese-European relations Britain was altogether absent. The earliest recorded Japanese encounter with the British occurred only in November 1587 and took place in neither Japan nor Britain but off the coast of Baja California, where the English navigator and privateer Thomas Cavendish captured a Spanish galleon, the *Santa Ana* (Lockley 2019: 86–7). Aboard, Cavendish found two teenaged Japanese converts, Christopher and Cosmus (presumably their baptismal names), whom he then brought to England. They arrived in 1588, staying initially in Plymouth and later in London. Conceivably they were glimpsed by a young William Shakespeare – but if so, it would have been the last such opportunity for almost 250 years; the next recorded Japanese visitor to Britain would not arrive until the 1830s. As for Christopher and Cosmus, in 1591 they accompanied Cavendish on his second, disastrous expedition and so sailed out of history (Lockley 2019: 128).

---

1 By 'Britain' and 'British' I refer, except where otherwise specified, to Great Britain or its constituent parts or (after its establishment) to the UK.

No Briton appears to have set foot in Japan itself until the beginning of the seventeenth century, when some limited trading began. The most celebrated British figure of this period was the Englishman William Adams, known in Japan as Miura Anjin, who arrived in 1600 as part of a Dutch expedition, settled in the country and eventually became a samurai and a close advisor of Ieyasu Tokugawa, then in the process of establishing the Tokugawa Shōgunate (Yoshizaki 2021: 10–11).[2] With Adams's help, an English trading station was later established at Hirado; however, it was abandoned in 1623 due to unprofitability, and in the following decade the third Shōgun, Iemitsu Tokugawa, banned all Europeans except the Dutch from visiting Japan, at the same time forbidding Japanese subjects to travel abroad. After less than twenty-five years, the nascent trading relationship between England and Japan was thus severed, and would remain so for more than two centuries.

The Shōgunate's isolationist policy, popularly known as *sakoku* (literally, 'chained country'), lasted until Japan was forcibly opened to foreign trade in the mid-nineteenth century. During that period, the sources of information about Japan available to Western writers were scant. Even the Dutch, confined as they were to a small trading post on an island off Nagasaki, had little access to intelligence about the wider country. In the British imagination, Japan began to drift from the everyday world of mercantile relationships towards the fantastic. It became an exotically inaccessible realm, a blank that could either be filled by unfalsifiable imagination or else used to mirror the preoccupations of European writers. Inevitably, it fulfilled both functions, as we can see by considering its appearances in the work of Jonathan Swift.

Japan as Lilliput

Swift's *Gulliver's Travels* contains what is undoubtedly English literature's most famous *sakoku*-era depiction of Japan. A satire on European (and specifically British) society, a spoof travel memoir and a philosophical fantasy, *Gulliver's Travels* is an astoundingly flexible text. It was an instant bestseller and was soon

---

2 The Tokugawa Shōgunate (1603–1867) was a military government in which supreme power was exercised by the Shōgun (or *generalissimo*), although the office of Emperor was retained as an essentially ceremonial position. Although repressive in its restrictions and social caste system, the rule of the Shōgunate (also known as the Edo period, after Tokugawa's capital) witnessed more than 200 years of peace and a flourishing of arts and literature.

adopted as, among other things, a children's book. Swift's friend, the writer John Gay, reported to him on 17 November 1726, within weeks of publication:

> From the highest to the lowest it is universally read, from the Cabinett-council to the Nursery . . . The whole town, men, women and children, are quite full of it. (Gay 1801: vol. 12, 214)

Of the four journeys related in *Gulliver's Travels*, the first, second and fourth find Lemuel Gulliver visiting just one country apiece: Lilliput, Brobdingnag and the country of the Houyhnhnms. By contrast, Gulliver's third voyage takes him to multiple countries in the eastern part of the globe – from the flying island of Laputa to the magicians of Glubbdubdrib and to Luggnagg, home of the immortal struldbruggs. Among these fantasy locations, Gulliver finds time to visit just one real country: Japan. Arriving towards the end of the book, he pretends to be a Dutchman to secure his safety and a passage back to England. The appearance of Japan among an assortment of invented places suggests the degree to which it had become a land of imagination in European minds, although Gulliver's brief stay there lacks the fantastic elements characteristic of his other destinations. At Yedo (Edo) he is admitted to the presence of the 'Emperor' (the title used for the Shōgun by all early English writers), who receives him courteously and arranges for him to be escorted to Nangasac (Nagasaki) and thence to Holland.

The sources of information available to Swift were not plentiful, but he seems to have attempted a fair degree of accuracy. He owned a copy of Samuel Purchas's 1625 compendium of voyages, *Hakluytus Posthumus or Purchas His Pilgrimes*, which includes the letters and history of William Adams (Tanaka 2009: 83–4), and it may be that the account of Adams's friendly reception by Ieyasu Tokugawa had some influence on his depiction of Gulliver's treatment at Yedo. It is likely that Swift had also read the account by the German botanist Engelbert Kaempfer of his visit to Japan with a Dutch trading mission in 1690–2, which would form the basis of European knowledge of the country for more than a century. Kaempfer's *History of Japan* was not published until 1727, the year after *Gulliver*, but had circulated in manuscript for some time before that. Swift at any rate demonstrates some awareness of the country's geography, including the locations of Edo and Nagasaki.

Swift's omissions are as interesting as what he includes. He might, for example, have used the episode as an opportunity to satirize the elaborate (and, to Western eyes, humiliating) rituals of abasement associated with the East. Kaempfer had written that he and his companions had been obliged to approach the Shōgun 'after the Japanese manner, creeping and bowing our heads to the ground' (qtd.

Markley 2004: 434), but Swift omits this, or rather displaces it to Gulliver's earlier visit to the court of Luggnagg, where supplicants are forced to approach the king on their knees while licking dust from the floor. Overall, his representation of the Japanese is markedly positive; however, it functions largely as a foil to his hostile portrayal of the Dutch as malicious, greedy and irreligious. For example, although the 'Emperor' graciously agrees to excuse Gulliver from the practice of *fumie*, or trampling on a sacred image, required of those suspected of being Christians in *sakoku* Japan, he expresses surprise at the request, no Dutchman having previously made such a scruple. The anti-Dutch barb is obvious, but Swift may also be making a more general point about European assumptions of moral superiority, as Robert Markley has argued:

> Gulliver's audience with the emperor, in effect, offers a fantasy – conniving with the Japanese against the Dutch – that discloses as fantasy Eurocentric discourses of economic imperialism, moral probity, and technocultural superiority. Gulliver's Japanese encounters mortify English pride by revealing the irrelevance of the assumptions, values, and logic on which the self-congratulatory rhetoric of Eurocentrism depends. (Markley 2004: 464)

Gulliver's Travels is of course one of the major canonical texts of English literature. That cannot be claimed for Swift's second Japan-related text, 'An Account of the Court and Empire in Japan'. This unfinished manuscript, dated 1728 and posthumously included in Swift's *Works*, is a transparent political allegory, which recounts a version of British politics in the first decades of the eighteenth century, using Japan as its nominal setting. It tells of the reign of the Emperor Regoge, who succeeded the Empress Nena – these being anagrams for Queen Anne and King George. The anagrammatic pattern continues: Whigs and Tories become the Husiges and Yortes factions, while the prime minister, Sir Robert Walpole, is Lelop-Aw.

'An Account' lacks the satirical brilliance of *Gulliver* but is important to the present study as the first text in which Japan and Britain are proposed as equivalents or mirror images of each other. Swift may have chosen Japan for this role in part because the very lack of information about the country made it a *tabula rasa* that could be easily adapted to his purpose, especially when addressing topics that might been politically dangerous if discussed directly. The remoteness and assumed otherness of Japan also served to heighten the piece's satire on the arbitrariness of social customs, as when Lelop-Aw, concluding a political speech, hits 'his forehead thrice against the table, as the custom is in Japan', and sits down 'with great complacency of mind' (278). However, Swift was clearly also struck by the similarities of the two island nations' geographical positions, each situated off a much larger continent. He writes that Regoge, 'before he succeeded to the empire of Japan, was King of Tedsu, a dominion seated on the continent, to the west-side of Japan' (102). Tedsu (i.e. Deuts, a name alluding to George's Germanic origins as Elector of Hanover) is of course on the continent to the *east* of Britain. In reflecting Europe in Asia, Swift turns Japan into Britain's mirror image.

This was to prove an enduring trope. In 1898, when Mary Crawford Fraser, then widow of the head of the British legation in Tōkyō, published her Japan memoirs, there was still a large disparity in power between the two nations, but Japan's development and its recent success in the Sino-Japanese War had convinced her and others of its potential to become the dominant force in East Asia. She summed up the position in an intensely imperialistic poem, published as an epigraph to her book:

> Two babes the mother bore at one rich birth,
> Twin hearts that beat to her low notes of love,
> Twin souls that leapt to each heroic call,
> As generous sword to snatch the Treasure-Trove
> Of hard-won honour. . . .
> Too great to rule together, worlds apart
> She set them, in the silver of the seas.
> Yet heart calls heart, as erst upon the breast
> That bore these glories, sovereign in their place,
> The Island Empires of the East and West. (Fraser 1904: vi)

As John L. Hennessey notes, Fraser reaffirms the equivalence of the two nations by depicting 'Japan as Britain's Eastern mirror image' (2018: 24) – a balancing power, on the opposite side of the globe.

By the mid-nineteenth century, the use of Japan as a convenient blank slate onto which to project satirical or other inventions had become increasingly untenable. As Britain and other Western powers grew in global reach and influence, Japan inevitably became better known to them, *sakoku* notwithstanding. Eventually, in 1853, the American naval commander Matthew C. Perry and his gunboats arrived in Edo Bay to demand that Japan engage in trade with the United States. Their superior firepower forced the Tokugawa government into a one-sided treaty, which was concluded in Kanagawa in March 1854 and soon replicated by the major European powers, including Britain. The demonstration of Japan's relative impotence against the technologically more advanced West played a catalytic role in hastening the fall of the Shōgunate and, after a period of turbulence, the restoration of the Emperor to effective political power for the first time in half a millennium. In 1868, the Emperor Meiji moved his capital from Kyōto to what had been the centre of government since the beginning of Tokugawa rule: Edo, now renamed Tōkyō (or 'Eastern capital').

The Meiji era (1868–1912) is of prime importance to this book, both as the time when British children's literature made its first appearance in Japan and as the point at which the image of Japan, long hazy in Western minds, rapidly took on a much more definite shape. That shape, I shall argue, was determined in significant part by the archetypes and images provided by children's literature.

One of the most prominent texts to be used in describing Japan was *Gulliver's Travels* itself. This was not in the form of Swift's explicit depiction of Japan in the third book but rather by way of Gulliver's earlier voyages, which took him to the countries of the minute Lilliputians and outsized Brobdingnagians. Both were regularly drawn on to suggest the striking difference in physical scale between Japanese people and their European visitors. As early as 1867, the French nobleman Ludovic de Beauvoir alluded to Swift in describing the small-scale precision of Japanese interior design: 'chaque maison est en sapin, sans un atome de peinture, un vrai bijou, un joujou, un petit chalet suisse lilliputien, d'un goût, d'une finesse, d'une propreté et d'une simplicité admirables' [each house is made of fir, without a speck of paint, a real jewel, a toy, a Lilliputian Swiss chalet, with admirable taste, delicacy, cleanliness and simplicity] (1874: 158). The English botanist, Marianne North, was another early visitor, arriving in Japan in 1875. In her autobiography she records her discomfort and sense of clumsiness on discovering herself suddenly large-bodied. On being taken to a tea garden shortly after her arrival this feeling was exacerbated by the tiny cups, delicate cakes and subtle flavours she encountered:

> The smell was delicious, the taste only fit for fairies, and very hard for big mortal tongues to discover. The tiny girls who served us were very pretty, and merry over our gigantic and clumsy ways. I felt quite Brobdingnagian in Japan. (North 1894: 215)[3]

Swiftian comparisons occur repeatedly in North's account of Japan (although nowhere else in her book, which describes visits to numerous other Asian

---

3 Thirty years later, portion sizes were still much on the mind of Bob Fawcett, the British hero of *Kobo*, by Herbert Strang (the pseudonym used by writing partners George Herbert Ely and Charles James L'Estrange), a Henty-esque adventure set in the Russo-Japanese War. Frustrated by the 'midget quantities' served at a feast in the house of a samurai, Bob is said to feel 'as Gulliver might have felt at a state banquet in Lilliput' (1905: 23).

countries): an interpreter is described as 'quite Liliputian [*sic*]', for example (220), while a temple rises above the surrounding single-storey houses 'like Gulliver among the Liliputians [*sic*]' (223).

The difference in average height between Japanese and Westerners is today less pronounced than in the mid-nineteenth century, but self-consciousness about one's physical size is something that many Western visitors to Japan (including the present author) have experienced (Holt 2017); it is one of the most immediate ways in which one's sense of normality may be destabilized. The same thing may also happen in reverse: a generation after North, the Japanese writer Sōseki Natsume experienced comparable disorientation while staying in London. As he wrote to his wife, Kyōko Nakane, on 22 January 1901:

> When I am seen as a short person, I feel humiliated. When I think I see a strange man coming towards me, it often turns out to be my own reflection in a big mirror – things like that happen a lot. I can't help the shape of my face, but I do want to be taller. (Natsume 2016: 19)

Natsume's account is evidence of the power of disparities of scale to trigger feelings of dissociation, whether from a 'Brobdingnagian' or 'Lilliputian' perspective – an experience for which *Gulliver's Travels* stands as an obvious point of reference. However, his being discomfited by the sight of his own reflection hints at an even more important literary source for Meiji-era Britons in Japan: Lewis Carroll's *Alice* books.

Japan as Wonderland

The radical politician, Sir Charles Wentworth Dilke, who had visited Japan in 1875, was perhaps the first person to draw a comparison between that country and Carroll's fantasies. Concluding an article in *The Fortnightly Review* the following year, he declared that Japan's 'rural districts form, with Through-the-Looking-Glass-Country and Wonderland, the three kingdoms of merry dreams' (Dilke 1876: 443). Dilke's sentimental allusion was soon to be elaborated in a more specific way, in the travel writings of Lady Annie Brassey. By the time Dilke's article appeared in late 1876, Brassey and her family, then engaged in a round-the-world trip on the steam yacht, 'Sunbeam', were already well on their way to Yokohama, where they arrived in January 1877. At that point, *Through the Looking-Glass* had been in print for barely five years, having been published at the end of 1871. Despite this, it and its predecessor, *Alice's Adventures in Wonderland*, were already sufficiently celebrated that Brassey, like Dilke, could be confident that a reference to Alice would be readily understood by her readers. *Alice's Adventures in Wonderland* shares with *Gulliver* an interest in disorientating changes of scale, and at least one children's writer of the Meiji era would later exploit that fact in drawing a comparison between Wonderland and Japan,[4] but it was to Carroll's second book that Brassey turned to convey her sense that Japan offered an apparently nonsensical (but perhaps just arbitrary) reversal of English life:

> There were many strange things upside down to be seen on either hand – horses and cows with bells on their tails instead of on their necks, the quadrupeds well clothed, their masters without a scrap of covering, tailors sewing from them instead of to them, a carpenter reversing the action of his saw and plane. It looked just as if they had originally learned the various processes in 'Alice's Looking-glass World' in some former stage of their existence. (Brassey 1984: 318)

The appearance of mirrors in these accounts should occasion no surprise. In their combined functions of replication and reversal they offer a powerful mechanism for conveying the combination of familiarity and alterity characteristic of British depictions of Japan. Nor was Brassey the only writer to reach for Carroll's texts in order to make the point. In 1882, D. C. Angus published *The Eastern Wonderland*, a volume in which he aimed to introduce modern Japan to 'English children – say from eight to fourteen years of age' (1890: v). Unlike Dilke, Brassey or North, Angus was not recounting a trip he had undertaken personally but attempting to describe the country and its recent dramatic history in a way that would be accessible to children. For this purpose, he invented a Japanese narrator for his story: a man born in 1850, who in relating the circumstances of his life could bear witness to the upheavals of the previous thirty years.[5] Angus's fictional narrator explains that he studied at University College, London, during which time he was introduced to *Alice in Wonderland* by his host family:

---

4 The American author Charlotte Gibson's 1908 narrative of a journey from the United States to Japan, *In Eastern Wonderlands*, centred her own Carrollian comparison on the question of scale:

> Did you ever go to sleep and dream you were in a doll's country, where you seemed like a giant? Alice [an American child] said she knew now just how that other Alice felt in her visit to Wonderland, for she never saw such tiny little people and such tiny little houses and even such tiny little trees. (Gibson 1908: 28)

5 Angus's solution was not unique. Edward Greey, an Englishman who had been a member of Lord Elgin's delegation to the Shōgun in 1855, used a similar device in his children's book, *Young Americans in Japan*, published in the United States in the same year that Angus's *Eastern Wonderland* appeared in Britain. In Greey's book, as Gregory Rohe explains, the Westernized Japanese character, Oto Nambo, who has studied in the United States, acts as a guide to the American protagonists touring Japan:

> This narrative convention allows Greey first to introduce aspects of Japan and its culture through the eager and curious eyes of the family, and then allows him to provide an explanation through the Nambo character. (Rohe 2015: 85)

The children were much given to talking about 'Alice in Wonderland', and one day I rashly said, 'I don't believe your Alice saw things a bit more wonderful than you would see if I could take you to *my* country. *That* is a wonderland if you like!' Then, of course, they began to ask how and why, and to set some startling incident of Alice's life before me, and ask if I could match that! And then I used to bring out the oddest things I knew (odd, I mean, to English people), and sometimes succeeded in beating Alice. . . .

So I said aloud, 'Well, in two years you may expect a book of pictures, with as many particulars as I can crowd into a little space, about –

'THE EASTERN WONDERLAND'.

Then they said, 'But there must be a little girl in it; there always is a little girl in "Wonderlands"'. But I didn't see how that could be done, unless I borrowed Alice from Mr. Carroll, who is not likely to wish to part with her. (Angus 1890: 9–10)

The children's reply that 'there always is a little girl in "Wonderlands"' suggests the extent to which Carroll's books had already established a genre, replete with recognized conventions. The Alice books were indeed much imitated, as one might expect of such immediate bestsellers, their influence being clear in children's stories such as Frederic Edward Weatherly's *Elsie's Expedition* (1874) and Clara Bradford's *Ethel's Adventures in the Doll Country* (1880), among many others. Before Angus, however, authors of children's fiction seem to have avoided the term 'wonderland' itself, perhaps because it was so closely associated with Carroll's work.[6] Writers on travel and geography showed no such reticence: Richard Meade Bache's *American Wonderland* (1871), John Tinne's *Wonderland of the Antipodes* (1873) and Edwin J. Stanley's *Rambles in Wonderland: Or, Up the Yellowstone, and among the Geysers and Other Curiosities of the National Park* (1878) were all published in the years between Carroll's and Angus's books. *The Eastern Wonderland* itself, being both a geographical text and a book that explicitly invokes children's fantasy, was thus taking advantage of not one but two fashions begun by the *Alice* books, even as it nominally set them at odds. Would its Japanese narrator be successful in proving the reality of Japan more wonderful than the fantasy of Wonderland?

Extending this device into the body of the text, Angus, like Brassey, picks up on the ways in which Japan offers a 'looking-glass' version of the world familiar to British readers. Describing a street of craftsmen, he has his Japanese narrator write to his young friends:

---

6 'Wonderland' was not Carroll's coinage – the *OED* cites an example from a 1790 satirical poem about the Scottish explorer, James Bruce – but he undoubtedly brought the word into common use.

> Carpenters make our shoes, and basket-makers our hats; and you would see the blacksmith pulling the bellows with his foot, the cooper holding his tub with his toes, the tailor sewing *from* him, and the sawyer pulling the saw *to* him, and many ways of doing things which would seem to you 'upside down' if you had walked through our streets and watched the people at work. (Angus 1890: 83)

When Angus became aware that Lady Brassey had used the same *Through the Looking-Glass* comparison, he used the preface to a later edition to acknowledge her priority but suggested that the association of Alice and Japan was a very natural one:

> I have only to add that the Introduction to 'The Eastern Wonderland' was written without any knowledge that the same idea had suggested itself to Lady Brassey (see 'Voyage of the Sunbeam') by the confusing effect of Japanese character and habit on her mind. It may well occur to more than one student of 'Alice in Wonderland' – and of Japan. (Angus 1890: vii)

In fact, neither Brassey nor Angus was the first to use the trope of Japan as 'essentially a country of paradoxes and anomalies, where all – even familiar things – put on new faces, and are curiously reversed'. Those words belong to Sir Rutherford Alcock, the British government's first diplomatic representative at the court of the Shōgun, where he served from 1859. In his 1863 account of his three years in Japan, Alcock provides an even lengthier list of examples, with such items as women blackening rather than whitening their teeth and wearing tight-fitting kimono rather than bulky crinolines, and old men flying kites as children look on (1863: 414). Annie R. Butler's *Stories about Japan*, too, boasts a substantial catalogue of such 'paradoxes', including the child-directed observations that 'if you went into a Japanese school, you would find the children reading down rather than across the page, and from the end instead of the beginning of the book; while their examinations are after, instead of before the holidays' (1888: 49–50). A similar list is given by Basil Hall Chamberlain in his 1890 book, *Things Japanese*, in a chapter entitled 'Topsy-Turvydom' (Chamberlain 1905: 480–2). Not all writers connected these phenomena directly to *Alice* – Alcock, writing in 1863, was of course not in a position to do so – but for Victorian Britons considering the trope of Japan as a country of reversals and reflections, Carroll's Looking-Glass country offered a natural comparison.

Alcock and the others were also drawing on a much more ancient tradition of reversal. Earlier catalogues of inversions of the natural order included those to be seen in Renaissance works such as Nicolò Nelli's sixteenth-century print, 'Il Mondo alla riversa' ('The World Reversed') and its successors. The depictions in such works of cattle walking behind men pulling ploughs, animal barbers or fish in trees do not lack humour, but they also point to a disturbing disruption of cosmic hierarchies and harmony, their *locus classicus* being Horace's evocation of civil war in the *Odes*:

> Proteus urged his whole herd to seek
> The heights of the mountain,
> And all kinds of fish clung to the highest elm,
> Which is known to have been seat to doves,
> And fearful deer float, sea having
> Covered the land. (*Odes*, 1.2 ll. 7-12)

In Horace such reversals are horrifying, but by the turn of the nineteenth century, with the authority of classical cosmologies considerably less secure, their latent comic aspects had begun to emerge. Even so, the anxious sense of a social order under threat might still be present. The children's book, *Signor Topsy-Turvy's Wonderful Magical Lantern; or, the World Turned Upside Down*, published in 1810 at the height of the Napoleonic wars, contains poems in which a horse turns the tables on its cruel owner ('She had trudged to this day / If he'd been a merciful master'), and fish, birds and hares (egged on by a rabble-rousing squirrel) begin to hunt the humans who had hitherto hunted them – a salutary warning for a revolutionary age (1898–9: 218–21) (Figure 1.1). By the 1860s, however, tropes of reversal could be regarded as amusing rather than shocking, and the context of Carrollian 'nonsense' offered scope for playful thought experiments. Indeed, having been invited to wonder at the strangeness of Japanese customs, the child reader of Angus or Butler might well go further and question whether such cultural differences were not, after all, purely arbitrary. Does it matter which way a tailor directs his needle? Why *should* the right-most page of a book be the 'end'?

Carroll uses the device of a dream to frame his fantasy within a more rational waking world. The inversions and contrary logic of Alice's interlocutors challenge her conventional habits of thought, but *Alice in Wonderland* culminates in her rejection of the kind of logical reversal that the book has flirted with throughout:

> 'No, no!' said the Queen. 'Sentence first – verdict afterwards.'
> 'Stuff and nonsense!' said Alice loudly. 'The idea of having the sentence first!'
> 'Hold your tongue!' said the Queen, turning purple.
> 'I won't!' said Alice.
> 'Off with her head!' the Queen shouted at the top of her voice. Nobody moved.
> 'Who cares for you?' said Alice, (she had grown to her full size by this time.) 'You're nothing but a pack of cards!' (Carroll 1962: 157)

Figure 1.1 From *Signor Topsy-Turvy's Wonderful Magic Lantern* (1810).

Alice's assertion of dominance over what is 'nothing but a pack of cards' marks the limit, at least in this book, of her willingness to accommodate fantasy-logic and the end of her tour of Wonderland. No such formula was available to Meiji-era British visitors to Japan, but their experience too, as we shall see, was from the beginning associated with a sense of Japan, not only as a topsy-turvy land but also as a two-dimensional one.

Two-dimensional Japan

By the time Western civilians began to arrive in Japan in any numbers, Japanese art and artefacts had already been exported in large quantities to Europe and America. The Meiji regime was keen to learn what it could of Western technology and political and military organization and pursued such knowledge vigorously, but it was no less committed to promoting its own products and exerting what would today be called 'soft power'. Indeed, such initiatives had begun even under the Shōgunate. Through Japan's participation in the Exposition Universelle in Paris in 1867 and the many national and international fairs that followed (Hennessey 2018: 26–8), as well as through the enthusiasm of private collectors such as Alcock, Japanese designs and aesthetics were widely propagated and soon became a feature of middle-class drawing rooms, in the form of prints, ceramics, lacquer work and relatively inexpensive objects such as folding fans. From the 1870s, Japanese aesthetics exerted a major influence on Western art and garden design, with Van Gogh, Manet and Whistler among the Western painters inspired by *ukiyoe* artists such as Hokusai and Hiroshige.

The fashion for *Japonisme* meant that Westerners who came to Japan during the Meiji period already had a store of associations and images from their previous encounters with Japanese art and artefacts. Marianne North, for example, recording her first impressions as she sailed into Yokohama, wrote:

> At daylight on the 7th of November [1875, we] found ourselves within sight of Fujiyama. I watched the sun rise out of the sea and redden its top, as I have seen so well represented on so many hand-screens and tea-trays. (North 1894: 213)

The immediate recourse to imported household goods as a means of understanding the physical reality of Japan is even more striking in the case of Annie Brassey and her family, who arrived at the same port fourteen months later. Her account is of particular interest, since it includes what may be the only record of a first encounter with Meiji-era Japan by British children – in this case, Brassey's daughters Mabelle and Muriel, aged eleven and four:

> [T]he people we met in the streets were a study in themselves. The children said they looked 'like fans walking about'; and it was not difficult to understand their meaning. The dress of the lower orders has remained precisely the same for hundreds of years; and before I had been ashore five minutes I realised more fully than I had ever done before the truthfulness of the representations of native artists, with which the fans, screens, and vases one sees in England are ornamented. (Brassey 1984: 306)

A little later in her account Brassey reiterates, writing about the countryside beyond Yokohama, that 'the whole landscape and the many villages looked very like a set of living fans or tea trays' (313).

Such similes indicate the relative paucity of comparators available to British visitors attempting to convey their experience to readers back home. If the most easily available pictorial representations of Japan in the West were such objects as 'fans or tea trays', it was perhaps inevitable that an encounter with the reality would prompt such associations. Indeed, the Chorus of Japanese nobles that opens

Gilbert and Sullivan's comic opera, *The Mikado* (1885), appears to satirize this reflex:

> If you want to know who we are,
> We are gentlemen of Japan:
> On many a vase and jar –
> On many a screen and fan,
> We figure in lively paint. (Gilbert 2006: 20–1)

A fan, in particular, was 'one of the cheapest Japanese objects available in the West and, for the average person, . . . possibly the only Japanese item they could hope to possess' (*Fan Circle International*). Fans might thus find their way into a nursery more easily than such prestigious and fragile wares as ceramics and lacquer work. Once there, as Etti Gordon Ginzburg has pointed out, they 'often functioned to inform and teach about Japan; many learned about Mount Fuji or the look of Japanese women from the painted images on the fans' (218: 385). Such scenes being part of the visual repertoire available to Western children, the remark of Lady Brassey's young daughters that the Japanese were 'like fans walking about' is an understandable, if rather dehumanizing, one.

These comparisons frame Japanese people in terms of the impression they make on Western viewers. The Japanese, seen through a Western gaze, are projected as if onto a flat surface, for aesthetic contemplation. The distance from 'nothing but a pack of cards' to 'like fans walking about' is not so great, especially when we remember that Japanese artistic techniques often shared with those of court playing cards the preservation of single plane of depth, a feature also deployed by John Tenniel in his illustrations of the playing-card characters for *Alice* (Figure 1.2). Pictorial representations of Japan might thus not only educate the viewer but also reduce their subjects to two-dimensional figures. The aestheticization of the Japanese landscape and its inhabitants and their imaginative reconstitution on a flat plane lend to both an estranging quality, in which they are perceived as simultaneously more exotic and less real than their British observers, who (like Alice in Tenniel's pictures) remain solidly three-dimensional. This touristic 'flattening' of experience is well captured, albeit in a different Asian setting, in E. M. Forster's *A Passage to India* (1924), when the new arrival from England, Adela Quested, remarks: 'I'm tired of seeing picturesque figures pass before me as a frieze. . . . It was wonderful when we landed, but that superficial glamour soon goes' (Forster 2005: 24).

The desire to go beyond 'superficial glamour' is familiar in a Japanese context, where finding 'the real Japan' remains even now a perennial quest of Western visitors. As Adele Quested later discovers, however, surfaces are not so easy to

Figure 1.2 A 3D girl in a 2D world: John Tenniel's illustration for *Alice's Adventures in Wonderland* (1865).

penetrate, in part because the tools available are calibrated to Western categories and perceptions. Even the fans exported to the West were adapted to their market, resulting in objects 'which Westerners considered to be wholly Japanese, but which could barely have been recognised as such by the Japanese themselves' (*Fan Circle International*). Failure might end in frustration and resentment, as in the case of Marianne North, whose inability to pierce the highly elastic but ultimately impenetrable layers of Japanese politeness and reserve led her to conclude: 'Everybody who has lived long among [the Japanese] seems to get disgusted with their falseness and superficiality' (1894: 225).

Nothing but a pack of cards, indeed.

Japan and childhood

One aspect of Meiji-era Japan with obvious relevance to the use of children's literature as an interpretative lens is the country's general association in Victorian minds with children and childhood. Western accounts frequently emphasized the indulged position enjoyed by Japanese children. The image of Japan as a 'paradise of babies' (Alcock 1863: 82) enjoyed wide currency, as for example in Annie R. Butler's evocation of the toy and sweet shops of Tōkyō:

> Japan has been called 'The Children's Paradise', and 'The Paradise of Babies', and so you would think it if you could see long streets with scarcely anything in them but stuffed and china animals on wheels, toy idols and idol cars, windmills and water-wheels, battledores and shuttle-cocks, sugary toys of all kinds and dolls of all sizes! (Butler 1888: 61–2)

The Swiss diplomat, Aimé Humbert, resident in Japan from 1863 to 1864, was an early observer of the extent to which Japanese children were indulged by their parents, a state of affairs he describes with approval:

> [I]t is granted by everyone that the child ought to have its own way. Fathers and mothers derive their pleasure from the observance of this natural law. Every means of enjoyment for children, every subject of their amusement, becomes a source of personal satisfaction to their parents; they give themselves up to it with all their hearts, and it suits the children admirably. Travellers who have said that Japanese children never cry, have stated with very little exaggeration of expression a perfectly real phenomenon. (Humbert 1874: 42)

Not only are Japanese children indulged, but their characters appear not to be adversely affected by the practice. This idea offered an obvious challenge to Western child-rearing precepts. The explorer Isabella Bird, during her 1878 overland journey through the interior of Japan from Yokohama to Yezo (Hokkaidō), remarked on how polite, unselfish and industrious the Japanese children she encountered were, despite being treated with what, by British standards, might be considered excessive lenience:

> I am very fond of Japanese children. I have never yet heard a baby cry, and I have never seen a child troublesome or disobedient. Filial piety is the leading virtue in Japan, and unquestioning obedience is the habit of centuries. The arts and threats by which English mothers cajole or frighten children into unwilling obedience appear unknown. I admire the way in which children are taught to be independent in their amusements. Part of the home education is the learning of the rules of the different games, which are absolute, and when there is a doubt, instead of a quarrelsome suspension of the game, the fiat of a senior child decides the matter. . . . They play by themselves, and don't bother adults at every turn. I usually carry sweeties with me, and give them to the children, but not one has ever received them without first obtaining permission from the father or mother. When that is gained they smile and bow profoundly, and hand the sweeties to those present before eating any themselves. (Bird 1984: 198–9)

Mary Crawford Fraser, likewise, reported enthusiastically on the behaviour of the Japanese children at the Christmas party over which she presided at the British legation in Tōkyō in January 1891:

> I feel that there must be a great deal to say for a system of education which, without robbing childhood of a moment's bright happiness, can clothe little children of every condition with this garment of perfect courtesy.... It is, to me, most comforting to see that all that is desirable in the little people's deportment can be attained without snubbings or punishments or weary scoldings. The love showered upon children simply wraps them in warmth and peace, and seems to encourage every sweet good trait of character without ever fostering a bad one. (Fraser 1904: 497)

The idea that treating children indulgently might be productive of thoughtful and unselfish behaviour must have been intriguing to Victorians interested in alternative approaches to child-rearing and education. However, the good behaviour of Japanese children could also be slightly estranging. 'They are gentle creatures, but too formal and precocious', Bird declared, adding:

> They have no special dress. This is so queer that I cannot repeat it too often. At three they put on the *kimono* and girdle, which are as inconvenient to them as to their parents, and childish play in this garb is grotesque. I have, however, never seen what we call child's play – that general abandonment to miscellaneous impulses, which consists in struggling, slapping, rolling, jumping, kicking, shouting, laughing, and quarrelling! (1984: 199)

Bird's attitude to 'child's play' in this passage is ambiguous, but it seems that the quiescent politeness of Japanese children, combined with the 'grotesque' restriction of the kimono that is its physical embodiment, is figured as less natural than the mental and physical freedom of their rough-and-tumble British counterparts, whose naughtiness and noise may be a price worth paying for health and high spirits. We may recall Catherine Sinclair's 1839 preface to *Holiday House*, which celebrates 'that species of noisy, frolicsome, mischievous children, now almost extinct, . . . when young people were like wild horses on the prairies, rather than like well-broken hacks on the road' (1856: vii). Nevertheless, in reworking Bird's words for a readership of British children ten years later, Annie R. Butler gave her description of the young Japanese a more straightforwardly positive cast:

> Perhaps it is partly their long dress, which prevents them from running about much, and makes them prefer quiet play; but certain it is, they are never rude

and rough and noisy when let loose from school, as our English children too often are. (Butler 1888: 63)[7]

For Butler, at least, the modest behaviour of Japanese children is an example to be followed. However, the sense that their undemonstrative good manners were unsettling and even slightly repellent is a persistent background note to many accounts, even where the overt theme is one of praise. Mary Crawford Fraser, though strongly approving the politeness of her young guests, notes that their education is one in which the virtues of filial duty and patriotism are taught with 'a good faith and solemnity which would send our English schoolboys off into fits of scoffing laughter' (1904: 497–8). Fraser may intend this as a positive reflection, but in drawing attention to an absence of ironic self-consciousness she underlines a perceived difference between Japanese and English sensibilities. For others, it is the lack of emotional spontaneity in Japanese children that is regarded as problematic. Isabella Bird, having been constantly followed in her travels through the interior of Tōhoku by crowds of Japanese to whom the sight of a foreign woman was an utter novelty, is at pains to stress that she never felt physically threatened, but conveys the disconcerting nature of the experience: 'These are such queer crowds, so silent and gaping, and they remain motionless for hours, the wide-awake babies on the mothers' backs and in the fathers' arms never crying' (1984: 151–2).

The image of Japanese children as uncannily quiet was epitomized by the figure of the non-crying baby. As Humbert had noted, the prevalence in Japan of this apparently paradoxical phenomenon was already a commonplace in the early 1860s, and so notorious did it eventually become that it was even made a target of satire, as in Anne St Vincent's poem, 'Japanese Babies', printed in the American children's magazine *St. Nicholas* in 1886:

A little bird sings from over the sea:
'I've been to a land that pleases me'
'Tis a fabulous land where babies don't cry
From the time they are born till the time they die!

You queer little baby, way over the sea,
Tell us, oh tell us, how can it be?

---

7   Bird's work is paraphrased and Bird herself named at several points in Butler's book, which relies on external sources for much of its material (Butler 1888: 5). There was also a closer connection, for Bird went on to marry John Bishop, an old friend of one of Butler's brothers (Stoddart 1906: 207). In early 1889, shortly after *Stories about Japan* was published, Bird (now widowed) arrived in Srinagar, India, where Butler's younger sister, Dr Fanny Jane Butler, was working as a medical missionary, and together they founded the John Bishop Memorial Hospital (Tonge 1930: 43).

Aren't Japanese baby clothes ever too tight?
Don't Japanese babies wake up in the night?

Do Japanese teeth come through without pain?
Or Japanese children tease babies in vain?
Don't Japanese pins have points that prick?
Won't Japanese colic make little folk sick?

You queer little baby, if secret there be,
Send it, oh send it way over the sea!
There is no such secret. Far off in Japan
Some babies *can* cry, and they'll prove that they can!
(1886: 948)

If Japanese children were too adult in their manners to be considered entirely childlike, the reverse was perceived to be true of their elders. Marianne North and D. C. Angus both assert the childish (or childlike) nature of Japanese adults:

> The Japanese are like little children, so merry and full of pretty ways, and very quick at taking in fresh ideas; but they don't think or reason much. (North 1894: 224–5).

> The Japanese are very fond of children; they are child-like themselves in many ways, and docile and obedient to 'superiors', and they teach their children as they were taught, with excessive indulgence and gentleness, but with great care and painstaking. (Angus 1890: 14)

Angus extends this observation to encompass the history of the country itself, which he sees as having a childlike simplicity and even a fairy-tale structure:

> there is something in its story which takes hold of the child and the childlike lover of the simple: the grotesque, the ceremonial and the beautifully natural, the improbable and the matter-of-fact, all mixed up together, as in a tale of homely ragged Cinderellas suddenly transported to Court balls and splendours by a sensible but wonder-working fairy godmother, or of the orphan Jack trying to help his mother, and assisted so unexpectedly in his rise in life by the magic bean-stalk. (Angus 1890: vi)

Annie R. Butler too draws on fairy tale, repeatedly comparing Japan to a Sleeping Beauty, one who had to be 'woken' twice, first by Portuguese traders in the sixteenth century and again (more roughly) by Commodore Perry and his gunships in the nineteenth (1888: 31, 34).

These authors' constructions of Japan as a country suitable for children because of its childishness, and as passively awaiting Western intervention, are problematic in obvious ways. The racist equation of non-Western peoples with children was of course a standard component of Orientalist and colonialist discourse, typically used to recast oppressive policy as a salutary discipline imposed for the victims' own good. A childlike nation, after all, could only benefit from the guidance of 'grown-up' countries such as Britain in managing its affairs. In February 1890, for example, Mary Crawford Fraser, whose husband was then renegotiating Britain's unequal trade treaty with Japan, commented on the Japanese wish to abolish the extraterritoriality provision that allowed foreign judges to sit with Japanese ones in trying foreign citizens: 'our own Government will not go back on the proposition, feeling that Japan is *still too young to the ways of justice* to be trusted blindly and entirely with the liberty, the property, perhaps the lives of British subjects' (1904: 251, my emphasis).

The fact that Japan was not a colony, but rather a country aiming to achieve parity with the Western powers with all possible speed, may have been a factor in the caution evident in many Western accounts of Japan's 'awakening' and precocious development during the Meiji era. Ambivalence about the transience of Japan's 'childhood' was easily accommodated by the structures of feeling evident in late Victorian and Edwardian children's books, where neo-Romantic yearning for the indefinite extension of childhood was fast becoming a prominent theme. Although some classic texts of this time, such as Frances Hodgson Burnett's *The Secret Garden* (1911), hailed the growth of children to healthy maturity as a wholly desirable outcome, many others, such as Kenneth Grahame's *The Golden Age* (1895) and J. M. Barrie's *Peter and Wendy* (1911), painted childhood as a prelapsarian state, departure from which was a matter for partial if not outright regret.

The opening paragraphs of *Peter and Wendy* exemplify some of these complications. They recount the incident of the infant Wendy Darling playing in a garden and winsomely handing her mother a plucked flower, which elicits the response: 'Oh, why can't you remain like this for ever!' Mrs Darling's delight in Wendy as a perfect Romantic girl child is inseparable from her regret that this condition cannot be permanent. Ironically, however, hers is a self-fulfilling presentiment, for it is Mrs Darling's own words that topple Wendy from her prelapsarian perch: 'This was all that passed between them on the subject, but henceforth Wendy knew that she must grow up. You always know after you are two. Two is the beginning of the end' (Barrie 1999: 69).

Western writing about Japan at this period often exhibits a comparably rueful sense that Japan has been spoiled by the West's own arrival and is losing its 'innocence' in consequence. Like Wendy Darling, the Japanese had lived in a state of unconscious bliss until hauled into the wider world by Perry's black ships. Visitors were torn between being impressed with the 'young' nation's precocity in learning Western ways and mortification at the speed with which it was losing – or wilfully discarding – its own. Repeatedly, British writers warn their readers that the Japan they have described is disappearing and is perhaps already submerged beneath the oncoming tide of Westernization. As early as 1867, the diplomat Laurence Oliphant gave an admiring account of Japanese generosity and sacrifice in *Blackwood's Magazine* but predicted that these qualities would not long survive exposure to the self-centred morality of the West, exclaiming in words that anticipate Mrs Darling's: 'Alas, alas! how long will they remain such?' (qtd. Yokoyama 1987: 86). A decade later, we find Annie Brassey concluding her discussion of the country with the urgent admonition that travellers who 'wish to see Japan should do so at once; for the country is changing every day, and in three years more will be so Europeanised that little will be left worth seeing' (1984: 360). D. C. Angus's Japanese narrator addresses his young English friend, Nelly, in similar terms: 'So, Nelly, my looking-glass is for you, and you are my Alice. And if you will make haste and come to Japan, you will see for yourself all the true wonders I have told. But you must be quick, or they will all have vanished away' (1890: 10).[8] Japan's past and vanishing present may be wondrous, and even its energy and adaptability in modernizing may be impressive, but as it comes to resemble modern Western nations its uniqueness and, in due course, its interest will diminish: 'In proportion as we drop our old civilisation we shall cease to be "The Eastern Wonderland," and little English children will need no magic looking-glass to see us by' (1890: 209).

Warnings of the imminent disappearance of Japan have been a persistent feature of Western writing on the country ever since. Almost a century after *The Eastern Wonderland* was published, Peter Milward was expressing his ambition to restore Japanese people's appreciation of their heritage 'before it disappears' (1980: v), and fifteen years after that Elizabeth Kiritani opened her book on Japan with the melancholy observation that 'Old Japan is vanishing' (1995: 7). Appropriately for a nation that has made awareness of transience an abiding aesthetic, Japan appears to many Westerners to be in a state of perpetual evanescence; where change happens it is, by implication, to be deplored. Nowhere is this view more strongly asserted than in the prefatory poem to the Japanese

---

8 In a revised edition, published some fifteen years later, the author evidently decided that it was already too late and changed this passage accordingly: 'even since these lines were written the changes have been going on and increasing every day. You must understand, therefore, that I am introducing to you, not the modern Japan, but the Japan of former days' (Angus *c.*1906: 3).

diaries of Marie Stopes, the palaeobotanist and birth-control campaigner, who spent eighteen months in the country from 1907. Stopes uses the familiar imagery of Japan as a recently wakened sleeper but casts its awakening in a much more negative light than had Butler. Although Japan's recent victory in the Russo-Japanese War had vindicated its claim to a place among the world powers, Stopes sees this in terms of loss rather than achievement:

> Dreamland of Beauty, girt by glowing seas!
> Thou didst appear unfitted for the storm
> That broke upon thee from the lowering West.
> 　Yet thou hast risen and conquered.
> 　Thou dost stand, armed as a modern People
> 　In the front rank – and yet I say, alas!
> 　Who could have wished, in waking thou should'st spurn
> 　The wondrous rightness of thy sheltered past?
> 　To be as others are thou seem'st to yearn,
> 　And for mere useful ugliness dost cast
> 　For ever from thee beauties unsurpassed.
> 　. . .
> 　O cherry flower of lands! I weep to see
> 　Thy falling blooms. The whole World's loss, thy 'gains'.
> 　(Stopes 1910: v)

Such sentiments were naturally unwelcome to those Japanese striving to create the modern industrialized state deplored by Stopes. The Japanologist Basil Hall Chamberlain relates the experience of the journalist and poet, Sir Edwin Arnold, who at a banquet held in his honour during his time in Japan made a speech praising the country for much the same qualities as those valued by Stopes. According to Arnold, Japan was:

> the nearest earthly approach to Paradise or to Lotus-land, – so fairy-like, said he, is its scenery, so exquisite its art, so much more lovely still that almost divine sweetness of disposition, that charm of demeanour, that politeness humble without servility and elaborate without affectation, which place Japan high above all other countries in nearly all those things that make life worth living.
> (Chamberlain 1905: 3)

The following morning, Arnold discovered from a newspaper report that, rather than being flattered, some of his audience had interpreted his speech as 'pitiless condemnation'. As Chamberlain paraphrases the reaction of a local newspaper: 'Why did not Sir Edwin praise us for huge industrial enterprises, for commercial talent, for wealth, political sagacity, powerful armaments?' (3). For the modernizers of Meiji Japan, to be appreciated only for aesthetics and good manners, and to have the colossal reforms of the Meiji regime ignored, could only be felt as an insult. Chamberlain pertinently adds that to focus exclusively on the ways that Japan might be appreciated and valued by the West, and to ignore the West's influence in inspiring Japan's own dreams and ambitions, was to miss half the picture. The West was itself, to Japanese eyes, an astonishing Other:

> Old Japan was to us a delicate little wonder-world of sylphs and fairies. Europe and America, with their railways, their telegraphs, their gigantic commerce, their gigantic armies and navies, their endless applied arts founded on chemistry and mathematics, were to the Japanese a wonder-world of irresistible genii and magicians. (1905: 4)

Chamberlain's Carrollian language of 'wonder-worlds' and his more general debt to the imagery of fairy tale are by now familiar, but he is less typical in the even-handedness with which he recognizes that Alice's looking-glass reflects both ways, and that the West might appear as strange and wonderful to the Japanese as Japan to the West. By contrast, the Japanese narrator of Angus's *Eastern Wonderland*, who has travelled in both the United States and Britain, does not mention finding either place strange; it is only his native land that he describes as 'upside down' and a 'Wonderland'. As a Christian convert and a student of English law, but especially of course as a fictional persona created by a British author, he has internalized a Western perspective.

The newspaper editorial cited by Chamberlain represented one Japanese point of view, but it would be misleading to suggest that the Japanese were monolithic in their attitude to the transformation of their country from semi-feudal state to industrial and military power. If Westerners were ambivalent about that transformation, attitudes among the Japanese themselves were even more sharply divided. To chart in any detail the tortuous and at times violent course of the Japanese adoption of Western technologies, institutions, fashion, arts and culture over the course of the Meiji period would be to exceed the scope of this chapter, but there were formidable forces aligned against it, from the discontented samurai who took part in the Satsuma Rebellion of 1877 to peasants burdened by taxation and conscription, and even in the positions of its most determined supporters there were some seeming contradictions. The phrase 'Meiji restoration' suggests to British ears an analogy with the restoration of the English and Scottish monarchy in 1660, but that is a misleading comparison.

For one thing, the position of Emperor had never been abolished, even though power had lain in the hands of military governments and warlords for much of the previous millennium. The Japanese word usually translated as 'restoration', *ishin*, suggests something closer to 'renewal' or even 'revolution' than the reversion to some *status quo ante*. On the other hand, the legitimacy of the new regime relied in large part on its ability to present itself as the re-emergence of a truer and older form of government, and was bolstered by an appeal to Japan's deep history, with Shintō as a state religion underscoring the Emperor's personal political authority.

Inevitably, a degree of compromise was reached regarding the extent and nature of Westernization. Japan had, after all, previously established a model for cultural fusion, when it had come under the influence of another powerful civilization. In the first millennium, when Tang-dynasty China had been culturally dominant in East Asia, Heian Japan had borrowed lavishly from it in areas ranging from religion and poetry to city planning. The doctrine of *wakon kansai* (和魂漢才, 'Japanese spirit, Chinese knowledge') had been developed as a way to acknowledge and accommodate Chinese influence without obliterating Japanese identity. In the Meiji era, the analogous concept of *wakon yōsai* (和魂洋才, 'Japanese spirit, Western knowledge') had a similar purpose, that of taking what was useful from the West but developing it in a distinctively Japanese way and in Japanese interests (Oguma 2002: 32).

Japan's attempt to build an empire of its own was driven by various internal and external political factors, but there is no doubt that the model offered by European empires, and particularly by Britain, inspired the form that Japan's own imperial ambitions would take, from the name of the empire itself – the Empire of Great Japan (*dai nippon teikoku*), which mirrored and perhaps imitated the 'Great' of Great Britain (Sladen 1895: viii) – to the imposition of an unequal treaty on Korea in 1876 very similar to those imposed on Japan by the Western powers barely twenty years earlier.

Japan as looking-glass

A key concern of Meiji-era Japan, as of any state, was control of its national narrative. Who got to tell Japan's story and interpret its image – Japan or the West? Whose culture constituted the normative standard from which departures might be regarded as deviant? Japan's government was alive to such questions from an early date. I have mentioned the dismay prompted by Sir Edwin Arnold's praise of Japanese culture, but even from the earliest days of interaction with the West the Japanese were vigilant in protecting their national image. In 1862, for the example, the so-called First Embassy of Japan to Europe visited the International Exhibition in London and witnessed there the collection of Japanese artefacts that Sir Rutherford Alcock had assembled during his time as consul general in Edo. This was the first substantial public display of such objects in Britain and played a significant role in igniting the public taste for Japan-related art and objects. The Shōgunate officials, however, were mortified by the poor quality of the goods chosen to represent their nation as well as by the Western taste for low-class *ukiyoe* woodblock prints showing common and vulgar subjects, which had been displayed in preference to nobler works. One member of the mission, Fuchibe Tokuzō, described Alcock's collection dismissively in his diary as 'a miscellaneous heap of objects from an antique shop' (qtd. Foxwell 2009: 40).

With the Paris Exposition Universelle of 1867 the Shōgunate began to participate in international exhibitions and fairs on its own account and thus to influence directly the impression made by the country in the West. The Meiji government continued the policy, taking a pavilion at the Vienna World's Fair six years later and thereafter becoming an enthusiastic contributor to such events, to which it would send parties of experts and technicians to ensure appropriate results (Hendry 2000: 55–6). However, it could not control the behaviour of foreigners, and it was with some dismay that it learned of a projected 'Japanese Village', to be installed at Humphreys' Hall in Knightsbridge, London. Opening in January 1885, this was the brainchild of a Dutch businessman, Tannaker Buhicrosan, and was designed to capitalize on the Japan craze in Britain. Buhicrosan's village was a purely commercial affair and did not rely on government approval or sponsorship, either from Tōkyō or London. The village was built on an ambitious scale. British visitors wandering down its 'street' of wood and bamboo buildings (with a painted backdrop of Mount Fuji) could see artisans in wood, ceramics and textiles, buy green tea and Japanese sweets at a teahouse, visit a Buddhist Temple and a Shintō shrine and watch demonstrations of traditional Japanese arts and crafts, as well as displays of *kendō* and *sumō*. The village was staffed by 100 Japanese men, women and children, most recruited directly from Japan. With one interruption due to fire, after which it was rebuilt on an even grander scale, it received visitors until June 1887, during which time more than a million people passed through its doors (Downer 2018).

The village was certainly effective in introducing many British people to Japanese life and culture with a vividness that, in a world before film or widespread foreign travel, was otherwise entirely unavailable. A writer in the periodical *The*

Children's Friend compared a visit to the village shortly after its opening to the magical journeys of fairy tale: 'I have paid a highly interesting visit to a foreign country this morning, without the aid of that "magic carpet" or "wishing ring" which, in fairy stories, is considered necessary in order to accomplish such an undertaking' (qtd. Williams 2020). The Meiji government was less enthusiastic. On the one hand, they feared that the kind of Japanese who would be tempted to leave Japan to participate in a foreign-made showcase would be unsuitable cultural representatives. To that extent, their disapproval resembled that of the Shōgun's representatives at the 1862 International Exhibition. In addition, however, there was discomfort with the idea of Japanese people, and Japan itself, being made objects of touristic display. Hirobumi Itō, soon to become Japan's first prime minister, is said to have complained, 'How can they take us seriously if we dress as novelty dolls?' (qtd. Downer 2018).

A looking-glass not only shows us a reversed reflection of ourselves, it also raises the question, who is reflecting whom? *Through the Looking-Glass* begins and ends with variations on this question. At the book's conclusion, Carroll challenges the reader to decide whether Alice dreamed the story or was herself part of the dream of the Red King, a matter Alice cannot determine (1962: 346). Moreover, shortly after she arrives in the Looking-glass country, Alice enters a garden of flowers and suffers the unaccustomed experience of their looking at and discussing *her*, rather than vice versa. As well as being judgemental about Alice personally, the flowers' remarks have a latent racial cast: "'Still, you're the right colour, and that goes a long way" . . . "If only her petals curled up a little more, she'd be all right"' (206–7).

The unsettling prospect of being the object of appraising stares from people one is more used to gazing *at* was anxiously depicted in a cartoon published in *Punch* magazine in January 1885. It marked the opening of the Japanese Village that month with yet another looking-glass reversal, imagining Japanese visitors to 'An English Village' in Tōkyō, where the scenes displayed include a drunken revel, a dogfight, a lazy policeman and a fairground freak show (Figure 1.3).

Was the effect of the Japanese Village to educate British people about Japan in an enjoyable and immersive way, or was it to hold the Japanese up, if not to ridicule, then at least to a kind of fetishized Othering? Probably both, but the display of foreigners for their interest *as* foreigners can never entirely escape the latter charge. Even if we acknowledge that there are significant differences between the Japanese Village in Knightsbridge and contemporary cultural showcases such as London's Hyper Japan, or the village of British

Figure 1.3 'An English Village from a Japanese Point of View', *Punch*, 24 January 1885.

Hills in Fukushima (discussed in Chapter 5 of this book), there are striking commonalities too.

The British reception of the Japanese Village, as reflected in press reports, appears to have been largely positive, if patronizing. Wendy S. Williams observes:

> Repeatedly, visitors to the Japanese Village used words that simplified and distanced the Japanese performers from their British spectators. The words 'strange', 'merry', 'content', 'little', 'childlike', 'simple-minded', and 'grotesque' appear again and again throughout Village descriptions. Reporters also simplified Japanese work and lifestyle by describing them as 'easy': 'free-and-easy system of living' ('Japanese Village', *The Times*) and 'Japaneasy going manner in which they toiled through their performances' ('Japanese Village', *Fun*). (Williams 2020)

Towards the turn of the twentieth century, ethnographic displays of human beings began to be seen with increasing frequency at international exhibitions, presented more or less explicitly in terms of race theory and social evolution. At the 1902 Exposition in Earl's Court, Japanese objections to the appearance of their citizens in a panorama with Chinese, Indians, Persians and Egyptians were based, at least in part, on the identity of their neighbours, as one correspondent pointed out in the *Ōsaka Mainichi* newspaper: 'because the Japanese were placed together with barbarians it was distasteful' (qtd. Ziomek 2014: 511). On the other hand, the plan to include Okinawans, Ainu, Koreans, Taiwanese and Chinese in the anthropological exhibition known as the Human Pavilion (*jinruikan*) at the Fifth National Industrial Exposition in Ōsaka in 1903 prompted similar objections from several of those groups. The Chinese, who were to have been represented by a woman with bound feet and a man smoking opium, succeeded in removing themselves from the anthropological gaze of the Japanese public after an official protest (Hur 2012: 58–64; Ziomek 2014: 505–6). Significantly, no mainland Japanese or Western nations were considered for inclusion.

I have lingered over these questions of representation and othering because they are inevitably entangled in the subject matter of this book, even if the exhibitions and expositions of the nineteenth century have little direct connection to children's literature. However, there is one pair of texts that provides a rather unexpected link: W. S. Gilbert and Sir Arthur Sullivan's comic opera, *The Mikado* (1885), and the children's book based on it, Gilbert's *The Story of the Mikado* (1921).

The Mikado was, from its first performance in March 1885, the most popular of the Savoy comic operas. Like Gilbert and Sullivan's other works, it combines memorable tunes, witty and satirical lyrics and a romantic plot of the utmost silliness. Earlier operas had been given a variety of settings, from a Royal Navy vessel to the Court of the Exchequer, and Gilbert's choice of Japan for *The Mikado* appears to have been prompted largely by his realization that there was a gap in the market for such a piece:

> A Japanese executioner's sword hanging on the wall of my library . . . suggested the broad idea upon which the libretto is based. A Japanese piece would afford opportunities for picturesque scenery and costumes, and, moreover, nothing of the kind had ever been attempted in England. There were difficulties in the way. Could a sufficient number of genuine Japanese dresses in good condition be procured in London? How would the ladies of our chorus look in black wigs? Could they be taught to wear the Japanese costume effectively? (Gilbert 1885)

Gilbert may not have chosen the subject matter of *The Mikado* on the basis of any deep knowledge of, or even interest in, Japan, but he was aware that a degree of authenticity would be necessary to produce a professional effect. He even employed the services of one of the teahouse waitresses at the Knightsbridge Japanese Village (which opened while the opera was in preparation) to train his female singers in dancing and deportment (Gilbert 1885). These efforts notwithstanding, the extent to which Japan is more than nominally the opera's setting has long been a point of debate. Gilbert made little attempt to find convincing names for his Japanese characters or places. Titipu, Pish-Tush and Yum-Yum, for example, all contain sound combinations that do not exist in Japanese and were evidently chosen for their comic effect in English. The Japanese language itself is largely absent from the libretto, although it does makes two appearances, most notably at the first entrance of the Mikado in Act II, which features a version of an imperial marching song from the campaigns leading to the Meiji restoration (Seeley 1985: 455). *The Mikado*'s plot is that of a generic romantic comedy rather than a story rich in specifically Japanese elements, and its satire is largely directed at universal human faults and foibles; Pooh-bah's excessive pride in his ancestry, for example, might apply as easily to an English as to a Japanese noble. There are also comically obtrusive Western details, such as Nanki-Poo's position as Second Trombone in a band.

That said, the story does not refrain from exploiting Orientalist stereotypes, such as the despotic habit of ordering painful executions for minor offences, which is as much a reflex response for the Mikado as for Carroll's Queen of Hearts. At a more abstract level, the image of Japan as an inversion or reflection of England may well have been part of the setting's satirical appeal to Gilbert, who had previously written a one-act operetta, *Topsyturveydom* (1874), about 'a country where everything is conducted on principles the very reverse of those that hold good [in Britain]' (Gilbert 1874), a description strikingly similar to Alcock's 1863 description of Japan as 'a country . . . where all – even familiar things – put on new faces, and are curiously reversed'. The observation of a Topsyturveydom native, that 'although everything here is the exact opposite of everything there, yet there isn't as much difference as you may think' (Gilbert 1874), may have resonated when writing about a country that, as Britain's mirror reflection, was both its opposite and its twin.

In the Britain of 1885 few people appear to have felt much queasiness about the opera's portrayal of the Japanese, although Japanese residents are said to have been shocked by it (Checkland 1989: 159); but, as Japan's international standing rose in the succeeding decades, with its military victories over China and Russia and the signing of the 1902 Anglo-Japanese Alliance, sensitivity to Japanese feelings became a matter of *Realpolitik*. The on-stage representation of an Emperor, however fictional, was always likely to cause offence, and indeed the opera was long banned in Japan, receiving its first mainstream production only many decades later (Brooke 2003; Rodman 2015: 288). When Prince Fushimi visited Britain in 1907, the British government took the pre-emptive step of banning *The Mikado* from the stage for the duration of his visit, along with the performance of any of the opera's songs or music. This censorship caused widespread outrage, prompting letters to the newspapers and questions in the House of Commons (Lawrence 1974: 153–8), but was effectively enforced, much to Gilbert's annoyance. His children's book, *The Story of the Mikado*, written in the wake of the visit, presented him with an opportunity to voice his resentment.

The exact date of composition of *The Story of the Mikado* is unclear, but it seems to have been a follow-up to Gilbert's earlier prose retelling of *HMS Pinafore* (1878), *The Pinafore Picture Book* (1908). In the event, publication was delayed until 1921, initially by the author's sudden death in 1911 and subsequently by the paper shortages of the First World War.[9] By the time *The Story of the Mikado* finally appeared, Gilbert's sarcastic references to what was by then a fourteen-year-old slight had lost much of their relevance and may well have puzzled child readers. The book begins:

> It has recently been discovered that Japan is a great and glorious country whose people are brave beyond all measure, wise beyond all telling, amiable to excess, and extraordinarily considerate to each other and to strangers. This is the greatest discovery of the early years of the twentieth century, and is one of the results of the tremendous lesson the Japanese inflicted on the Russians, who attempted to absorb a considerable portion of Manchuria a few years ago. . . . It is important to bear this in mind, because our Government being (in their heart of hearts) a little afraid of the Japanese, are extremely anxious not to irritate or offend them in any way lest they should come over here and give us just such a lesson as they gave the Russians. (Gilbert 1921: 1–2)

The Story of the Mikado is in most respects a faithful retelling of the plot of the opera and includes the lyrics of many of its songs, although with some alterations in consideration of a child readership. For example, the song of Koko, the Lord High Executioner, describing the 'little list' of people he wishes to see beheaded, has been modified to focus on those likely fall under the condemnation of children: 'The teacher who for hours keeps you practising your scales / With an ever-aching wrist – *she* never would be missed' (15). At times, Gilbert reverts to a type of satire that had surfaced in earlier works such as *Patience* (1881), on what he saw as the faddish reverence paid to Japanese art and poetry by British aesthetes at the height of the Japan 'boom'. In discussing the etymology of the name, 'Yum-Yum', he mocks the idea of Japanese as a language uniquely

---

9   The latter is the explanation given by the publisher, Daniel O'Connor, in the book's foreword (Gilbert 1921: vii).

capable of succinctly capturing complex emotional and spiritual states, a quality associated in British minds with minimalist forms such as haiku:

> 'Yum-Yum' means, when translated, 'The full moon of delight which sheds her remarkable beams over a sea of infinite loveliness, thus indicating a glittering path by which she may be approached by those who are willing to brave the perils which necessarily await the daring adventurers who seek to reach her by those means', which shows what a compact language the Japanese is when all these long words can be crammed into two syllables – or rather, into one syllable repeated. (3–4)

In satirizing a variety of targets – British images of the Japanese, homegrown institutions in Japanese disguise, the pusillanimous stance of the British government and the Japanese themselves – Gilbert was sending a complex and perhaps confusing message. As one might expect from a proponent of topsyturveydom, British and Japanese identities are wittily mixed in both *The Mikado* and the children's book it inspired, and E. P. Lawrence is no doubt correct in stating that Gilbert meant to pose the question: 'Are you any less ridiculous than you think the Japanese to be?' (1974: 161). However, the implication that to see one's reflected image in Japanese cultural garb is to make oneself ridiculous cannot be separated from the sense that there is something ridiculous about Japan in the first place.

Seeing ourselves as others see us

In this chapter I have discussed British reactions to Meiji-era Japan and some of the ways in which they were inflected by the metaphors and narratives available from children's literature. These discourses form part of my own cultural inheritance and have influenced my habits of thought as a twenty-first-century British writer. By discussing them I hope, as well as bringing to light a history interesting in its own right, to reduce the likelihood of replicating the same stereotypes unconsciously in this book. However, the ways of thinking about Japan that I have described are not the preserve of Western writers alone; this final section will peer into the looking-glass one more time, to consider the double perspective of modern Japanese people looking back at their own Meiji-era history.

Both Britain and Japan have undergone huge changes in the last century and a half, including major wars and social upheavals, but the transformation that characterized Japan in the Meiji era, with the wholesale importation of foreign systems of government, education, military organization, technology and cultural production, was especially dramatic. It has become a cliché that 'the past is a foreign country', but the British past is arguably more accessible than that of Japan, in terms not only of the continuity of institutions but also of the built environment – points with implications both for the Japanese consumption of British children's literature and for the writing of Japanese literature in British-inspired genres, as I shall show in later chapters. I have noted that a common trope of Western writing is that Japan, like the Cheshire Cat, is liable to be caught in the act of disappearing. I am wary of adding my voice to this chorus, but radical change has undoubtedly been a prominent feature of Japanese history since the Meiji restoration. Time has proved quite as effective an estranging agent as distance in making it a 'foreign country', and the Japan described in this chapter has become almost as alien to the modern Japanese as it was to the British who travelled half the globe to see it. Indeed, contemporary Japanese readers encountering the Japan of the 1870s may find that in many respects they have more in common with those Western observers than with the Japanese of the time.

The cultural distances imposed by geography, on the one hand, and history, on the other, form the explicit and implicit themes of Taiga Sasa's manga, *Bird in Wonderland* (*fushigi no kuni no bādo*), a text that combines many of the concerns of this chapter. Beginning publication in 2015, *Bird in Wonderland* is an adaptation of Isabella Bird's *Unbeaten Tracks in Japan* (1880). In Japan as well as in the West, *Unbeaten Tracks* has rightly become a classic of Japanese travel writing and a valuable historical source for a period when rural Japan was still in transition from the feudal culture of the Edo period. Sasa's Bird is considerably younger than the middle-aged adventurer of reality, but his manga is otherwise quite faithful to her narrative.

Sasa's decision to write a historical manga about Japan from a foreigner's rather than a Japanese perspective may seem counterintuitive, especially when the foreigner did not understand Japanese. Indeed, this makes the process of reading the manga slightly disorientating at first. Bird's own words are written in Japanese, which in the manga is used to represent English, while the Japanese used by other characters is shown as a series of illegible squiggles, reflecting her incomprehension. The technique has the effect of wrong-footing the reader's sense of what counts as a 'foreign' perspective.

One way to understand Sasa's choice of Bird as a point-of-view character might be as an exercise in empathetic and imaginative distancing, providing a 'Martian' view of a world otherwise familiar to the manga's readers. In interview, however,

Sasa has stressed that it is Bird, not the Meiji-era Japanese she encounters, whose mental world more closely resembles that of contemporary Japanese readers:

> When I read accounts by Westerners with modern values of travelling to and staying in pre-modern Japan, they were very convincing and I could empathise with them. Since the West at that time had already modernised, their values were similar to those of us today. In short, although we are Japanese, we can sympathize with the feelings of Westerners at that time more easily than with the feelings of Japanese people before Westernisation. (Sasa 2021)

Western writers on Japanese culture typically have to tread a line between the twin dangers of exoticization and erasure – that is, between giving undue prominence to features that contrast with the customs and perspectives familiar to them and glossing over those differences entirely. For Sasa, however, maximizing the element of unfamiliarity in his portrayal of Meiji-era Japan is a deliberate strategy, aimed at conveying the sense of that world as a lost civilization. He therefore discards familiar aspects and foregrounds those most alien to contemporary Japanese sensibilities:

> To allow readers to have the same experience as Bird, the behaviour and ways of thinking of the Japanese people who appear are deliberately selected and drawn to be completely different from what we are today. There are customs from that time that still remain in modern Japan, but I selected and added emphasis in order for readers to have the feeling of being lost in a 'wonderland' (*fushigi no kuni*) and to have a sense of the 'things that have been lost' (*ushinawareta mono*) through the destruction of a civilization. (Sasa 2021)

One constant, however, is that Lewis Carroll remains a touchstone for this experience of cultural disorientation. Like D. C. Angus before him, Sasa draws on the *Alice* books through the very title of his manga. In this, he is far from alone among Japanese authors, as we will see later in this book. In the meantime, I have shown that children's literature held an important place in the Victorian British imaginary where dealings with Japan were concerned, whether manifesting in anxieties about physical scale, a fascination with mirror images or ambivalence about Japan's development expressed in terms of regret at the passing of the country's 'innocence'. Behind the last of these, especially, lay the uneasy realization that the understanding of Britain's relationship with Japan as one of adult and child, observer and observed, active and passive could not long be sustained, and that the Japanese were in turn developing their own views of the West and their relationship with it. The part played by children's literature in that story will occupy us from this point on.

2

Britain and the origins of Japanese children's literature

Children's literature in the modern sense did not exist in Japan before the beginning of the Meiji era. That is probably a reasonable statement, but it inevitably invites questions of definition. There had long been an extensive oral literature of folk and fairy tales, after all, for which children were an important (though not the only) audience. The Edo period (1603–1867) had also seen written materials such as the woodblock-printed *akahon* (red books), which typically told illustrated traditional stories, although their use had declined well before the end of the Shōgunate (Wakabayashi 2008: 227–8). What was new to the Meiji era, however, was the kind of children's literature that had developed over the previous century in Europe and North America: that is, a significant corpus of original short- and long-form texts, written as literary productions by named authors who had child readers as their intended readership and entertainment as well as education as their end.

The development of such a literature over the course of the Meiji era and beyond makes for a fascinating story. As one aspect of Japan's modernization during this time, the various debates and developments that attended it paralleled those in other areas of Japanese life and culture. Whether Western models should be copied or adapted; whether they should replace, or be integrated into, Japanese traditions – such issues were live ones throughout the period. They inevitably interacted with wider political concerns about the perceived need for Japan to hold its own with the West. Part of the Meiji government's programme involved the introduction of universal schooling, including compulsory primary education, and this naturally opened up space for debate about what the purpose of a children's literature should be. My focus in this chapter is on the part played by British children's books in the development of children's literature in Japan, but wider developments in politics and culture will inevitably feature in that account.

Years before Japanese writers turned their hands to original fiction for children, Western children's literature was being published in translation and thus providing a set of potential models for what a native children's literature might look like. The books selected for translation were of numerous kinds, but I will begin by noting three categories prominent in the early days of Japanese children's literary encounters with the West, though relatively marginal to children's literature as defined earlier: religious books promoted from within the Christian missionary movement; books originally published for adults that had come to capture a child readership; and books of traditional stories.

An example that fits the first two categories is John Bunyan's *The Pilgrim's Progress* (1678). This Puritan allegory of Christian's redemptive journey from the City of Destruction to the Celestial City had long been a staple of English Protestant literature. Although it was by no means solely a children's text, its exciting narrative, plain style and striking evocation of places and people had captured a child readership from the start, as Bunyan himself noted in his prefatory verses to the second part in 1684:

> The very children that do walk the street,
> If they do but my holy Pilgrim meet,
> Salute him will, will wish him well, and say,
> He is the only stripling of the day. (Bunyan 1996: 138)

The appeal of *The Pilgrim's Progress* to young readers continued well into the nineteenth century, as the book's famous appearance in the opening chapter of Louisa M. Alcott's *Little Women* (1868) illustrates. In that novel, Mrs March reminds her teenaged daughters of their childhood love of the story, and Alcott apparently assumes that her readers too will be familiar with it:

> Do you remember how you used to play *Pilgrim's Progress* when you were little things? Nothing delighted you more than to have me tie my piece bags on your backs for burdens, give you hats and sticks and rolls of paper, and let you travel through the house from the cellar, which was the City of Destruction, up, up, to the housetop, where you had all the lovely things you could collect to make a Celestial City. (Alcott 2014: 14)

In Japan, the Meiji era saw several translations of *Pilgrim's Progress*, all successful enough to require multiple editions. The first, by Yoshimine Satō, appeared in the mid-1870s and was taken from a Chinese translation, from which it borrowed what became the book's enduring Japanese title: *Ten Ro Reki Tei* (天路歴程; *Journey on the Road to Heaven*) (Takano 2020: 38). However, the second – the

Figure 2.1 Christian at the Wicket Gate, *Pilgrim's Progress* (Yokohama 1886).

first direct translation from English and the first accompanied by illustrations – is perhaps more noteworthy. It was published in Yokohama in 1886 and was credited to the English missionary William John White,[1] although Michiyo Takano has plausibly suggested that he had assistance from native speakers, the resulting book being written in accomplished literary Japanese (2020: 38). Probably the most striking thing about this edition is the illustrations, which (unlike any subsequent translation of this period) gave Christian's adventures a Japanese setting. Christian himself appears with a topknot and everyone he encounters is in Japanese dress, with architecture and landscape to match. The fight with Apollyon takes place against the placid backdrop of Mount Fuji, and the Wicket Gate by which Christian enters the road to the Celestial City has 'Knock, and it shall be opened unto you' written above it in Japanese (Figure 2.1). As Annie R. Butler acknowledges in *Stories about Japan*, these choices were a deliberate attempt to boost the book's proselytizing power:

The Japanese understand their meaning much better, and the book much more easily, than they would if the pictures were English. Missionaries tell us that the

1 Takano refers to White as an American (2020: 43), but in fact he was born and brought up in Hampshire and received his theological training from Charles Spurgeon at the Pastors' College in Croydon (*Proceedings of the General Conference of Protestant Missionaries* 1901: 739).

people of Japan are getting to be just as fond of Bunyan's wonderful book as the people of England are. (Butler 1888: 102)

Bunyan's text is set in an allegorical dreamscape, albeit one drawing on seventeenth-century Bedfordshire. The kind of cultural domestication attempted in White's edition may thus have been less challenging than in a text with a more historically and geographically specific setting. Here and elsewhere, early translators had to decide between a strategy of domesticating the setting to facilitate understanding and one of preserving the source material as accurately as possible. In an evangelical work such as *The Pilgrim's Progress* the case for domestication might seem compelling, although the Japanese illustrations in White's edition drew some criticism, for example from the later Bunyan translator, Unshū Matsumoto (Takano 2020: 44n.5).

Bunyan's was far from the only text with a dual audience of adults and children to find its way into Japanese in the Meiji era. Such works appeared in a variety of settings, sometimes reflecting the inexact fit between Western and Japanese genre categories. For example, in 1894 a Japanese version of Daniel Defoe's *Robinson Crusoe* (1719), translated by Yūhō Takahashi, appeared as part of the publisher Hakubunkan's World Library (*sekai bunko*), a series focused on accounts of adventure and exploration that indiscriminately mingled fiction and non-fiction. *Robinson Crusoe: Desert Island Castaway Tale* (*robinson kurūsō zettō hyōryū ki*) was thus placed alongside such works as Henry Morton Stanley's *In Darkest Africa* (1890) and Albert Hastings Markham's account of his Arctic voyages, *The Great Frozen Sea* (1880), as well as Miguel de Cervantes's *Don Quixote* (1605) and H. Rider Haggard's *King Solomon's Mines* (1885).[2] Nor was it only books with an appeal to both adult and child audiences that might appear in unexpected contexts. Japan's love affair with Beatrix Potter's *The Tale of Peter Rabbit* (1902) began in the surprising setting of the *Journal of Japanese Agriculture* (*nihon nōgyō zasshi*), which in 1906 published the book's first translation into any foreign language, by Jirō Matsukawa (Kawano 2007).

Among those works translated in the Meiji era with a child readership in mind, the most popular genres were folktales and fairy tales, a literature of

---

2 It is unclear how important the distinction between fiction and non-fiction was regarded as being in the compilation of the World Library series. An earlier translation of *Robinson Crusoe* via Dutch by Kikuro Kuroda, published in 1872 (although written in the 1840s), appears to have been made in the belief that it was a factual account. However, Yoshikiyo Yokoyama's 1857 translation, 'the first published translation of a European work to target a readership of children', was made in the knowledge that it was a novel (Wakabayashi 2008: 232–3). Defoe did not help matters in the lengths he went to in order to give an impression of verisimilitude, which included putting Crusoe's name on the book's title page as its author.

which Japan already had a rich store and thus perhaps more easily assimilated by publishers and readers alike. Hans Andersen and the Brothers Grimm were especially popular and were translated multiple times (Wakabayashi 2008: 237–40). The name most strongly associated with this kind of production was that of Sazanami Iwaya, probably the dominant figure in children's literature in Meiji Japan. At twenty, he was already a rising literary star and a member of the influential Kenyūsha literary club, when he produced what is widely credited as the first original work of children's fiction in Japanese, the anthropomorphic novella *Kogane-maru* (1891), about a dog who avenges the deaths of his parents at the hands (or paws) of a tiger. Iwaya, who was born into a wealthy family and had learned German with the intention of becoming a doctor (German being the language of medicine and science), had been sent a volume of Otto Sutermeister's *Märchen* by his older brother as a child and was soon hooked (Ōsaka International Institute 1993: vol. 1, 97). He explains in his preface to *Kogane-maru* that he was influenced not only by Andersen and the Grimms but also by Goethe's *Reineke Fuchs*, as well as traditional Japanese stories such as 'The Peach Boy' (*momo tarō*) (Iwaya 1891; Ortabasi 2008: 183–4).

Kogane-maru became the first in Hakubunkan's 'Children's Literature Book Series' (*shōnen bungaku sōsho*), but Iwaya was also an indefatigable collector and reteller of folk and fairy tales, which he published in various series, including *Old Tales of Japan* (*nihon mukashibanashi*) (1894–6) and *Fairy Tales of Japan* (*nihon otogibanashi*) (1896–8), each running to twenty-four volumes, and the 100-volume *Fairy Tales of the World* (*sekai otogibanashi*) (1899–1908). *Otogibanashi* is usually translated as 'fairy tale', but the stories included some material that would not be conventionally classed as such in the West. Among the rest, Iwaya published a children's version of the first voyage of Swift's *Gulliver's Travels*, dealing with Gulliver's visit to Lilliput. He was aware that this was a literary and satirical work, as his preface attests, but felt able to include it in his collection, perhaps because it featured diminutive people and could therefore be assimilated to the existing Japanese folk tradition of 'little people's islands' (Tanaka 2009: 79–80).

As well as producing original fiction and anthologies, Iwaya was an active and influential editor of children's literary magazines, a type of publication that began to appear in Japan from the 1880s.[3] These were typically general-interest magazines and included readers' letters, poems and articles as well as

---

3　Earlier magazines had in fact existed, such as the missionary-published *Happy Visit* (*yorokobi no otozure*), which began publication in December 1876 (Chimori 2005: 95), but this was a more evangelical affair than the kind of general-purpose magazine that followed.

material provided by the editors. The earliest such publication was *Children's Garden* (*shōnen en*), published from 1888 under the editorship of Teizaburō Yamagata. They quickly proliferated, however, usually in monthly or bimonthly formats, and *Children's Garden* was soon joined by *Young Citizens* (*shōkokumin*, 1889–95), *Japanese Children* (*nihon shōnen*, 1906-38) and *The Girls' Friend* (*shōjo no tomo*, 1908–55), among others. The publication with which Iwaya is particularly associated was *Children's World* (*shōnen sekai*), which he edited from its foundation in 1895 until 1917. The word *shōnen*, which in modern Japanese means specifically 'boy', at this period referred to children in general, but before long *Children's World* gave rise to two spin-off magazines, also edited by Iwaya: *Infants' World* (*yōnen sekai*, from 1900) and *Girls' World* (*shōjo sekai*, from 1906). *Shōjo* was a recent coinage (Monden 2014: 266), but a notion of gendered reading for children was evidently already becoming established.

Children's magazines were popular and relatively affordable, and their proliferation, along with the expansion of their potential audience with the introduction of compulsory primary school education from 1872 and the attendant increase in literacy rates, created a benign environment for the growth of children's literature. Much of the magazines' content was naturally comprised of original Japanese material, but they also provided a setting for the publication of Western literature in translation. The range was international: Jules Verne's adventures, Hector Malot's sentimental novel *Sans Famille* (1878) and literary fables such as Leo Tolstoy's 'Ivan the Fool' (1886) were all popular, along with Andersen and the Grimms. In the 1870s and 1880s, English-language texts enjoyed no particular prominence in Japan; however, as the common tongue of two of the Western powers with which Japan had the closest dealings, and of many of the missionaries active in its schools, English enjoyed a structural advantage that only increased over time (Nakata 2000: 63–78).

An important case in point is that of Shizuko Wakamatsu, one of the foremost female writers and translators of the era, who is remembered among other things for her translation of Frances Hodgson Burnett's novel, *Little Lord Fauntleroy*. Born in 1864, Wakamatsu was the daughter of a samurai who found himself on the losing side in the civil wars of that decade and whose family was consequently stripped of its wealth and position when Wakamatsu was still a young child. Having spent some time with a merchant's family in Tōkyō, she was placed in a Presbyterian mission school in Yokohama, where she eventually became a Christian. Wakamatsu thrived at the school, being valued for her intellectual ability and especially for her unusual talent in English. She went on to become a teacher and from 1886 began to publish work in the magazine, *Women's*

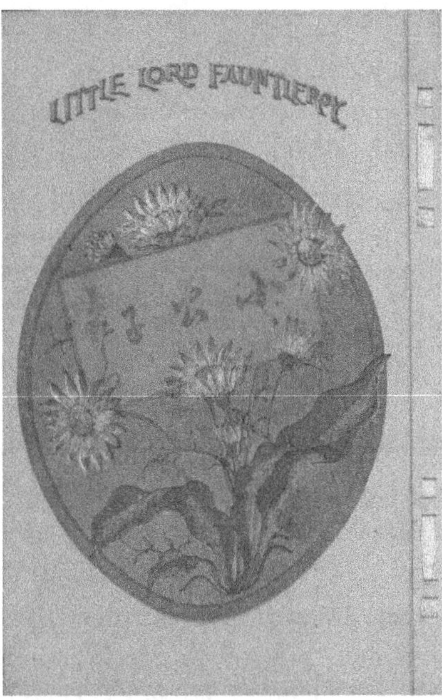

Figure 2.2 Cover, Shizuko Wakamatsu's *The Little Lord* (*shōkōshi*), volume 1, 1891. Original in the possession of Ōsaka Prefectural Central Library.

Education Journal (*jogaku zasshi*), eventually marrying its editor, Yoshiharu Iwamoto. Her translation of *Little Lord Fauntleroy* appeared in instalments in *Women's Education Journal* from March 1890 to January 1892 (Copeland 2000: 129), with separate publication in book form following shortly after (Figure 2.2).

Burnett's *Little Lord Fauntleroy* was published as a book in 1886, having likewise been published in instalments the previous year in the American children's magazine, *St. Nicholas*.[4] Burnett is now probably better known for her later novels, *A Little Princess* (1905) and *The Secret Garden* (1911), but *Fauntleroy* was her breakout book. It is the story of Cedric Errol, a boy born in New York to an English father and an American mother (now widowed), who unexpectedly finds himself heir to an earldom and is obliged to travel to England to be prepared for his role. Through his good nature, honesty and unaffected charm he gradually wins over his hard-hearted grandfather, the current earl, and brings about a reconciliation between him and his mother, who had been rejected because of the earl's anti-American prejudice. The book was wildly

---

4　A native of Manchester, Burnett lived a transatlantic life, with long periods spent both in Britain and the United States.

popular, and the signature Fauntleroy 'look', with long hair, velvet suit and lace collar, became a fashion sensation.

Fauntleroy's popularity may account for Wakamatsu's choice of it as a book to translate. However, despite its initial appearance in *St. Nicholas* and the age of its title character, *Fauntleroy* is not obviously a children's book. Anne Thwaite has stated that 'Cedric . . . is always seen from the outside, from the adult point of view' (qtd. Copeland 2000: 137), and, while this is an overstatement, Burnett (at the time known primarily as a writer for adults) spends as long describing the impression made by Cedric on others as theirs on him. Moreover, the Fauntleroy suits inspired by the book appear to have been more popular with parents than with the boys forced to wear them. That said, there is little point in imposing a procrustean categorization that will place the novel neatly on one side or other of a child-adult divide. Like many of the books already mentioned in this chapter – *Pilgrim's Progress*, *Robinson Crusoe*, *Gulliver's Travels* – *Fauntleroy* enjoyed a mixed audience. In Japan, Wakamatsu's translation, *The Little Lord* (*shōkōshi*), appeared in a magazine aimed at women readers, but in 1890 there were as yet few alternatives. The first children's magazine, *Children's Garden*, had appeared less than two years previously, and it was natural that Wakamatsu would continue to publish in the journal where she was a regular contributor and of which her husband was editor. About halfway through the serialization, *The Little Lord* moved from the main pages of *Women's Education Journal* to its new 'Children's Column' (*jiran*), although whether that was because it was regarded as having a potential child readership or because of its narrative concern with parenting is uncertain. As Milek Ortabasi notes, a dual readership of mothers and their children was not regarded as mutually exclusive:

> The column was to 'provide mothers with information about raising children, as well as to offer stories that parents could read to their young'. In other words, children themselves were not intended as the immediate audience for *Shōkōshi*; rather, their female parents were defined as the conduit through which material for children should be disseminated. (Ortabasi 2008: 181)

Wakamatsu's work was pioneering in several respects. Burnett's brisk, straightforward narrative style had no obvious parallel in Japanese literature. In developing a vernacular equivalent, Wakamatsu was undertaking a task that went well beyond conveying the meaning of the text; she was also helping to create a literary space that later writers of original fiction could exploit in their development of the Japanese children's novel. Accustomed as we are to reading children's fiction, it is easy to forget that its conventions are the result of choices made by writers rather than an inevitable development. When Iwaya wrote *Kogane-maru*, for example, he adopted a classical style of literary expression (*bungotai*), in the belief that this would be easier to understand for children whose education had been in that kind of literature. Wakamatsu, making her translation at around the same time, wrote *The Little Lord* using a more colloquial Japanese influenced by conversational speech patterns. The *genbun icchi* movement, which aimed to bring spoken and written Japanese closer together, was controversial at the time, and Wakamatsu's adoption of it was a risky strategy. However, as Nobumichi Ueda comments, Wakamatsu's 'selection, which should have been irrational (*hijōshiki*) from a common-sense perspective, turned out to be ahead of its time, and gained the attention of the world' (Ueda 2002). It would be several more decades before *genbun icchi* became the norm for published literature, but Wakamatsu's choice was ultimately vindicated; even later editions of *Kogane-maru* were edited to approximate spoken language more closely.

Wakamatsu's immersion in Western culture was such that she was able to portray with conviction and authenticity the kind of child that Burnett had created in Cedric Errol, a boy whose virtue had the power to melt the heart and change the character of his grandfather and who exemplified innocent adherence to the principles of fairness and justice rather than any internalization of Neo-Confucian ideals of familial obligation. He was an early Japanese example of the kind of pure-hearted child who would come to prominence in the literature of the Taishō era (1912–26), when childlike innocence would become a prized characteristic. Wakamatsu believed strongly in the potential of children's literature to effect moral education and clearly saw Cedric Errol as a potential role model for her child readers. As she wrote in *Women's Education Journal* in 1890, the year *The Little Lord* began publication:

> I think the novel is not unlike a child's toy. Many people will tell you that the wares offered in a toy store lack value – and I think some will make similar statements about the novel. But the fact of the matter is, toys do have value. They play an important role in a child's education, proving to be far more effective at instructing the child on how to make and use items than are textbooks and teachers. Novels, too, have a similar role to play in moral reform and education.
> (Wakamatsu, quoted Copeland 2000: 135)

The Western-inflected moral sensibility implied here becomes more apparent when Wakamatsu's version of *Little Lord Fauntleroy* is contrasted with a second translation – or rather, adaptation – that also appeared in 1890, this time in the explicitly child-facing pages of *Children's Library* (*shōnen bunko*), a magazine created as a spin-off from *Children's Garden*.[5] The writing of *Neikeiji* (roughly, 'An Extraordinary Child') was credited to Ryōshi Shūko, but this was a pseudonym of Isō Yamagata, the brother of *Children's Garden*'s editor. In writing his version, Yamagata made the significant decision to move the story's action from the United States and Britain to Japan. Cedric becomes Kiyō, and rather than New York his mother is widowed in the commercial city of Ōsaka, whence she and Kiyō are recalled to the Tōkyō compound of the aristocratic Count Sano. Yamagata's story was not carried through to completion, so we can only speculate as to how it would have been concluded, but the extant part reveals notable differences of emphasis from Wakamatsu's text. As Ortabasi points out:

> Kiyo'o may be charming and sweet (*kawaiirashii*, as we are told repeatedly), but his superior moral qualities are not enough to inspire the grownups around him to treat him as a social peer. In *Neikeiji*, the child protagonist is a model of Meiji schoolboy virtue: the narrator makes sure to comment that he excels at his Chinese and English studies. However, he is not the powerful mediator between social classes – and even nations – that he is in Burnett's and Shizuko [Wakamatsu]'s versions. (Ortabasi 2008: 189)

The transplantation of a story from one country and culture to another always brings complex consequences in its wake. The substitution of Ōsaka for the United States and Tōkyō for England is in many ways astute; in both cases, an energetic, 'brash' commercial culture is set against one that piques itself on its sophistication and civilized values. The Ōsaka-Tōkyō contrast would surely have been more readily legible to the average 1890s Japanese child reader than the America-Britain contrast of Burnett's novel. But such surface similarities are inevitably accompanied by deeper and less visible differences such as those noted by Ortabasi.

Issues of localization are apparent once again in the two British nineteenth-century children's books that were to have the greatest long-term impact on Japanese culture, Lewis Carroll's *Alice's Adventures in Wonderland* and *Through the Looking-Glass*. Both books have been translated into Japanese many times – more than 400 in total, according to Amanda Kennell (2017: 7) – and *Alice's Adventures in Wonderland* has reportedly had more than 1,200 Japanese editions (Lindseth and Tannenbaum 2015: 22). *Alice* has been influential on Japanese creators in a variety of media, and Tenniel's illustrations have become

---

5 Although, as the title implies, *Children's Library* was intended as a children's publication, its age profile gradually expanded, to the point where it was renamed simply *Library* (*bunko*).

universally recognized icons, quoted and referenced in fashion, advertising, music and other facets of Japanese popular culture, as I will discuss in the next chapter. Even Alice's cat, Kitty, a very minor 'character' in *Through the Looking-Glass*, achieved her own immortality by inspiring the designer Yūko Shimizu to name her Sanrio character Hello Kitty – a quintessentially Japanese figure who is nevertheless officially stated by Sanrio to be an English child, Kitty White, living in the suburbs of London (Rubin 2014).

Although they have been published in more than 174 languages, the *Alice* books are a perpetually challenging choice for translation. With their innumerable puns and dense references to, and parodies of, sometimes obscure English poems and nursery rhymes, they depend to an unusual degree on just the kind of cultural and linguistic context that the process of translation tends to strip out and that a readership of children can least be relied on to supply for itself, especially in a country with as little shared culture as Meiji-era Japan had with Victorian Britain. The differences between the languages themselves are another potential barrier. Mikiko Chimori notes:

> While the large number of homophones in Japanese facilitates the creative translation of puns from English, the lack of phonetic variety to which it is due has the opposite effect on attempts to reproduce onomatopoeic and other kinds of soundplay from English. (Chimori 2005: 76)

As well as these phonemic difficulties, Chimori further notes the mismatch between the languages' grammatical structures, with the highly contextual nature of Japanese linguistic praxis tending to run Carroll's logic-chopping into the quicksands of vagueness and ambiguity (Chimori 2005: 76–7).

The *Alice* books were also difficult for early translators to appraise in terms of genre. They were not novels in the sense that *Little Lord Fauntleroy* was, but neither were they literary fairy tales in the tradition of Hans Andersen. There were also aspects of Alice's behaviour that must have seemed jarring in Meiji-era society. Alice is independent, unafraid and at times quite assertive in the face of adult authority. It has been suggested that the canonical six months between the events of the two books (one taking place when she is seven, the other when she is seven and a half) evidence a degree of socialization: *Looking-Glass* Alice is politer and more solicitous, and her hitherto unruly hair has been tamed by the acquisition of a hairband (Labbe 2003: 26–8). However, such changes are relatively slight, and even *Looking-Glass* Alice falls well short of the polite deference and physical timidity expected of a well-brought-up Meiji girl.

Japanese translators of the *Alice* books did have some advantages. Like *The Pilgrim's Progress*, Carroll's books are dream narratives, and this fact provides some hedge against the necessity to render the material world entirely realistically. Only the very beginnings and endings of the two stories are set in Victorian England, and then only in two limited locations: the bank where Alice and her sister are sitting in *Alice's Adventures in Wonderland* and the drawing room of Alice's house in *Through the Looking-Glass*. Again, although Japan did not have a tradition of nonsense literature in the style of Carroll's books, stories in which a protagonist gains temporary access to another world were not unfamiliar. This might happen through the intervention of magical or supernatural powers, as in the ancient tale of Tarō Urashima, but it could also come about through a dream.

The traditional story, 'The Dream of Akinosuke' (based on a Chinese tale and later collected by Lafcadio Hearn), provides some intriguing parallels to that of Alice. It begins with the protagonist, Akinosuke, falling asleep while sitting with friends under a tree in his garden. On waking, he is greeted by a procession of richly dressed attendants, who escort him to the palace of their king. The king welcomes him warmly, marries him to his beautiful daughter and makes him the governor of a nearby island province. Akinosuke rules the province in peace and prosperity for some years, his wife bears him seven children and all is well. One day, however, his wife dies suddenly. The grieving Akinosuke builds her an opulent tomb, and soon after, the king commands him to return to his own country. When he wakes – this time in reality – his friends tell him that he was asleep for only a few minutes, but that during that time they saw a yellow butterfly, perhaps his soul, emerge from his nostril, where it was captured by an ant and dragged into its nest, then ejected a little later. On digging out the nest, Akinosuke and his companions find that it is laid out just like the country of his dream, with a large central chamber that might be the king's palace, a subsidiary nest like the island province and a stone resembling a burial monument. Beneath the stone, they find the clay-interred body of a female ant.

The differences from the *Alice* books are obvious, but the parallels are also striking. Not only do both protagonists fall asleep while sitting outside with companions, they then follow a creature down a hole into an alternative underground world in which they consort with nobility and royalty. Moreover, on waking they find that their real-life surroundings – the ants' nest in 'Akinosuke', the chess pieces in *Through the Looking-Glass* – recall the contents of their dream. I point out these parallels, not to suggest any direct connection between these very different stories but only to note that in some respects the structure of the *Alice* books was not entirely alien to existing Japanese story traditions.[6]

Although only a few pages of the *Alice* books are set in England, one should not exaggerate the freedom this affords a translator. Victorian society is a strong influence on both Wonderland and the Looking-Glass Country, its conventions defining by their very absence or inversions what makes something 'nonsensical' in the first place. As Sadie Stein puts it:

> a nonsense world requires a kind of straight man – a sense world – to function as the opposition. [Carroll] placed Alice in a world that was a stark contrast to the rigors and rules of Victorian England. What happens when you take that Englishness away? (Stein 2015)

The answer to Stein's question, as far as Meiji Japan is concerned, is provided by the first translations of the books, made for a Japanese readership that as yet had only a limited context of reception through which to understand them.

Appropriately, perhaps, the Alice books were translated in reverse order, with *Through the Looking-Glass* appearing first. A version by Tenkei Hasegawa, titled *Mirror World – A Western Fairy Tale* (*kagami sekai – seiyō otogibanashi*), was published in 1899 in the magazine, *Children's World*. *Alice's Adventures in Wonderland* was not translated until 1908, when two chapters appeared in *The Girls' Friend*, in Shizuo Nagashiro's translation. Nagashiro later expanded this to a complete version, *The Story of Alice* (*arisu monogatari*), published in 1912; but in the meantime no less than three other translations had appeared, of which the first, in 1910, was *The Story of Ai's Dream* (*aichan no yume monogatari*), by Eikan Maruyama. Maruyama's therefore stands as the first complete translation of *Alice's Adventures in Wonderland* into Japanese.

The word 'translation' suggests a close correspondence between source and target texts, but this is far from the case for all these versions. In part, this is the result of the practical obstacles to translation noted earlier. However, it also reflects the fact that the popular Western conception of translation, as a self-effacing procedure on the translator's part, designed to give as clear and undistorted a view of the original text as possible, was far from universal in Meiji Japan. Isō Yamagata, for example, referred somewhat disparagingly to direct translations as 'dry and tasteless' in justifying his changes to *Little Lord Fauntleroy* in *Neikeiji* (qtd. Ortabasi 2008: 188). Translators might expect to stamp their own imprint

---

6　There has in fact been a recent suggestion that Hearn's narration of the story – although not the body of the story itself, which dates to the Tang dynasty – was influenced by his reading of *Alice* (Nasuno 2020: 38–9).

on the texts passing through their hands and – especially in the case of children's texts – to take an active part in adapting them to the needs of their local readers, providing children with a story easily comprehensible within their existing context of knowledge and conformable to Meiji-era norms and values.

This process can be seen to various degrees in the translations of the *Alice* books, as Chimori's comparative discussion demonstrates (Chimori 2005: 115–40). Hasegawa's *Mirror World*, for example, is not a straightforward translation of Carroll's *Through the Looking-Glass*, from which it diverges in many respects, both major and minor. The renaming of Alice to something more recognizably Japanese (Mī) and the replacement of the book's game of chess with a similar Japanese game, *shōgi*, are hardly surprising, but Hasegawa's alterations are far more thoroughgoing. As Chimori puts it, Hasegawa's is 'neither a complete translation nor an adaptation, but an amalgamation of Japanese and Western narrative forms, which made it possible to transplant a work of imagination from its Victorian origins to a Meiji setting' (Chimori 2005: 118). One can see this cultural transplantation at work in the depiction of Mī, now a suitably decorous and appealingly incapable Meiji maiden. Where Alice runs downhill and jumps a stream without difficulty, Mī stumbles, tumbles and lands repeatedly on her bottom as she gingerly makes her way down the slope (Chimori 2005: 123).

The most notable of Hasegawa's changes concerns the story's conclusion. The scene in which Alice is promoted from pawn to queen is one that could not have been translated directly, *shōgi* having no such piece available, but in fact Hasegawa completely removes the book's last five chapters, replacing them with material of his own invention. The episode of Tweedledum and Tweedledee concludes with Mī running into the woods and undergoing a series of startling and at times terrifying adventures, including one in which she finds herself in the house of an ogre (*oni*) and is served a severed human arm. Such incidents may not be very Carrollian, but they are effective in assimilating Mī's world to that of the Japanese fairy tales familiar to Hasegawa's readers. The claim of Gorō Niwa, one of the Meiji-era translators of *Alice's Adventures in Wonderland*, that 'the bones [of the story] are foreign, and the flesh local' (Niwa 1911: 1), is widely applicable to Meiji-era translations of Carroll and other Western authors.

Hasegawa's translation, despite its departures from Carroll's text, was to some extent constrained by the magazine's use of Tenniel's illustrations, or rather a set of copies incorporating some slight elements of domestication, for example in the depiction of Alice's facial features (Vaclavik 2019: 104–5). Other Japanese publishers of the *Alice* books commissioned homegrown artists and were thus potentially freer to introduce changes. Shōtarō Kawabata's pictures, which accompanied Nagashiro's 1908 translation of *Alice's Adventures in Wonderland* in *The Girls' Friend*, for example, while clearly influenced by Tenniel in terms of subject and composition, depict an Alice who is much easier to conceive as a dark-haired Japanese girl in Western-style clothes, one considerably older than the seven years of Carroll's protagonist. In the West at this period, Tenniel's vision of Alice was competing with those of other artists, such as those in the editions illustrated by the Americans Blanche McManus (1899), Fanny Cory (1902), Maria Kirk (1905) and Bessie Pease Gutmann (1909). However, in both Japan and the West, it was Tenniel's original that had the most staying power and is most readily associated with Alice today, beyond even the popular instantiation by Walt Disney in 1951.

It is a similar story when it comes to the title of *Alice's Adventures in Wonderland*, where a bewildering array of variations appeared before the now standard version, *Fushigi no Kuni no Arisu* (不思議の国のアリス), was coined in the late 1920s and confirmed in Toshio Tanaka's 1955 Iwanami Shōnen Bunko translation. Before that, Carroll's book had been published as *The Story of Ai's Dream* (*ai-chan no yume monogatari*, 1910), *Long Fairy Tale about a Child's Dream* (*chōhen otogibanashi kodomo no yume*, 1911), *The Story of Alice* (*arisu monogatari*, 1912) and *Mari's Journey through Dreamland* (*mari-chan no yume no kuni ryokō*, 1925), among other variants. It is a salutary reminder that the apparent solidity and self-evidentiality of canonical texts, and of canons themselves, is often contingent on factors that may be relatively arbitrary – a point to which I will return in the next chapter.

The invention of childhood

If the Meiji era saw the beginnings of children's literature in Japan, both in translation and in the form of original Japanese texts, the succeeding Taishō era consolidated it. There is of course something artificial about treating the transitions between imperial eras as though they were sharp cultural divisions, but here it has some justification. The tone of the Meiji era had inevitably been set by the manner of the regime's foundation, which was effectively as a revolutionary government, particularly in its early decades. It overturned a societal structure that had lasted more than 250 years and imported Western technology, science, fashions, customs and organizational structures on a scale never before seen, while at the same time working vigorously to reinforce its own legitimacy by an appeal to Japan's deep past, centred on the person of the

Emperor. No aspect of cultural life was exempt from its mission to foster a sense of Japan as a people united in the common purpose of national renewal, and education was a special focus of government attention. The Imperial Rescript on Education, issued in 1890 and thereafter recited daily in all schools until 1945, emphasized the selfless values to be applied in daily life to family, friends and strangers as well as the duty to offer one's life to the state should circumstances require it (Oguma 2002: 32). In such an environment, children's literature was naturally valued for its didactic potential.

The emergence of children's literature in the Meiji era signalled that children were an audience worth addressing; however, its emphasis was generally on preparing those children for adulthood by providing them with factual knowledge and instilling in them moral and social values, exemplified in the plots and characters of fiction. Stories that rewarded good and punished evil (*kanzen chōaku*) or that featured exemplary characters who conformed to slogans such as 'good wife, wise mother' (*ryōsai kenbo*), a four-character phrase coined in 1875 by the educationalist Masanao Nakamura, tended to meet with approval. Didacticism has been a perennial feature of children's literature the world over, but the tradition of evaluating a book's worth by the extent to which it offered suitable models for emulation was particularly strong in Meiji Japan and had a lasting effect on the Japanese children's literature canon.

By the time the Emperor Taishō ascended the Chrysanthemum Throne, a place of relative constitutional stability had been reached, and the country had successfully established itself as a modern industrial state and a regional military and imperial power. Attention began to shift from the public aspects of life that had dominated the previous decades to the family and the domestic sphere (Jinnō 2017: 84–6). In children's literature, one aspect of this change was greater emphasis on children as people with unique qualities and virtues, rather than as half-formed adults. In Western terms, we might see this as analogous to the move from the Lockean view of children as *tabula rasa* to be shaped by adult guidance towards something more akin to the Rousseauian conception of children as enjoying access to a purity of experience and consciousness inaccessible to their elders. In British children's literature, the latter conception reached its zenith in the years immediately prior to the Taishō era, in the so-called Golden Age books of the decades either side of the turn of the twentieth century. The First World War dealt the Golden Age valorization of childhood innocence a severe blow in the West, but Japan, which had only limited involvement in the conflict, continued to develop the principle throughout the Taishō era. Rebecca Copeland, paraphrasing the children's literature historian Michimasa Satō, notes that children's literature 'does not consist of stories and verses handed down to children from above but, rather, works that explore a child's world from a child's perspective. Before such works could be created, of course, "the child" had to be invented' (Copeland 2000: 137–8). In Japan, that invention can be dated to the Taishō era.

The influential children's magazine *Red Bird* (*akai tori*), which was first published in July 1918 under the editorship of Miekichi Suzuki, was explicit in positioning itself as a periodical of higher literary quality than had hitherto appeared for children. Its contributors included Ryūnosuke Akutagawa, Junichirō Tanizaki, Kan Kikuchi and many other luminaries of the Japanese literary world. (Anglophone readers are invited to imagine W. B. Yeats, T. S. Eliot, Ezra Pound and Ernest Hemingway all rolling up their sleeves to create a children's magazine.) Along with his attempt to raise the literary tone, Suzuki was a vocal advocate of the more elevated conception of childhood mentioned earlier:

> *Red Bird* . . . is in the vanguard of an epoch-making movement to conserve and develop the purity of children by gathering together the sincere efforts of the best writers and illustrators of today and encouraging the creative work of young writers for children. (Suzuki 1918)

This passage, drawn from the magazine's manifesto, combines both an end – to conserve and develop the 'purity of children' (*kodomo no junsei*) – and a means, the fostering of high-quality, contemporary children's literature. The aim has subtly changed from that of the Meiji era; now the focus is less on the literature's power to lead children towards maturity and an adult role in society and more on the promotion of a refined form of childhood itself, through the provision of a space where children can imaginatively explore and express their own natures. Suzuki's project fostered a generation of Japanese writers of stories, songs and literary fairy tales in which childlike innocence (*dōshin*) was a prominent quality, many of whom were published in his magazine and in others that participated in the *Red Bird* 'movement' (*undō*). Kazue Kawahara suggests that the prominence of the ideal of *dōshin*, and of the *dōwa* (fairy stories) and *dōyō* (children's songs) that were produced under its influence, was a reaction to the rapid sociological changes of the previous generation:

> Modernisation and industrialisation, taken up and driven forward by the government, had wrought great changes in private life by the end of the Meiji era . . . One consequence was an increasing receptivity to modern Western ideas of people as citizens rather than subjects, but another was an increase

of utilitarianism and hedonism in private life. . . . It is natural that innocence, idealism and unselfishness grew more venerated in reciprocal relation to the growing inclination towards insular 'success', and children's souls became the central focus of this veneration. (qtd. Chimori 2005: 90)

What was the place of British children's texts in this changed environment? To answer that question, we must bear in mind both the position of the texts themselves and also their indirect role as influences on, and models for, native Japanese literary productions. As Judy Wakabayashi notes, the latter was a function that they had fulfilled from the start:

Many works now regarded as classics of children's literary heritage were translated in the Meiji period, not only extending the canonization of these works beyond their original borders but also helping to shape Japanese concepts of what constitutes a canonical work for children. Translations presented models of well-written and interesting works, waking Japanese writers to the possibility of creating their own works that might appeal to children. (Wakabayashi 2008: 245)

The manifesto that Suzuki published in the first issue of *Red Bird* compared the state of Japanese children's literature unfavourably with that in the West, lamenting that 'unlike Westerners, we Japanese have, sadly, almost never been proud of any true artist producing pure reading matter for children' (Suzuki 1918). Given this judgement, it is not surprising that among the magazine's early publications was a twenty-four-page narrative version of J. M. Barrie's 1904 play, *Peter Pan*, perhaps the most celebrated British text to explore the *dōshin* conception of childhood. Appearing in 1921, the story was introduced by Suzuki as a 'purely Western tale' – one moreover that his readers were expected already to be aware of, being, '*needless to say*, the famous fairy tale play (*dōwageki*) by the British author, Barrie' (Suzuki 1921, 3, my emphasis).

Japanese writers and editors at this time were clearly well aware of British children's literature. In general terms it seems fair to speak, as Wakabayashi does, of its role in modelling what a literature for children might look like and even in contributing to the Japanese conception of childhood itself. More specific influence is often harder to pin down, but plausible cases can nevertheless often be made. Amanda Kennell, for example, argues persuasively that Ryūnosuke Akutagawa's late novella, *Kappa* (1927), which has been linked with various literary works, notably *Gulliver's Travels*, also bears the strong imprint of *Alice's Adventures in Wonderland* (2017: 94–104). Early in 1927, Kan Kikuchi, who, like Akutagawa, was one of Suzuki's *Red Bird* contributors, commissioned him to undertake translations of both *Alice's Adventures in Wonderland* and *Peter Pan* for a series of books that he was editing for primary school pupils. The task was forestalled by Akutagawa's death, although Kikuchi himself completed and published both translations, with *Alice* appearing late in 1927 and *Peter Pan* eighteen months later (Kennell 2017: 89). That Akutagawa wrote *Kappa* while working on his *Alice* translation lends plausibility to the suggestion of some seepage from one text to the other, conscious or otherwise. Certainly, there is circumstantial evidence: the narrator of *Kappa* begins his story by following a strange creature – a *Kappa* (a type of supernatural creature, or *yōkai*) – down a hole and, after an extended fall, arrives in a world where he meets a variety of characters who invert and satirize the familiar world. Madness is of course a major theme of Carroll's text, but in the hands of Akutagawa, whose own mother suffered from mental illness and whose fear that he would take after her may have been a factor in his suicide in July 1927, it assumes a much darker inflection.

Lewis Carroll and Kenji Miyazawa

Kappa was not a children's book, but another writer on whom *Alice* appears to have had considerable influence was Kenji Miyazawa, perhaps the most celebrated children's writer of the Taishō and early Shōwa periods. Miyazawa was born in 1896 in Hanamaki, in the large and sparsely populated northern prefecture of Iwate. A polymath with wide knowledge of literature, languages, music and the natural sciences, he produced his first *dōwa* in August 1918, perhaps inspired by Suzuki's manifesto in the inaugural issue of *Red Bird* the previous month. However, whether because he lacked connections or because of a difference of artistic approach, he never succeeded in having his work published in that magazine, the exception being an advertisement for his self-published collection of stories, *The Restaurant of Many Orders* (*chūmon no ōi ryōriten*) (1924).

The tales in that collection, like Miyazawa's other stories, often feature uncanny encounters with nature, talking and otherwise anthropomorphised creatures and dreamlike events. Although his characters say and do things that may provoke approval or disapproval, Miyazawa (like Carroll) refrains from the kind of neat reduction to a moral associated with the fabular form. Many of his stories were inspired by Iwate Prefecture itself, which Miyazawa transformed into a fictionalized personal 'dreamland' (*dorīmurando*) named 'Ihatov'.[7] Ihatov

---

7　The full title of Miyazawa's collection is *Ihatov Dōwa: The Restaurant of Many Orders*.

is Iwate, in fact, seen through the glass of fantasy, as Miyazawa explains in his *Red Bird* advertisement:

> Īhatov is a place name. If you want to find the place, the fields are the same that Big and Little Claus farmed. It's in the same world as the Looking-Glass Land that the girl Alice found her way to. It is said to be far northeast of the Tepantar Desert, and far to the east of Ivan's Kingdom. Indeed, it is Japan's Iwate Prefecture, as it actually existed as a dreamland in the imagination of the author. (Miyazawa 1925)

Miyazawa was the right age to have grown up on the Hakubunkan 'Children's Literature Book Series' and magazines such as *Children's World,* and in this passage he shows how his childhood reading (including of Carroll) became a means to enchant the landscape of his home. Īhatov is constructed by mixing the real Iwate with imaginative elements drawn from world literature. Of the texts alluded to here, three were published in Miyazawa's childhood. The earliest is Hans Andersen's 1835 story, 'Little Claus and Big Claus', which was translated into Japanese in 1884 as the second volume of Hakubunkan's 'Children's Literature Book Series', immediately after Iwaya's *Kogane-Maru.* 'Ivan's Kingdom' refers to Tolstoy's 1886 literary fairy tale, 'Ivan the Fool', which had been translated for *Children's World* by Tenkei Hasegawa in 1902, as 'Big Devil and Little Devil' (*daiakuma to shōakuma*), three years after the same translator's version of *Through the Looking-Glass.*

The remaining reference, to the Tepantar Desert, is an outlier, since it is taken from a text that Miyazawa could not have read in childhood. The phrase appears in the poem, 'The Land of Exile', in Rabindranath Tagore's collection of children's poems and stories, *The Crescent Moon* (1913). In 'The Land of Exile', a young boy repeatedly asks his mother to tell him about the Tepantar Desert – a place that may be their lost homeland, or a land of story, or an evocation of the elusiveness of childhood itself. The poem concludes:

> The shepherd boy has gone home early from the pasture, and men have left their fields to sit on mats under the eaves of their huts, watching the scowling clouds.
>
> Mother, I have left all my books on the shelf – do not ask me to
>
> do my lessons now.
>
> When I grow up and am big like my father, I shall learn all that
>
> must be learnt.
>
> But just for to-day, tell me, mother, where the desert of Tepantar in the fairy tale is? (Tagore 2012: 25)

Tagore was already celebrated by the time *The Crescent Moon* was published in 1913, becoming the first Asian to win the Nobel Prize for Literature in that same year, but Miyazawa's interest may have been piqued by the poet's appearance as a guest lecturer at Japan Women's University in Tōkyō in July 1916, as part of his first visit to the country. Miyazawa's younger sister Toshi, with whom he had an especially close bond, was a student there at the time, and it seems likely that she would have attended the event and reported back to her brother (Yamane 2003: 51–2). In any case, the poem's plangent melancholy, its call for the postponement of adulthood and its desire to use imagination to transform dull reality into something luminous and magical were all qualities to which Miyazawa would have responded strongly.

Carroll's Looking-Glass Land is one element among many in Miyazawa's description of Ihatov. However, there is evidence that Britain loomed particularly large in his conception of that country. His 1923 essay, 'The English Shore', recounts how, as an agricultural student, he found himself visiting a stretch of the Kitakami River near his home town. The riverbank contained pale slabs of mudstone that made him think of the White Cliffs of Dover and – along with a periodic rising and falling of the river that was actually caused by local conditions but could be read as a kind of 'tide' – led him to dub the place 'The English Shore' and to incorporate it into his dream version of Iwate (Figures 2.3 and 2.4). On this stretch of the river, he 'had the feeling that [he] was walking along the English coast, near the white cliffs' (Miyazawa 2003). Perhaps, in the words of the Hanamaki Tourist Association website, Miyazawa was writing out of 'longing' (*akogare*) ('The English Shore'). It seems fair to say, at least, that in Miyazawa an

Figures 2.3–2.4 (*Left*) 'The English Shore': the Kitakami River near Hanamaki, 2022, with the water level higher than in Miyazawa's time (photograph by the author). (*Right*) The Kitakami river and mudstone as it would have appeared to Miyazawa (photograph by the author).

intense consciousness of physical remoteness combined with narratives he had encountered in childhood to create a unique literary sensibility.

That Lewis Carroll was a particular influence on Miyazawa's writing has been widely acknowledged, with the parallels between his stories and elements of the *Alice* books being cited by numerous scholars.[8] As is often the case, however, suggestive parallels are easier to find than conclusive evidence of influence. For example, in chapter 3 of *Through the Looking-Glass* ('Looking-Glass Insects'), Carroll includes a scene in which Alice suddenly finds herself in a train, along with a man dressed in white paper, a goat, a beetle, a horse and a gnat. A guard demands their tickets, and only Alice is unable to produce one, after which her fellow passengers criticize her and discuss whether she will be able to proceed with her journey (Carroll 1962: 220–4). This use of a train carriage as a heterotopia or transitional space (it is carrying Alice from one square of the chessboard to the next) is perhaps the earliest of its kind in children's literature and inaugurated a significant *topos* that thrives to the present day, in books ranging from *The Polar Express* (1985) to *Harry Potter and the Philosopher's Stone* (1997) (Jenkins 2013). The scene's influence was soon felt; in 1874, Frederic Edward Weatherly set almost half of his avowedly Carroll-inspired *Elsie's Expedition* in a railway carriage, with the eponymous Elsie encountering a succession of bizarre passengers, including Jack Horner, the Knave of Hearts and a set of German officers of graduated size.

In this light, it is easy to see how a line can be drawn from *Alice* to what became one of Miyazawa's most famous stories, 'Night on the Milky Way Train' (*ginga tetsudō no yoru*), which he began in 1923 and worked on for the rest of his life, before it finally saw posthumous publication in 1934. The story involves two schoolboy friends, Giovanni and Campanella. Despite the protagonists' names, the setting does not appear to be Italy; the railway of the title was inspired by a line in Iwate, but the train's journey carries the characters through the stars to regions above and beyond earth. The adventure proper begins when Giovanni, staring at the night sky on the night of a star festival, suddenly finds himself in a train with Campanella, much as Alice found herself unexpectedly in a train after leaping a small brook in Carroll's story. Like Alice, the pair encounter several unusual fellow passengers, including a lighthouse keeper, a palaeontologist, a group present at a disaster resembling that of the Titanic and a man who catches herons before turning them into sweets.

---

8 For a useful digest of suggestions from the critics Asaichirō Suda, Taijirō Amazawa and Dō Fukushima, as well as some of her own, see Tamaki Horie (1999).

Giovanni differs from Alice in that, when the conductor asks for tickets, he finds after a moment's panic that he has one in his pocket, but his fear that he may be ticketless inevitably recalls the equivalent exchange in *Through the Looking-Glass* (Miyazawa 2020: 36).

Miyazawa's train journey shares with Carroll's its dreamlike transitions, unquestioned bizarreness and cryptic yet opinionated conversations. Yet this is not an exercise in nonsense writing. Miyazawa's train is a conveyance of the dead. The shipwrecked passengers alight at the Christian heaven, and a little further Campanella too, having glimpsed his mother in a field between the stars, disappears from view. Giovanni awakes, as Alice did after her first adventure, in the open air. Returning home from the hill where he had gone to view the stars, he learns that Campanella has died that evening, drowned while saving another boy's life. 'Night on the Milky Way Train' is thus revealed as a story about grief, perhaps rooted in Miyazawa's response to the death of his beloved sister Toshi, who had succumbed to tuberculosis in November 1922, shortly before he began work on it. In this case, although Carroll likely provided some of the raw materials for Miyazawa's story, if anything the similarities serve to highlight the writers' differences of purpose and tone.

Another example in which similarity of form accompanies profound philosophical differences is discussed in Ryō Ueno's essay, 'Alice in Īhatov' (*īhatovu no arisu*), included in his 1978 book, *The Peter Pan of Our Time* (*warera no jidai no pītā pan*). Ueno compares the *Alice* books to Miyazawa's short story, 'Night in the Oak Grove' (*kashiwabayashi no yoru*), in which the protagonist, Seisaku, encounters a dishevelled painter who – like the White Rabbit – leads him to a kind of wonderland in a nearby oak grove, where he meets talking animals and trees. However, although both writers animate nature, in Ueno's opinion Carroll's interest is only superficial; nature in his books is a cypher for the human world or a medium for the cerebral play of language and logic, rather than something to be acknowledged in its own right:

> Certainly, insects, flowers and animals also appear in *Alice's Adventures in Wonderland*. However, they do not make you feel the 'fear' or 'shiver' that envelops the protagonist. It is not that kind of 'nature'. It is 'observed nature', as a numerical value assigned by the mathematician, Lutwidge Dodgson. Rather, you might call it British nature, which, while it too is an island country, did not have the idea of *kachō fūgetsu*[9] (empathy for nature).

9 *Kachō fūgetsu* (literally, 'flowers, birds, wind, moon': 花鳥風月) is a set phrase referring to the traditional Japanese aesthetic appreciation of nature.

By contrast, Kenji's nonsense tale has the idea of a large life form that envelops humans, trees and birds alike. It is not, as in Alice's story, nature seen on equal terms, nature artificially controlled . . . this is nature as a maternal body, from which human beings are born and to which they return. (Ueno 1978)

Ueno's suggestion that British literature does not engage with nature in sublime or organic terms suggests some important omissions in his reading, but few people seeking those qualities would make Lewis Carroll their first port of call, and his observation is a useful reminder of the limitations of source studies as a tool of critical analysis, even where intertextual influence can be demonstrated.

Overall, Miyazawa appears to have learned numerous techniques from Carroll, for example about the narration of dream narratives; but he was not a nonsense writer, and it is important to bear in mind the differences as well as the similarities between the two authors. To place a text like Weatherly's *Elsie's Expedition* alongside 'Night on the Milky Way Train' is to be made aware of the gulf between a writer self-consciously imitating 'a successful style of Nursery Literature' (Weatherly 1874: ix) and one prosecuting his own vision and drawing on all the resources of his experience and imagination – of Īhatov – in order to do so.

Momoko Ishii and the growth of British children's book translation

The Shōwa period (1926–89) continued the consolidation of children's literature seen during the first quarter of the twentieth century. Over the course of the Emperor Shōwa's six-decade reign, native Japanese children's literature developed rapidly, and most well-known British texts from the early and middle part of the twentieth century found their way into the language. However, translation remained in some ways unsystematic, relying on the enthusiasms of individual editors or translators – a point to which I will return in the following chapter. Increasingly, too, the international outlook often found among such figures came into conflict with the Japanese government's turn towards militaristic nationalism in the first two decades of the period.

The career of the writer, translator and editor Momoko Ishii can stand as representative of the fortunes of Japanese children's literature in the twentieth century; she not only lived through almost its entire duration but was also in contact with most of its major figures, as well as becoming one in her own right. Born in 1907, Ishii was brought up in Saitama Prefecture, near Tōkyō. While still at high school, she worked part-time for Kan Kikuchi, reading and summarizing English-language books and magazines, and in 1928, on graduating from Japan Women's University with a degree in English literature, she joined Kikuchi's publishing company, Bungeishunjū. It was through Kikuchi that she met the writer and politician Takeru ('Ken') Inukai and his young family. Inukai had been the son of the prime minister, Tsuyoshi Inukai, whose assassination by a group of young naval officers in May 1932 was a key event in Japan's descent into militarism in the 1930s (Mori 2017). After Tsuyoshi Inukai's death, Kikuchi recommended Ishii to Ken Inukai as a suitable person to organize the deceased prime minister's library, but Ishii soon became a family friend as well.

On Christmas Eve in 1933 Ishii, then aged twenty-six, visited Ken Inukai's house in Shinanomachi, Tōkyō. She was greeted by his two children, Michiko and Yasuhiko (aged twelve and five), who were excited to have been given a copy of A. A. Milne's *The House at Pooh Corner* (1928) as a Christmas present by another friend, Kinkazu Saionji, who had returned to Japan two years earlier after studying at the University of Oxford.

In later years, Ishii, Michiko and Yasuhiko each described the reading that followed when, urged by the children, Ishii took the book from under the Christmas tree and began to translate it for them. As is often the case with events that assume mythic status, the details of their accounts differ. Was the book inscribed to Michiko or to Yasuhiko? Did the reading take place while leaning against the stove or cosily at the living-room *kotatsu*?[10] What is not in doubt is the effect of the occasion on Ishii. In her own words:

> At that time, I didn't know anything about the book's author, nor about Christopher Robin, Pooh or Piglet, who appear in the book. I didn't know anything. So, without giving any explanation in advance to my young listeners, I dived straight in: 'One day, Pooh Bear . . .'
>
> Just then, something strange happened to me that I have never experienced before or since. I entered a kind of mysterious world together with Pooh, a creature drawn to look like a cross between a bear and a pig. I really felt it physically, a feeling like making one's way through mist as warm as (or a little warmer than) body temperature, or pushing aside a soft curtain. . . . Pooh's story has a lot of loyal readers all over the world, but among them I flatter myself that the listeners and reader that night weren't at all bad. Anyway, as we pushed through the mist, I think that both I and my pair of young listeners accurately tuned in to the book's wavelength. . . .

---

10 For a collection of their accounts, and of other details concerning Ishii's life, see Numabe (2007/2014).

That night, saying that I wanted to read the rest of the story, I borrowed the book and took it home, and finished it in a daze. However, I didn't know anything about the author or how he came to write the book. In any event, from this book I first realised that there was a world of enjoyment, able to fill me with satisfaction. (Ishii 2014: 10–12)

The 1930s were a febrile time in Japan, and the circle of liberal intellectual friends that frequented Ken Inukai's house – including Saionji and Hotsumi Ozaki – was out of step with the increasingly bellicose government. The environment became dangerous, even for a figure such as Ishii who was not overtly political. Meanwhile, her new-found love of children's literature, particularly in English, dominated her activities. She continued to translate *The House at Pooh Corner* for the Inukai children and to entertain her soulmate Fumiko Ori, who was gradually dying of tuberculosis. After working as an editor in the mid-1930s with the writer and anti-war campaigner Genzaburō Yoshino, in 1940 Ishii opened a children's library in a room at the Inukai house. There, in quick succession, she published the first Japanese edition of Kenneth Grahame's *The Wind in the Willows* (1908), translated by Yoshio Nakano, and Masuji Ibuse's translation of Hugh Lofting's *The Story of Doctor Dolittle* (1920), both under her own imprint, Hakurin Shōnenkan – a name borrowed from the Inukai country villa. In December, Iwanami Shoten published her own translation of Milne's *Winnie-the-Pooh* (1926).

At this point, it may have seemed that Ishii's ambition to popularize modern Anglophone children's literature in Japan was destined for success. However, in October 1941 Ken Inukai's friend Hotsumi Ozaki was arrested as a Soviet spy, followed the next spring by Saionji and then Inukai himself. It became impossible for Ishii to continue her work from the Inukai residence. In 1942, with everything collapsing around her, Iwanami Shoten finally published *The House at Pooh Corner* (*pū yokochō ni tatta ie*), the book that had started it all; but the disintegration of the world she had built, coming shortly after the deaths of her parents and of Fumiko Ori, surely marked the lowest point in Ishii's life (Nakagawa et al. 2014: 57).

Ishii moved to Miyagi Prefecture and worked as a farmer for several years. It was only after the war that she was enticed back to Tōkyō by her former boss, Genzaburō Yoshino, who was now working for Iwanami Shoten. There, Ishii became the editor-in-chief of a series of classic children's texts in translation: Iwanami Shōnen Bunko (Figure 2.5). It was a defining moment, both in the creation of the modern Japanese children's literary landscape and in cementing British children's literature's place within it.

Figure 2.5 Momoko Ishii in about 1953. ©Tōkyō Children's Library.

Iwanami Shōnen Bunko was far from being the first attempt to produce a 'library' of recommended reading for children; it was not even the first in which Ishii had been involved. This kind of enterprise had a history going back at least to Sazanami Iwaya's various series, which Ishii had read as a child. In the late 1920s, Kan Kikuchi's 'Complete Collection for Primary School Students' (*shōgakusei zenshū*), on which she worked after graduation, was one of many 'libraries' that sprang up in response to the destruction caused by the Great Kantō Earthquake of 1923. By no means all these so-called one-yen-per-book (*en pon*) collections focused on children's literature, although Kikuchi's enterprise had a significant rival in the 'Japanese Children's Literature Library' (*nihon jidō bunko*), produced in seventy-six volumes between 1927 and 1930 by the publisher Ars (*arusu*). As Amanda Kennell observes, such collections were presented 'with the implication that an educated person (or child) has read all of them and the implicit promise that a less-informed parent can simply buy all of the books in the series should he wish to ensure that his child is properly educated' (Kennell 2017: 51).

When Ishii had worked for Genzaburō Yoshino in the mid-1930s, it was as an editor for Yūzō Yamamoto's 'Japan Young Citizens' Library' (*nihon shōkokumin bunko*), which was established in 1935 with the idealistic mission to nurture 'hope for the future of boys and girls, to protect children from vulgar readings and foster progressive ideas and rich emotions' (qtd. Mori 2017: 6). At the time, such ideals had run against the prevailing political tide in Japan, but in the post-war era Iwanami Shōnen Bunko offered a fresh start. This was the spirit that shaped the imprint's founding statement in 1950, in which Yoshino identified the rising generation with the resurrection of war-torn, firebombed Tōkyō itself:

> In a city where everything was burnt, grass began to sprout; young branches grew towards the sky from the ravaged roadside trees. The striking appearance of vegetation everywhere after the war teaches us what to value and what we can expect. Those who are spending their childhood in today's Japan, which has undergone an unprecedented collapse and still has not recovered, are truly our society's blades of fresh grass and young branches.
>
> This library was born out of profound expectation for these new seedlings of Japan. Its purpose is to cultivate the young shoots, with abundant water and bright sunlight. (Yoshino 2021: 100)

Under Ishii, Iwanami Shōnen Bunko differed from earlier 'libraries' in several respects. The books she published were small in format and printed in paperback, which allowed them to be sold fairly cheaply – an innovation paralleling that of Puffin in the UK. Just as importantly, Ishii's policy was to use direct translations of the original texts, rather than continue the practice of abridgement and 'retelling' (*saiwa*) common in Japanese versions of foreign-language texts at the time (Tanaka 2008: 96–9). In the Meiji era, Isō Yamagata had been able to refer to direct translations such as Wakamatsu's *The Little Lord* as 'dry and tasteless' in their servility to the source text, but the boot was now on the other foot, and it was the looser retellings that were liable to be disparaged as inaccurate and misleading.

In its early years, Iwanami Shōnen Bunko struggled to compete against the more traditional 'libraries' being produced by rivals such as Kōdansha, which was publishing the kind of standardized, hardback, multivolume editions of world classics to which schools and libraries were accustomed. However, in the long run Ishii's editorial policy, and the view of literature that informed it, prevailed, and the principle of accurate translation was accepted as the industry standard. Today, Iwanami Shōnen Bunko remains a flourishing imprint, more than seventy years after Ishii launched it.

While still in Miyagi, Ishii had become an author in her own right, writing the novel *Non-chan Rides the Clouds* (*non-chan kumo ni noru*), which was first published in 1947 and became a classic of the post-war era. As a campaigning critic and translator of criticism, she led a group devoted to the creation of a modern Japanese children's fantasy literature and in 1958 opened a home library, Katsura Bunko, from her house on a residential street in Ogikubo in west Tōkyō, a building that still operates as part of the Tōkyō Children's Library. A 'pioneer writer, editor, translator, librarian and reviewer', she remained active for the rest of her long career, publishing books well into her nineties (Tanaka 2008: 296). The list of titles – British and otherwise – that Ishii brought into Japanese is an extensive one and effectively constitutes a personal canon of children's books from the first half of the twentieth century. Her own translations of British books include Grahame's *The Wind in the Willows* (1950), Hilda Lewis's *The Ship That Flew* (1953), Eve Garnett's *The Family from One End Street* (1957), J. M. Barrie's *Peter and Wendy* (1957), E. Nesbit's *Five Children and It* (1959), Elizabeth Goudge's *The Little White Horse* (1964), John Masefield's *The Midnight Folk* (1973) and *The Box of Delights* (1975), Rumer Godden's *The Mousewife* (1977) and Beatrix Potter's *The Tale of Peter Rabbit* (1971), as well as several of Alison Uttley's books for younger readers. In the 1950s, she made a particular discovery of Eleanor Farjeon, then as now a largely unfashionable writer in Britain, and (having translated several individual books) went on to publish her collected works in six volumes. As a result, Farjeon is certainly a more canonical writer in Japan than in her homeland.

By the time Ishii died in 2008, aged 101, she was nationally celebrated as a writer, critic and translator of books for children, and there can be few Japanese who grew up in the second half of the twentieth century who were unaffected by her activities. The animator Hayao Miyazaki, born in 1941, has written:

[Momoko] Ishii and [Rieko] Nakagawa:[11] I feel these are 'women beyond compare'. . . .

Many works became masterpieces owing to Ishii's translations. [Eleanor] Farjeon is completely forgotten in her home country of England, but it is because of Ishii that she is still read. Should I say 'because of', or 'thanks to'? Due to Ishii's translation, I too wanted to go to Sussex to see the apple orchards and the flowers in bloom.[12] That's what it is to be a great translator.

In Japan, translated literature has a lot of power, so if translators really show the range of their talents and work from their heart, they will get deep readers. (Miyazaki 2011, 94–5)

---

11 Rieko Nakagawa, a well-known Japanese children's writer and lyricist for the theme song of Miyazaki's 1988 film, *My Neighbour Totoro*, was a protégée of Ishii's (Miyazaki 2011: 94; Nakagawa et al. 2014).

12 The reference is to Ishii's translation of Farjeon's *Martin Pippin in the Apple Orchard* (1921).

In an article celebrating Ishii's centenary, Shinichi Numabe (born in 1952) expressed his generation's gratitude even more eloquently, drawing on John 12.24:

> What a blessed life!
>
> However, there were also hard times and unknown adversities. She tasted the despair of losing everything.
>
> 'Unless a grain of wheat dies . . .' said the ancient writer. A tiny grain of wheat must fall into the earth and die, but thus it will in time bring forth a great harvest.
>
> Every one of us lives in a vast wheat field grown from a seed called Momoko Ishii – and it is abundant with grain. (Numabe 2014)

This moment of gratitude and the sense of copiousness it records offer a fit point at which to pause this story. Influential as Ishii was, no literature is the creation of one individual. There were other major translators of British children's literature among her contemporaries, such as Teiji Seta, who introduced J. R. R. Tolkien's Middle-earth and C. S. Lewis's Narnia to Japan; Teruo Jingū, whose translations included work by Arthur Ransome, Alan Garner and Richard Adams; and Ishii's colleague at Tōkyō Children's Library, Kyōko Matsuoka, translator of Michael Bond's *Paddington* stories. The list could be extended, but it is time to move the discussion beyond its current focus on the historical circumstances of significant individuals and to consider some of the larger structural forces that have shaped the canon of British children's literature in Japan and that literature's wider place in Japanese culture.

3

Canons to the West, canons to the East

British children's books in Japan

British books played a critical role in the establishment and early history of Japanese children's literature, but what of their continuing presence? Whether considered from the perspective of individual texts or of broader genre traditions, Japanese approaches to understanding and using British books exhibit significant differences from those current in Britain, reflecting yet another of the present volume's Looking-Glass relationships. In this chapter, I describe the development of a Japan-specific canon of British children's literature, noting the motives and mechanisms underlying its divergence from that in its home country, and explore some of the ways – not all literary in character – in which British children's books have remained visible and influential in Japanese culture.

Canon divergence

I ended the previous chapter with the heartfelt tributes paid to Momoko Ishii by Hayao Miyazaki and Shinichi Numabe. For a children's book translator to be venerated in this way in the Anglophone world is, sadly, unheard of; but, as Miyazaki observed, the situation in Japan is different. While Japan has many excellent children's writers of its own, it also publishes a large number of translated books, and the creation of a flourishing literature for children in Japanese over the last 150 years has been the achievement of translators, editors and publishers as much as of novelists, with numerous individuals taking on many or all of these roles. To that extent, the star status of a figure such as Ishii need cause no surprise. However, the fact that the development of the field depended on the efforts of a relatively small number of people, particularly in its early days, has several corollaries, not least for the establishment of a canon of international children's literature in Japan.

One consideration is the role of chance. It is a sobering reflection that, if Tsuyoshi Inukai had not been assassinated, Momoko Ishii would not have become close to Ken Inukai's family, would not have found the copy of *The House at Pooh Corner* under the Christmas tree and would quite possibly never have pursued a career in children's books. To suggest that the world of Japanese children's literature therefore owes Inukai's assassins a debt would be perverse, but it is a striking example of the arbitrary consequences of human actions, especially when large enterprises depend disproportionately on the actions of a few individuals.

The example of Ishii should also make us aware of the extent to which personal taste can shape the wider field. I have already mentioned Ishii's support for Eleanor Farjeon's writing. Without it, it is unlikely that Farjeon would be available in Japanese translation today; but that is just one instance of a broader influence that inevitably favoured texts with settings, values, characters, styles and genres congruent with Ishii's tastes and talents. Her preference for fantasy literature is an obvious example. Of the British books she translated into Japanese, only Eve Garnett's *The Family from One End Street* (1937) is a non-fantasy work. Any Japanese reader who knew British children's literature solely through Ishii's translations might imagine it to be far more dominated by fantasy than is really the case. More generally, Ishii's role as an English-language translator, combined with her position at Iwanami Shōnen Bunko, may have worked to increase the reach and number of translated English-language children's books, as compared with works translated from other languages. (Of course, this was only one of several factors tending to promote the translation of English-language texts, another being the American dominance of the country after the Second World War.) To point this out is by no means to criticize Ishii; it is natural for creative people to work on the projects that inspire them. However, in a field where the number of active translators and editors is small, the preferences of influential individuals will inevitably be amplified to a greater extent than in a more diverse, populous and well-established literary ecosystem.

Another way in which a focus, not just on English-language texts but specifically on British ones, has historically been perpetuated is through academic criticism. English-language children's literature is now taught in many Japanese universities, not least to prospective schoolteachers, and the selection of the texts that form the subject's backbone is thus influential on future child readers as well as on students. The Japan Society for Children's Literature in English was established in December 1970 by a group of scholars from Shizuoka University, and it remains a flourishing body, having grown from an initial 80 to some 250 members. It organizes conferences, produces a refereed journal and newsletter, and has overseen the publication of several scholarly volumes. Its journal, *Tinker Bell*, which began publication in 1971, is one of the oldest academic journals devoted to children's literature. Although the Society has always taken the whole of English-language children's literature as its province, British literature received particular attention from the beginning and has been the subject of the lion's share of those articles in *Tinker Bell* devoted to specific texts or authors. In 2001, the Society published a student guide, *Anglo-American Children's Literature Guide: Works and Theory* (*eibei jidō bungaku gaido: sakuhin to riron*), edited by the Society's four original mainstays, Shinichi Yoshida, Shō Hara, Okiko Miyake and Seigō Tanimoto. Seventeen chapters are devoted to individual children's texts, and of these all but three are British, the exceptions being Mark Twain's *Tom Sawyer* (1876), L. M. Montgomery's *Anne of Green Gables* (1908) and Margaret Mahy's *The Haunting* (1982): one apiece from the United States, Canada and New Zealand. The same guide also includes a thoroughly international timeline of twentieth-century books (Yoshida et al. 2001: 255–68), but the central position of Britain in the English-language children's literature tradition is clear and has remained an implicit feature of much Japanese scholarship. Indeed, it was only in April 2020 that the Society changed its Japanese name from 日本イギリス児童文学会 ('Japan British Children's Literature Society') to 英語圏児童文学会 ('Anglophone Children's Literature Society').[1]

Beyond the activities and preferences of influential individuals and institutions, there are several mechanisms by which a translated literary canon may come to diverge from that of the originating culture. One occurs when a translated text appears early in the formation of a literature or genre, at a time when it has few competitors and can thus establish itself to a degree that it was unable to do in its home territory. A striking example is the English writer Diana Coles's story, *The Clever Princess* (1983), about a princess who rises to the challenges of living in a patriarchal society through a combination of intelligence and female solidarity. *The Clever Princess* is in many ways typical of the wave of feminist fairy tales that

---

1 This British emphasis is also reflected in the reading choices of the fictional Professor Amemiya, protagonist of Hisa Takano's manga, *Professor Amemiya's 3pm Teatime* (*gogo sanji amemiya kyōju no ocha no jikan*) (2019–2022), which describes a university teacher's hobby of making baked goods and desserts mentioned in British books (primarily books published for children). Amemiya's culinary choices, for which recipes are included, are sometimes easy to predict: marmalade for Michael Bond's *A Bear Called Paddington* (1958), jam tarts for *Alice's Adventures in Wonderland*. Fewer people might expect a reading of K. M. Peyton's *Flambards* (1967) to prompt a foray into sausage rolls; but, taken together, Professor Amemiya's selections too constitute an informal British children's literature canon, approximating but not replicating that in Britain itself.

appeared in the West at the turn of the 1980s as part of a conscious attempt to counter the prevailing image of fairy-tale heroines as passive figures dependent on supernatural aid or male rescue.[2] It was published by a small collective, Sheba Feminist Publishers, and in Britain appears never to have gone to a second edition. However, the following year it was spotted at a women's centre by four visiting Japanese feminists. Calling themselves 'Group Women's Space' in 1989 the quartet published a Japanese translation under the title, *Princess Arete's Adventure* (*arīte hime no bōken*). As *Princess Arete's Adventure*, the book was highly successful and gained much positive attention, including a picture book spin-off, appearances in school textbooks and eventually a feature-length anime adaptation directed by Sunao Katabuchi, *Princess Arete* (*arīte hime*) (2000). In contrast to its fate in Britain, where *The Clever Princess* rapidly sank from initial obscurity into utter oblivion, *Princess Arete's Adventure* became, as Hideko Taniguchi notes, 'one of the most widely-read feminist fairy tales in Japan' (2010: 131). It is impossible to account with certainty for this disparity in fortunes, but it seems likely that *The Clever Princess* was squeezed out of the English-language market by competition from the other unconventional princesses thronging bookshops at the time, most backed by far larger marketing budgets than that available to Sheba Feminist Publishers. In Japan, not only was there less competition, but as a heroine who uses her wits rather than weapons, Arete may have been welcomed as an alternative to the 'beautiful fighting girl' figures then in vogue (Saitō 2011: 89–118).

Canon formation can also work in the opposite direction, with a work accorded classic status in its own country finding less acceptance in the target culture, at least until societal norms or market conditions change in a way that allows it to thrive. E. Nesbit's comic fantasy, *Five Children and It*, gained immediate popularity in Britain on its publication in 1902 and has remained in print ever since, but it had to wait until 1959 to be translated into Japanese by Momoko Ishii as *The Sand Fairy* (*suna no yōsei*). One possible reason for the book's relative neglect is the unashamed fallibility of Nesbit's child protagonists. As Nesbit put it in the sequel, *The Phoenix and the Carpet* (1904), her 'children were not particularly handsome, nor were they extra clever, nor extraordinarily good. But they were not bad sorts on the whole; in fact, they were rather like you' (Nesbit 1959: 21). Anthea, Cyril, Robert and Jane quarrel, behave foolishly and are altogether unsuitable role models for the child readers of the Meiji or

---

2 Precursors include Jay Williams's *The Practical Princess and Other Liberating Fairy Tales* (1979) and Jeanne Desy's *The Princess Who Stood on Her Own Two Feet* (1981).

Taishō eras. However, the episodic structure of Nesbit's book, in which each adventure with the wish-granting Psammead is neatly concluded at sunset, the day's magic undone and the situation essentially reset ready for next time, made it an excellent fit for the requirements of television anime. Nesbit's book had eleven chapters and was initially serialized in *The Strand Magazine* over the course of 1902, but the makers of the 1980s NHK series *Please, Psammead!* (*onegai! samia-don*) realized that the model could be extended much, much further. The resulting anime, directed by Osamu Kobayashi, ran to seventy-eight episodes and was broadcast from April 1985 at the rate of two episodes per week. The story was updated to a contemporary English setting but otherwise used the same premise and to a large extent the same characters as Nesbit's book. Placed in a Japanese television context, the Psammead became recognizably a figure in the tradition of anime such as *Doraemon* (1970–). Just as the time-travelling robot cat Doraemon uses his endless store of futuristic devices to help his hapless young friend Nobita out of trouble (or get him into it), so the Psammead grants wishes for the 'Turner' children in *Please, Psammead!* (Sasada 2015a). Even now, Nesbit's book is not regarded as a classic in Japan to the extent that it is in Britain, but when the appropriate cultural niche presented itself, it was able to fill it.

A third occasion for canon divergence occurs when a book enjoys a degree of success on first publication but, due to a change in taste, comes to be forgotten in its native land, while surviving in translation elsewhere as a kind of 'living fossil'. Maria Nikolajeva gives a pertinent example of translation from English into Russian:

In Russia, one of the most beloved children's classics is a book entitled *The True History of A Little Ragamuffin* by a certain James Greenwood. It is a sentimental story that takes place in the slums of London, somewhat in the style of *Oliver Twist*. However, the book is not mentioned in any British reference source on children's literature, the reason being that the work, published in 1866, was never intended for children, was never reprinted and in Britain was never regarded as a children's book. Not many experts on British nineteenth-century literature have even heard of it. But in Russia the book was retold for young readers only a few years after the appearance of the original. In the 1920s the great Russian children's writer and educator Kornei Chukovsky made a new version which secured the book a prominent place in Russian children's reading. It has been reprinted in more than forty editions totalling more than twenty million copies. A third-rate British adult text has thus become a children's classic and a component of Russian childhood reading. (Nikolajeva 1996: 18)

Lack of competition is not the only factor in the survival of such texts. They may also acquire powerful patronage, as *A Little Ragamuffin* did from Chukovsky, or exemplify values (moral or aesthetic) that accord with those of its adoptive culture but from which its home culture has diverged. Greenwood's sentimental story was written in a sub-Dickensian style that was fashionable enough in 1866 but had become a relic by the turn of the twentieth century. Oscar Wilde's remark about Dickens's *The Old Curiosity Shop* (1841), that 'one must have a heart of stone to read the death of little Nell without laughing', may be apocryphal, but it is indicative of a real change in British literary taste. In Russia, the taste for sentimental reading endured, while the popularity of Greenwood's book in the early years of the Soviet Union may also have been bolstered by its focus on the plight of the poor.

In Japan, too, sentimental tales of virtuous-but-oppressed children have enjoyed a long shelf life. Given that these selfless protagonists tend to exemplify the qualities seen as exemplary from the point of view of Meiji-era educationalists, this may be accounted for in part by their didactic potential as role models for their young readers. Hector Malot's *Sans Famille* (1878), for example, which was published as *Nobody's Boy* in English and *Homeless Child* (*ie naki ko*) in Japanese, is, like *Oliver Twist* and *A Little Ragamuffin*, the story of a poor young boy who goes through a series of adventures in different milieux before finally finding happiness. While still known in its native France, it has steadily dwindled in popularity there but continues to lead a far more vigorous life in Japan (and indeed in Russia) and has received multiple film and anime adaptations.

In the case of British literature, there is no better example of this phenomenon than Ouida's 1872 novella, *A Dog of Flanders*. This book is almost as obscure as *The True History of a Little Ragamuffin* in Ouida's homeland, and its author is scarcely better known, but there are few Japanese over the age of thirty unfamiliar with Nello and his faithful dog Patrasche. Ouida was the pen name of Maria Louise Ramé, also known as Marie Louise de la Ramée, born in Bury St Edmunds in 1839 to an English mother and French father. As a child, she found Suffolk suffocating and longed for a more elevated social and artistic life. In her late twenties she moved to London, becoming the centre of a literary salon where many well-known writers of the period were regular visitors, before relocating to the continent (primarily Italy) in the 1870s. In her prime, Ouida was a successful novelist, but by her death in 1908 her star had already set, and she died in straitened circumstances. There was a small revival of interest in her among feminist critics in the early years of this century, spurred by the emerging body of scholarship on the 'New Woman' movement of the 1890s, a phrase

Ouida had popularized in an essay of 1894 (Ouida 1987). Ouida, however, was a vocal opponent of the movement, and her politics, being aristocratic and anti-suffrage, meant that she was never going to be unreservedly embraced. As Pamela Gilbert puts it, her 'antifeminism, combined with stylistic extravagance, has contributed to render Ouida invisible within today's canon, in which she can be classified neither as canonical nor as a feminist foremother' (2010: 170). Ouida was, however, passionately interested in animal welfare, and it is in part owing to this concern that her work (or rather, one of her works) lives on in Japan.

A Dog of Flanders was initially published as one of a collection of four stories for adults, and this is reflected in its brevity; the entire text is barely 14,000 words long. The story concerns Nello, a boy living with his elderly grandfather, a disabled Napoleonic War veteran, in a village outside Antwerp. At the beginning of the story, they are poor but contented: 'they were happy on a crust and a few leaves of cabbage, and asked no more of heaven or earth' (1872: 4). One day, they discover a dog, of a Flemish breed used as beasts of draught, which has been abused by its owner and left for dead. They nurse it back to health and name it Patrasche. Patrasche repays them by faithfully pulling their milk cart the few miles into Antwerp every day, where Nello earns money by selling milk to the citizens. Meanwhile, Nello has a secret passion. He is in fact an artist of genius, albeit untutored, and his twin ambitions are to become a professional and to see the two Rubens paintings housed in Antwerp Cathedral, which are revealed by the cathedral staff only on payment of a franc. Such a fee is beyond Nello's means, but he maintains his hopes and practises his art, not least by sketching his young friend Alois, the daughter of the local miller, Baas Cogez, the richest man in the village.

At length, things begin to unravel. Baas Cogez fears that his daughter will fall for Nello and make an unsuitable match and forbids her his company. When a fire breaks out at the mill, Nello is unjustly blamed, and Baas Cogez ensures that the other villagers withdraw their custom from him and his grandfather. Shortly after, the grandfather dies of old age and indigence. Their landlord evicts Nello and Patrasche (by now also old and infirm) from their peasant hut on Christmas Eve, with snow thick on the ground. An art competition that Nello had entered, success in which would have assured his future, is awarded to an inferior but better-connected candidate. Through all this accumulation of sorrows, Nello maintains his nobility and honesty. As he wanders in the snow, he discovers a packet containing 6,000 francs that Baas Cogez has accidentally dropped and conscientiously returns it. He then makes a final journey to the cathedral, where, finding the Rubens paintings without their customary curtain, he cries out, 'I have seen them at last! . . . O God, it is enough!' (1872: 61). Putting his arms around Patrasche, he dies of exposure on the cathedral floor. The next morning boy and dog are discovered by Alois and an artist who has recognized Nello's genius from his competition entry and wishes to tutor him, but: 'the young pale face, turned upward to the light of the great Rubens with a smile upon its mouth, answered them all, "It is too late"' (Ouida 1872: 63). Where Dickens's Oliver, Greenwood's Jimmy and Malot's Rémi all get the happy endings they deserve, Nello's story is a tragic one.

Throughout *A Dog of Flanders*, Ouida stresses the plight of unrecognized and unrewarded genius, a subject evidently close to her heart. As if to vindicate her theme, in Britain her own story soon sank without trace; there appears (with one exception) to have been no British edition later than 1893. It fared better in the United States, where several film adaptations were made in the twentieth century, including one in 1924 starring Jackie Coogan as Nello, which, like almost all American adaptations, changed the story's ending to ensure Nello's and Patrasche's survival. Interest prompted by Coogan's performance may have moved Ouida's London publishers, Chatto and Windus, to bring out that exceptional twentieth-century British edition, which appeared the following year.

However, it was in Japan that *A Dog of Flanders* was to find its most devoted admirers. The first Japanese translation was made in 1908, the year of Ouida's death (Figure 3.1). Masujirō Honda, a Japanese journalist with an interest in animal rights, who was living in the United States at the time, proposed *A Dog of Flanders* as a suitable candidate for translation, having read her obituary in the *New York Times* (Voickaert and Van. Diendeveren 2007). A translation by a Japanese Christian, Hidaka Kakiken, duly appeared less than ten months later, along with a message from the publisher, Naigaishuppan, expressing the hope that the book would increase Japanese children's love of animals. In this first translation, Nello's name was changed to the more Japanese Kiyoshi – a choice that, like Kiyō, the name assigned to Cedric Errol in *Neikeiji*, the Japan-set adaptation of *Little Lord Fauntleroy* discussed in the previous chapter, derives from a *kanji* (清) with connotations of purity and nobility (Ouida 1908).

A Dog of Flanders enjoyed moderate success in Japan for several decades, but after the Second World War there was a flurry of new translations, perhaps under the influence of the American occupation forces, including one in 1952 by Hanako Muraoka, whose celebrated translation of L. M. Montgomery's *Anne of Green Gables* appeared the same year. Unlike the Hollywood film

Figure 3.1 Cover of the first Japanese edition of *A Dog of Flanders*, 1908. Original in the possession of Ōsaka Prefectural Central Library.

versions, most Japanese editions retained Ouida's tragic resolution, although one *kamishibai*[3] published in the 1960s cannily printed two endings, one in which Nello and Patrasche die and another in which they survive, allowing performers to adjust the telling according to their audience (Voickaert and Van. Dienderen 2007). Despite this, the book gained nationwide fame only in 1975, when it was made into an anime by Nippon Animation for the television series, *World Masterpiece Theatre*. Hayao Miyazaki has written of its status prior to that point:

> *A Dog of Flanders* and the like were already archaeological items when they became animations. I remember reading it as a sad story when I was a kid, and there were also versions that had been given a happy ending, but it was already completely a thing of the past. . . . There must have been a classic translation of the work from the Meiji era, but at that time only a few people read it. So, only the name was handed down as a masterpiece. (Miyazaki 2011: 74–5)

3 *Kamishibai* (literally, 'paper drama') is a form of storytelling employing pictures and oral narration. Originally used by Buddhist monks as a preaching aid, by the mid-twentieth century it had become a popular form of street entertainment for children.

What does it take to qualify as a 'masterpiece' (*meisaku*)? The preface to the 1908 translation of *A Dog of Flanders* had referred to it hyperbolically as 'counted among the "hundred best volumes in the world"' (Ouida 1908: 2), and in 1957 the publisher Kōdansha included the story in its multivolume *Complete Collection of World Masterpieces* (*sekai meisaku zenshū*). Was that enough for the accolade to be passed down to children of Miyazaki's generation and beyond? The distinction between literary evaluation and commercial advertising can become blurred in such cases, but, however motivated, the repetition of a word such as 'masterpiece' tends to cement a work's status, especially in a culture as alert as Japan's to the importance of consensus and authoritative validation.

As Sylvie Geerts and Sara Van den Bossche have noted, the role of adaptation in canon formation is frequently a crucial one, both in underlining a work's standing and in disseminating it to a larger audience, and this was certainly the case with *A Dog of Flanders* (2014: 10). *World Masterpiece Theatre*, a series of television anime adaptations of international (but in fact almost exclusively Western) children's classics, had been running for some years under the aegis of Fuji TV when Nippon Animation took it over in 1975, and its format had to some extent been established. The show was broadcast early on Sunday evenings, one of the few times when a family audience could be expected, and its appeal was thus to adults as well as children. Each 'masterpiece' was spread over many episodes; by 1975 a standard length of fifty-two had become the norm, meaning that each story ran for an entire year. The series immediately preceding *A Dog of Flanders* had been a celebrated production of Johanna Spyri's *Heidi* (1881), *Heidi, Girl of the Alps* (*arupusu no shōjo haiji*), in which Miyazaki and his future Ghibli-founding partner, Isao Takahata, were both deeply involved. *Heidi*, like *A Dog of Flanders*, was a nineteenth-century story of an orphan living with her grandfather in the European countryside. Whether or not this fact affected the selection of Ouida's book, the choice was a happy one in that *A Dog of Flanders* was able to slot directly into the gap left by its successful predecessor. How to stretch a 14,000-word story into a fifty-two-episode anime series was a more difficult question. Ouida's text provided only about ten words per minute of animation, and it is not surprising that the director, Yoshio Kuroda, bulked it out with numerous extra incidents and characters, such as a subplot in which Patrasche's original abusive owner returns and accuses Nello of theft. As for the ending, the then president of Nippon Animation, Kōichi Motohashi, has reported that there were many requests to give Nello and Patrasche a reprieve, but that the show's sponsor (the soft drink company, Calpis), which was then headed by a Christian, insisted on the tragic ending being retained (Voickaert and Van. Dienderen 2007). In fact, the final scenes of the anime are considerably more religious in tone than Ouida's text, which is frequently bitter against the hypocrisy and cruelty of the Church and ends with the surviving characters feeling shame and remorse at their treatment of Nello. The anime, by contrast, has Nello and Patrasche (along with the milk cart) carried joyously into heaven by a flock of cherubs, while a voice-over assures the viewer of their happiness in the afterlife.

That final episode was watched by approximately 33 million people (Voickaert and Van. Dienderen 2007), around 30 per cent of the Japanese population, and remains well known to this day. Its appeal appears to have been primarily moral and emotional rather than religious. Nello, a boy who was cheerful, loyal and pure hearted to the end, was a role model whom both parents and children could approve. As viewer Noriko Takamiya, then five years old, later put it: 'My parents were relieved when we cried at the sad story. They realised that we were growing up really well' (qtd. Voickaert and Van. Dienderen 2007).

The tone set by *Heidi* and *A Dog of Flanders* established the later course of *World Masterpiece Theatre*. Four out of the next five seasons would showcase nineteenth-century stories about orphans or children separated from their parents. As Shōji Satō put it: 'The main character, a boy or girl, acts in a so-called moving way while going through a hard time. That was the image of a masterpiece' (qtd. Shimizu 2019: 183). Another desirable characteristic was the inclusion of a model child, and on occasion the source material might even be modified so as to make a story's protagonist conform more closely to that expectation. Yuri Shimizu gives the example of *Little Princess Sara* (*shōkōjo sēra*), an adaptation of Frances Hodgson Burnett's *A Little Princess* (1905), which aired in 1985 and illustrates the gendered aspects of this process:

There are two areas in which specific changes were made to Sara's character to make it 'exemplary' (*mohanteki*). One is that there are almost no scenes where Sara talks back to adults. This is illustrated in the scene where Minchin tells Sara, who is all alone in the world, to work as a servant instead of staying at the academy. When the original Sara is told to thank Minchin for her kindness, she says, 'You are *not* kind, and it is *not* a home'. By contrast, anime Sara just says 'Thank you', while weeping. The second is the significant deletion of Sara's monologue, another feature of the original. From the moment she sets eyes on Minchin, the original Sara describes her in her mind as 'tall and dull, and respectable and ugly', and thereafter continues to criticise her behaviour inwardly. However, from what the anime version of Sara says she appears to have almost no feelings about Minchin or indeed anything else. Instead, the viewer sees Sara's expressions, especially her wide eyes, the tears that flow from them, and the shoulders that tremble as she cries. In other words, anime Sara loses the autonomy of behaviour and mind that was the greatest feature of the original. As a result, the focal point of the original story's development, how the main character reacts to and deals with her change in circumstances, becomes rather how the other characters treat the innocent girl, Sara. (Shimizu 2019: 184–5).

It seems that, more than eighty years after Tenkei Hasegawa had young Mī stumble her way through Looking-Glass Land, female protagonists of Western texts were still being given makeovers to render them more appealingly helpless.

The huge success of Kuroda's *A Dog of Flanders*, and of later screen versions of the story, led in time to a touristic interest in its setting, and as Japan grew richer and international travel more affordable, *Dog of Flanders*-inspired tourism to Belgium became an increasing phenomenon. The various paradoxes and literary ramifications of what would later become known as contents tourism are a subject for a later chapter, but it is worth noting, as an eloquent demonstration of the mutual illegibility of national literary canons, that in the 1980s, when Japanese tourists arrived in Antwerp seeking the locations of the various incidents in *A Dog of Flanders*, the city authorities were at a loss. The book was entirely unknown to them; it had never been translated into Dutch, and would not be until 1985, stimulated by Japanese interest. Since Ouida herself had spent at most a few days in the city, it proved unsurprisingly difficult to map the book's events onto the geography of Antwerp and its surroundings. Nor had her portrait of Flanders been a flattering one, either physically ('Flanders is not a lovely land, and around the burgh of Rubens it is perhaps least lovely of all' (Ouida 1872: 15)) or in terms of moral character. Nevertheless, to oblige Japanese visitors, the city authorities identified Hoboken as the likely site of Nello's home and commissioned a statue of him and Patrasche, although this bore little resemblance to the characters described in the book (Voickaert and Van. Dienderen 2007).

Since the 1980s, although *A Dog of Flanders* remains obscure in Britain, the three-way relationship between Ouida's text, Antwerp and Japan has grown ever more entrenched. For example, the cover of Kaori Chiba's *Journeys to World Masterpiece Theatre* (*sekai meisaku gekijō e no tabi*) (2015), a book featuring many of the places featured in that programme's long run, is dominated by a full-page photograph of Antwerp Cathedral, superimposed with a line drawing of Nello and Patrasche and a flight of cherubs borrowed from the anime's iconic final scene. In 2016, the artist Batist Vermeulen created a new, substantial sculpture in front of the cathedral to memorialize the connection, incorporating the cobblestones as a blanket drawn over the recumbent figures of Nello and

Figure 3.2 Statue of Nello and Patrasche by Batist Vermeulen, in front of Antwerp Cathedral (photograph by the author).

Patrasche, asleep in peaceful death (Figure 3.2). Meanwhile, the city's tourism website has fully domesticated their story, suggesting relevant landmarks, recommending the 'Nello and Patrasche' chocolates for sale at the Kiosk bakery in Hoboken and referring to *A Dog of Flanders* as 'famous all over the world' ('Nello and Patrasche').

It gives no hint that it was ever otherwise.

Influence and genre: time-slips and magical schools

How should we assess the influence of British children's books on Japanese children's literature and culture? We have seen that they played a significant part in establishing a Japanese children's literature and perhaps even the concept of 'the child' as a person for whom a bespoke literature was warranted; but this is to characterize 'influence' in very general terms. Conversely, we can note the inspiration found by individual Japanese authors in the work of specific texts and predecessors. Kenji Miyazawa acknowledged the role of *Through the Looking-Glass* in the creation of Īhatov, while Noriko Ogiwara became a fantasy author after reading C. S. Lewis's Narnia books, for example (Ogiwara 2006: 181–222). Other examples could be adduced, but the effect of such encounters, while undoubtedly important for the authors concerned, is quite local in character.

An approach that sits between the abstractness of 'children's literature' and the specificity of single-author studies is that of genre. Several genres now well-established in Japan gained popularity after being introduced through British models; for the current purpose, time-slip fantasies and magic school stories will serve as indicative examples. The arrivals of these genres are conveniently spaced chronologically and are associated with specific books – Philippa Pearce's *Tom's Midnight Garden* (1958) and J. K. Rowling's Harry Potter series (1997–2007), respectively – that in Japan have acquired the effective status of foundational texts, although neither is the earliest example of its type in Britain.

By 'time-slip fantasies' I mean here not time travel stories in general but the subgenre in which the protagonist's movement through time is (at least initially) largely accidental and unintentional. This does not apply to the majority of British children's time fantasies from the first half of the twentieth century, which generally drew on the powers of magical devices, such as the amulet in E. Nesbit's *The Story of the Amulet* (1906), or magical creatures, such as Puck in Rudyard Kipling's *Puck of Pook's Hill* (1906) or Mouldiwarp in Nesbit's *The House of Arden* (1908) and *Harding's Luck* (1909) – all of which could be variously controlled, commanded or importuned. A major exception was Alison Uttley's *A Traveller in Time* (1939), which has a strong claim to be the first time-slip novel in children's literature. Uttley's protagonist, Penelope Taberner, slips back and forth between contemporary England and the 1580s without any control over whether or when it happens, or certain knowledge of why. This was to become the characteristic mode of later time-slips such as *Tom's Midnight Garden*, Lucy M. Boston's *The Chimneys of Green Knowe* (1958)[4] and Penelope Farmer's *Charlotte Sometimes* (1969). Rather than a supernatural creature or device, the movement through time in such stories is usually triggered by the interaction of the protagonist's emotional state with a significant setting, typically a historical building or garden such as Penelope Taberner's Thackers, the ancient manor of Green Knowe, the Victorian house of *Tom's Midnight Garden* or the school where Charlotte is a boarder in *Charlotte Sometimes* (Butler 2021: 43).

Among these, *Tom's Midnight Garden* has been widely recognized in Britain as pre-eminent, for its emotional wisdom and for its rich depiction of the

---

4   The first in Boston's series, *The Children of Green Knowe* (1954), was written as a ghost story. For more on the generic differences between the Green Knowe books, see Butler (2021).

Victorian house and garden into which the modern protagonist, Tom, steps each night when the grandfather clock in the hallway of the house where he is staying strikes the impossible hour of thirteen. Pearce's novel duly won the Carnegie Medal and was translated into Japanese by Ichirō Takasugi (*tomu wa mayonaka no niwa de*) in 1967, before any of the other time-slip fantasies mentioned earlier. The undoubted literary qualities of the book thus combined with a somewhat exaggerated sense of its innovativeness, considering that it post-dated *A Traveller in Time* by almost twenty years and appeared in the same year as *The Chimneys of Green Knowe*. In Japan, Pearce's eschewal of the supernatural meant that her book was embraced by critics who (following Momoko Ishii) were attempting to develop a modern children's fantasy literature independent of the *dōwa* tradition, while children's authors saw in it a challenge to find new means of expression. As Mihoko Tanaka puts it, *Tom's Midnight Garden* was 'not only the first time-fantasy but also the first fantasy without any fairies or magic to be translated in Japan' (2009: 66), and its impact was correspondingly great. It may even have become more popular than it was in Britain (Ogawa 2009: 54).

Tanaka has detailed the immediate impact of *Tom's Midnight Garden* in Japan. This included, in the years following the publication of Ichirō's translation, the appearance of plainly derivative works, such as Miyoko Matsutani's *The Two Īdas* (*futari no īda*) (1969), which recounts a boy's encounter with the same girl in two different time periods through the medium of a chair in an old house, and Naoko Awa's story, 'The Time Nobody Knows' (*daremo shiranai jikan*) (1972), in which a boy and girl meet at thirteen o'clock. As *Tom* was joined by translations of other British time-slip fantasies, including those by Uttley, Boston and Farmer, a more substantial body of native Japanese time fantasies also began to emerge, many employing words such as 'time', 'garden' or 'door' in their titles (Tanaka 2009: 266). Along with *Tom*, Uttley's and Boston's books proved especially popular and enduring. Boston's home at Hemingford Grey Manor, which was the model for Green Knowe and at 800 years old has a claim to be the oldest continually inhabited house in Britain, continues to attract Japanese visitors, and her books are regularly discussed by Japanese scholars (e.g. Watson et al. 2021).

Having reached a critical mass in Japan, the time-slip genre became to an extent self-sustaining. Nevertheless, the contrasting circumstances of Britain and Japan in the second half of the twentieth century inevitably meant that there were differences in the ways that time fantasies could be written. As Tanaka points out (2009: 277–83), the standard locus of the British time-slip story, an ancient house in which many successive generations have lived, was rare in Japan, where older buildings are generally made of perishable materials such as wood, houses depreciate with age and are frequently rebuilt, earthquakes are frequent and the damage caused by wartime bombing was even more extensive than in Britain. There was no Japanese Hemingford Grey to serve as the setting for an equivalent of the Green Knowe books. Another important distinction is that British time-slip books, not least *Tom* itself, often portrayed the past in a more positive light than the present. *Tom*'s post-war England is grey and dreary: the beautiful Victorian garden has been built over, the house converted into stuffy flats, the river polluted. Japan's historical circumstances were different, certainly as regards the past of living memory; neither the Second World War nor the military-dominated regime of the 1930s was likely to be portrayed in an idealized manner by Japanese authors, and this gave some Japanese time-slip fictions a darker tone.

One Japanese author who has struggled very consciously with the tensions between the genre's British origins and the desire to give it an authentically Japanese instantiation is Kaho Nashiki. Born in 1959, as a student Nashiki became a protégée of the Jungian psychologist and children's literature advocate, Hayao Kawai, who influenced her to take an interest in British children's books. On graduating from university, Nashiki stayed for some time with the children's novelist Betty Morgan Bowen in Saffron Walden, during which period she also visited Hemingford Grey and got to know Lucy Boston.[5] Her experiences, both of Britain and of the tutelary influence of these mentors, had a powerful effect on her literary sensibility. Nevertheless, she was also conscious that, as a Japanese woman, there was a limit to how far she could participate in Western culture or use it to make art that would be culturally legible in her own country. She recounts:

> when I was turning over the pages of *The Wonderful Wizard of Oz*, suddenly, a line, 'the witch of the West is dead,' jumped out at me. I was so shocked that I fell into a chair nearby and pondered for a while. At that time, my life had been focused on Western culture for a long time, but I sensed my limitations at that point. (Qtd. Isobe 2018)

Nashiki's first novel, duly titled *The Witch of the West Is Dead* (*nishi no majo ga shinda*) (1994), is not a time-slip fiction but, as Satomi Isobe has noted, it shares the emotional structure of time-slips such as *Tom's Midnight Garden* and the Green Knowe books, being the story of an isolated child who stays at the house of a relative and is mentally and spiritually healed by the experience (Isobe 2010). The protagonist, Mai, is Japanese but has an English grandmother living in the Japanese countryside. Her own parents, unable to understand or relieve her unhappiness, send her to stay there, and the pair become close. The grandmother

---

5 I am grateful to Satomi Isobe for this information.

teaches her such British domestic arts as jam-making, nurtures her awareness and appreciation of nature, teaches her mental and physical self-care and slowly coaxes her back to happiness, a process framed in terms of training her to be a witch. Their fond, teacher-apprentice, slightly teasing relationship is at times reminiscent of that of Mrs Oldknow and her great-grandson Tolly in *The Children of Green Knowe* and may have been informed by Nashiki's own British experiences. In her next novel, *Back Garden* (*uraniwa*) (1995), Nashiki created a fantasy based around a Western-style villa, once owned by an English family called Burns. When the protagonist, Terumi, enters it she finds a mirror through which, like Alice, she is able to pass into a fantasy world and undergo experiences that help her and her family come to terms with the death of her twin brother. The description of the villa, as Isobe notes, seems an acknowledgement of the parts played by both Britain and Japan in the creation of the book and its world (Isobe 2018):

> The stone wall is constructed in a unique way passed down from ancient times in that region. Because it is a Western-style house, from a specialist's point of view its Japanese construction might seem strange, but to come into contact with its imposing presence is to feel that it doesn't matter whether it is Eastern or Western. (Nashiki 2016: 7)

Time fantasies gradually waned in popularity in Britain over the course of the 1970s, and in Japan too they no longer have the currency they once enjoyed. Nevertheless, one subtle acknowledgement of the continuing influence of *Tom's Midnight Garden* is to be glimpsed in Mamoru Hosoda's 2018 anime feature, *Mirai* (*mirai no mirai*), about a four-year-old boy's difficulty in coming to terms with having a baby sister and his encounters with the same sister when she visits him from the future. At one point the boy, Kun, looks through his picture books. The camera lingers over one called *The Wonderful Garden* (*fushigina niwa*), on the cover of which are depicted a girl in a Victorian pinafore dress and a boy in pyjamas. It is a clear allusion to the picture of Tom and his friend Hatty drawn by Susan Einzig for the first edition of *Tom's Midnight Garden*, which was also used for the Japanese translation. Given that *Mirai* is a time-slip story in which Kun, like Tom, learns to value humanity across multiple generations, and that in both stories the two central characters are older and younger than each other at various points, this graceful tribute from Hosoda is very apt. In interview, he has cited Pearce's book, among other Western children's classics, as one of his inspirations:

> [*Mirai*] really is a story about a child, through a mysterious garden, finding out about his family's secrets – and I feel like that is actually a theme or style that is explored a lot in Western literature. There's *Tom's Midnight Garden*, and *Narnia*, and *The Secret Garden*. (Grobar 2018)

In 1999, thirty-two years after *Tom's Midnight Garden* was translated into Japanese, the first translation of J. K. Rowling's 1997 fantasy *Harry Potter and the Philosopher's Stone* (*harī pottā to kenja no ishi*) appeared in Japan. Like *Tom*, it made a huge impression, and like *Tom* it precipitated numerous imitators. Rowling's was not of course the first British book about a magical education, nor even the first to blend the conventions of boarding-school fiction and witchcraft. Mary Stewart's *The Little Broomstick* (1971), Jill Murphy's *The Worst Witch* (1974) and its numerous sequels and Anthony Horowitz's *Groosham Grange* (1995) were among its predecessors (Pinsent 2002). *The Little Broomstick* and *The Worst Witch* had even been translated into Japanese before Rowling's books, in 1975 and 1987, respectively, although they made relatively little impression at the time. The global success of Harry Potter changed the landscape entirely, however, and Japanese magic school stories soon began to appear, not only in novels but also in manga, anime and other media.

Some Japan-made magic schools were located in Japan itself. Tsutomu Satō's *The Irregular at Magic High School* (*mahōka kōkō no rettōsei*), a light novel series published between 2008 and 2011, and Kazue Katō's manga, *Blue Exorcist* (*ao no ekusoshisuto*) (from 2009), both created Japanese settings for their magical schools. However, Britain has often been seen as the natural home of such establishments. Type-Moon's *Fate* franchise, for example, which has produced multiple stories in visual novel, computer game, manga and anime formats, generally sets its stories of multi-participant mage battles for the 'Holy Grail' in Japan, but the headquarters of the international Mages' Association is in the so-called Clock Tower school, located under the Houses of Parliament in London.

A useful insight into Japanese awareness of British boarding-school settings is provided by Yana Toboso's popular manga, *Black Butler* (*kuroshitsuji*) (from 2006). Its protagonist, Ciel Phantomhive, is a Victorian child from a noble English family, who has inherited the duty of protecting the realm from supernatural attack, which he does with the aid of his demonic butler, Sebastian. The story's primary setting is not a school; however, in volumes 14–17 of the manga (2012–13) Ciel's duties lead him to infiltrate a public school called Weston College. In the 'Below Stairs with the Black Butler' section at the end of volume 15, Toboso describes the research for this public school arc, which she carried out with the aid of Riko Murakami and which involved reading a variety of books with public school settings, including Thomas Hughes's *Tom Brown's Schooldays* (1857), James Hilton's *Goodbye, Mr Chips* (1934), Julian Mitchell's play, *Another Country* (1981) and Kiyoshi Ikeda's account of his time at the Leys School in Cambridge, *Freedom and Discipline* (*jiyū to kiritsu*) (1949). Toboso was amazed to find that many of the bizarre rituals, structures (such as colour-coded school houses) and uniforms that she had encountered when reading about 'a certain magic school' (*bō mahō gakkō*) were genuine features of public school life, exclaiming: 'Boarding school really is a fantasy!' (*kishuku gakkō maji fantajī*) (Toboso 2012: 174).

Of the Japanese works that have built on the foundation of that fantasy, one of the most notable is director Yō Yoshinari's anime franchise, *Little Witch Academia* (*ritoru uitchi akademia*) (2013–17), which is set in a witch school in southwest England. The anime does not disguise its debt to Harry Potter (Luna Nova Academy is even powered by a Sorcerer's Stone (*madō ishi*)), but it also draws on the broader traditions of British boarding-school fiction, such as Enid Blyton's *St Clare's* (1941–5) and *Malory Towers* (1946–51), Murphy's *Worst Witch* and perhaps even Elinor Brent-Dyer's *Chalet School* series (1925–70), given the decidedly international character of Luna Nova's intake. Like Murphy's Mildred Hubble, the Japanese protagonist, Akko, is a seemingly incompetent witch, who relies on the support of two female friends: Lotte Jansson, a kindly girl with glasses (like Murphy's Maud Spellbody), and Sucy Manbavaran, who is fond of practical jokes (like Murphy's Enid Nightshade). Other familiar 'types' include the snobbish Diana Cavendish, an accomplished pupil from an illustrious British witch family, whose initial disdain for Akko gradually gives way to respect.

Non-literary British influence is also evident. Blytonbury, Luna Nova Academy's neighbouring town, alludes to Blyton through its name but is also recognizable as a lightly disguised version of Glastonbury in Somerset, with Glastonbury's distinctive Tor and abbey ruins often visible throughout the series. The choice of location shows some sophistication, since, outside the realm of fiction, Glastonbury is Britain's most famous centre for Wicca, paganism and alternative spiritualities. When Akko arrives in Blytonbury from Japan, declaring, 'I'm going to become a witch here!' ('Starting Over', 2017), she is echoing the sentiments of many a modern Glastonbury pilgrim. For viewers aware of that context, the setting significantly modifies the experience of watching the show, evoking not only the magic of Hogwarts but also the esoteric and occult traditions of Glastonbury, particularly in the story's use of 'Earth mysteries' concepts such as leys.[6]

---

6 Alfred Watkins's foundational book on leys, *The Old Straight Track* (1925), is referred to as early as the *Little Witch Academia* franchise's first outing, in a short film of 2013, where it is referred to in a lecture by one of Luna Nova's teachers. For a Japanese perspective on Glastonbury's alternative religions, see Kawanishi (2015).

Literary versus cultural influence

So far, this discussion has considered the influence of British children's books in Japan in terms of conventional literary influence, with genres, tropes, plots, settings and characters being adapted and repurposed by Japanese writers and other artists in the production of new texts. Important as such activity is, some books have achieved a different kind of presence in Japanese culture, running at right angles (as it were) to the first, through their availability for iconic and allusive use. Texts used in this way may also be influential in a literary sense, but this is not necessary for them to make their presence felt in the culture at large, sometimes in radically transformative ways.

For example, few children's authors can claim to stand entirely outside the shadow of Lewis Carroll, given that his books were in many ways constitutive of the field. However, purely from a genre point of view, his influence is now relatively slight. 'Nonsense' novels in the Carroll tradition, though common in the decades after his books' publication, are today rare in English and Japanese alike. This is not to say that the *Alice* books are no longer influential, however. On the contrary, their hypercanonicity has made them open to allusion and quotation both within and beyond the domain of children's literature. It is to this more pervasive cultural presence that I now turn, taking Carroll as an initial case study.

Even a relatively slight acquaintance with Japanese popular culture will bring home how frequently Alice is alluded to in manga, anime, television, music and advertising. Sometimes the allusion is explicit, as in the 'Sakura and *Sakura in Wonderland*' (*sakura to fushigi no kuni no sakura*) episode of the magical-girl anime, *Cardcaptor Sakura* (broadcast 2 November 1999), in which the protagonist finds herself cast as Alice in a Wonderland created by the Chinese-English magician, Clow Reed, and encounters her friends and family in roles taken from Carroll's books. Comparably direct uses of *Alice* can also be found in more recent works, such as Mai Mochizuki's light novel, *Alice in Kyoto Forest* (*kyōraku no mori no arisu*, 2018), about an *Alice*-obsessed girl in an alternative version of Kyōto; but elsewhere, and perhaps more typically (as Amanda Kennell has argued), there is a degree of obliquity, with Alice being 'silhouetted' rather than represented directly or in detail. Kennell discusses numerous examples drawn from manga (2017: 138–42), but I will briefly note here two fairly recent television shows that perform this manoeuvre in very different, adult-orientated series.

The more oblique is the 2017 romantic comedy drama, *Tokyo Alice* (*tōkyō arisu*), based on a manga by Toriko Chiya originally published in *Kōdansha*

'Kiss' (2005–15). *Tokyo Alice* refers to Alice in its title and in the name of its protagonist, a young Tōkyō salarywoman named Fū Arisugawa. The opening credits show Fū and her friends falling through a space filled with fashionable clothes, shoes, lollipops and toys – a version of Alice's rabbit hole that manages to be simultaneously both more adult and more infantilized than the original. However, beyond the implication that adult life (and Tōkyō in particular) is the kind of environment that might leave a young woman as bewildered as Alice was in Wonderland, the analogy is not significantly elaborated. The silhouette of Alice flashes before us as barely more than a subliminal cue.

In a contrasting genre, *Alice in Borderland* (*imawa no kuni no arisu*) (2020–2), a Netflix series based on a 2010–15 manga by Haro Asō, has a male protagonist, Ryōhei Arisu.[7] Arisu and his friend Usagi ('Rabbit') find themselves forced to take part in a series of deadly games, played out in a transformed and weirdly deserted Tōkyō. Other *Alice* references include the prominence of playing cards, a climactic game of croquet in a rose garden and the presence of characters called Chishiya ('Cheshire') and the Hatter (*bōshiya*), but again there is no systematic development: these touches function as stylistic flourishes, drawing on an established lexicon to add texture to a story that has its centre of gravity elsewhere.

As the number of Japanese editions of *Alice's Adventures in Wonderland* testifies, Carroll's remains a widely read book, but for many Japanese, Alice is primarily a visual rather than a literary reference point (Ichikawa 2016: 30). The text itself, notoriously resistant to adequate translation because of its heavy reliance on culturally specific references and English-language wordplay, can be rather impenetrable to Japanese readers, and it is often Tenniel's illustrations rather than Carroll's text that act as the primary signifier of 'Alice' (Monden 2014: 271). Tenniel's images are instantly recognizable icons, widely found in advertising and as decorative motifs in shops and restaurants. *Alice's* influence has also been felt in fashion, notably as a component of what has become known as the Lolita style, after the title character of the 1955 novel by Vladimir Nabokov.[8]

The route by which this came about is not straightforward, but Jun Ichikawa has plausibly suggested that Tenniel's drawing style may have been one factor (2016: 34). Tenniel, being a political cartoonist, was not accustomed to depicting children, and his Alice is a curiously affectless, at times doll-like figure. Mikiko

---

7   The English title is a loose translation of the Japanese. A more literal one might be, 'Alice in the Land of the Hour of Death'.

8   For Nabokov's own career as an *Alice* translator, see Park (2018).

Chimori, describing Tenniel's picture of Alice holding a pig in *Alice's Adventures in Wonderland*, suggests that, although his depiction captures some aspects of Carroll's protagonist ('her air of unperturbed calm, with its suggestion of deliberately controlled sexuality, her decisive expression, and her tightly closed lips' (2005: 99)), it gives little impression of the liveliness or curiosity of the girl described in the text. Such a figure was liable to have fantasies projected onto it: indeed, the 'deliberately controlled sexuality' identified by Chimori is already a quality more likely to be perceived by an adult viewer than possessed by a seven-year-old child. In Japan, this process was expedited through books such as the photographer Hajime Sawatari's *Girl Alice* (*shōjo arisu*) (1973). Using sets loosely inspired by Carroll's text, Sawatari showcased a blonde, twelve-year-old British model named Samantha (Ichikawa 2016: 32). Samantha was photographed in various soft-focus erotic scenes, sometimes in white, frilly dresses, sometimes without.

The invitation to paedophilic fantasy in such a work is overt. However, Alice was also co-opted by young Japanese women of a later generation for their own purposes (Hinton 2013). Combining the doll-like Alice 'look' with lace- and frill-heavy styles inspired by French rococo, they created the Lolita fashions associated with the Harajuku district of Tōkyō in the 1990s and 2000s. *Alice* was only one element in the mix that made up Lolita fashion, and it was already a mediated version that had travelled some distance from Carroll's text, but it was an important and foundational element nonetheless. So, when a character in Asari Endō's light novel series *Magical Girl Raising Project* (*mahō shōjo ikusei keikaku*, 2012–) is introduced as 'Hardgore Alice' (*hādogoa arisu*) and we see a sinister, blank-eyed girl carrying a stuffed white rabbit toy and dressed all in black but for the Victorian lace in her headband, we need have no difficulty in reading her as a version of Alice, reconfigured within a gothic Lolita frame of reference. Overall, it seems reasonable to conclude, with Zoe Jaques and Eugene Giddens, that in Japanese appropriations of Alice the 'mixture of child and adult, eroticism and playfulness, crosses boundaries that are kept in fairly strict binaries' in the West (Jaques and Giddens 2016: 227).

It is possible to trace a route (however indirect) from Carroll's Alice to her manifestation on the streets of Harajuku as a component of Lolita fashion; but there are times when the appearances of children's literature figures in Japan seem entirely removed from their original context. Advertising, especially, is a form of display that will often utilize a character design or other form of iconic imagery simply on the basis of recognition value, positive associations and the ability to capture a viewer's attention, rather than relevance to the product

Figure 3.3 Peter Rabbit acting as the emblem of Daitō Bunka University on a bus at Takasaka Station, Saitama, 2022 (photograph by the author).

being sold. Compare the adoption of Peter Rabbit as an official emblem by two Japanese institutions: Daitō Bunka University in Saitama and the financial giant, Mitsubishi UFJ Trust and Banking (Figures 3.3 and 3.4). Daitō Bunka's use of Peter occasions no surprise, since it advertises the university's position as Japan's premier centre for Beatrix Potter research and the home of the Beatrix Potter Reference Library. At first sight, Mitsubishi's use of the same iconic picture is more puzzling. A fictional character whose main narrative action is to break into a householder's property and commit theft might not seem an ideal representative for a trust bank, but in practice this is not a problem. Posters such as that in Figure 3.4, which advertises a Mitsubishi subsidiary offering estate agent services, incorporate Peter essentially as a logo, making no reference to him in the accompanying text. From Alice and Peter Rabbit to Paddington Bear and Thomas the Tank Engine, the function of such high-recognition children's literature characters is often associative rather than semantic. Iconic advertising of this kind is not of course unique to Japan, but it is particularly deeply embedded in Japanese culture. Every city and prefecture, as well as many companies and individual products, will have a bespoke mascot, while Sanrio characters such as Hello Kitty can flourish largely free of narrative context, giving them maximum flexibility to bestow desirable associations (such as cuteness) on the widest possible range of products. Stripped of the context of Potter's story, Peter's image is similarly free-floating.

British children's literature and Japanese culture touch at many points, and this discussion can only hope to give an indicative sense of that larger landscape,

Figure 3.4 Peter Rabbit advertising an estate agent, Nakano Station, 2018 (photograph by the author).

although Chapter 5 will offer the opportunity to return to some of these questions in the rather more specialized domain of tourism. Meanwhile, Japan's unique history and context of reception have given rise to a canon and a cultural economy of British children's books significantly different from that in the UK. That economy is engaged in a constant negotiation with Japan's own literature but is no less involved in its wider culture, notably through the iconic uses made of British characters and imagery. Although some of these uses may appear more significant than others viewed through the prism of literary critical discourse, all have their own place and value in Japanese culture, even when that value lies partly in their capacity to surprise Western expectations.

4

Hayao Miyazaki and British children's literature

In the previous chapter, I discussed the cultural presence in Japan of numerous animated adaptations of British children's books, from classics such as *World Masterpiece Theatre*'s *A Dog of Flanders* to more ephemeral productions such as *Please, Psammead!*. Although such works remain well known in Japan, and some have even enjoyed international success, in terms of global fame they cannot be compared with the work of Hayao Miyazaki. Miyazaki is not a children's novelist, editor, publisher or scholar. He reads English-language books only in Japanese translation. Nevertheless, he has had a unique role in popularizing British children's literature in Japan, both through direct advocacy and through his animations, notably at the company he co-founded in 1985, Studio Ghibli. This chapter will discuss not only that contribution but also the wider context within which Miyazaki has worked, his part in influencing the Japanese reception of British children's books and the implications of his activities for the adaptation of literature across cultural, national and linguistic borders.

Miyazaki was born in Tōkyō in 1941. Growing up in post-war Japan, he was a book-loving child and read widely in Japanese and foreign literature, as well as manga. This interest continued at university, where he studied politics and economics but was also a member (at times the sole member) of a children's literature study group (Napier 2018: 11). He was a precocious artist and as a young graduate soon made his way into the anime industry. There is an obvious affinity between anime and literature for children, especially in a land where manga (a form in which Miyazaki would become an accomplished practitioner) offers unparalleled opportunities to combine words and pictures in storytelling; however, Miyazaki's devotion to children's books was driven by more than a professional interest. His reading of children's literature was, and remains, eclectic and omnivorous. It encompasses many classics, as we shall see, but also extends to more unexpected texts and writers. Laura Cecil, Diana Wynne Jones's literary agent, recalls meeting Miyazaki in Tōkyō while negotiating the film rights to *Howl's Moving Castle* and being surprised when the director asked her opinion of a book he admired, *The Grange at High Force* (1965), an almost entirely forgotten novel by an equally obscure English writer, Philip Turner. Luckily, Cecil had represented the rights for one of Turner's other works and was able to answer knowledgeably (Cecil 2020).

Miyazaki's reading taste is by no means exclusively British, but he has always had a particular affinity for British children's literature. This was demonstrated most clearly in 2010, when he was invited to select fifty children's books, from all periods and nationalities, for an exhibition celebrating the sixtieth anniversary of the Iwanami Shōnen Bunko imprint. If we include British-born Frances Hodgson Burnett and Hugh Lofting, twenty-two of the fifty titles were by British writers, far more than those of any other nation. France and the United States followed at six titles apiece, then Russia with three, with the remaining ten countries included boasting just one or two titles. (Japan's representatives were Miyazawa's *The Restaurant of Many Orders* and the Heian-era collection of myths, legends and folktales, *Nihon Ryōiki*.) The British books were, in chronological order: Daniel Defoe, *Robinson Crusoe* (1719); W. M. Thackeray, *The Rose and the Ring* (1854); Lewis Carroll, *Alice's Adventures in Wonderland* (1865); Robert Louis Stevenson, *Treasure Island* (1882); Frances Hodgson Burnett, *Little Lord Fauntleroy* (1886); Arthur Conan Doyle, *The Adventures of Sherlock Holmes* (1892); Kenneth Grahame, *The Wind in the Willows* (1908); Frances Hodgson Burnett, *The Secret Garden* (1911); Hugh Lofting, *The Voyages of Doctor Dolittle* (1922); A. A. Milne, *Winnie-the-Pooh* (1926); Arthur Ransome, *Swallows and Amazons* (1930); J. R. R. Tolkien, *The Hobbit* (1937); Eleanor Doorly, *The Radium Woman* (1939); Hilda Lewis, *The Ship That Flew* (1939); Elizabeth Goudge, *The Little White Horse* (1946); Cecil Day-Lewis, *The Otterbury Incident* (1948); Mary Norton, *The Borrowers* (1952); Rosemary Sutcliff, *The Eagle of the Ninth* (1954); Eleanor Farjeon, *The Little Bookroom* (1955); Joan G. Robinson, *When Marnie Was There* (1967); K. M. Peyton, *The Flambards* series (from 1967); and Philippa Pearce, *What the Neighbours Did, and Other Stories* (1972) (Miyazaki 2011).

Powerful as this list is as evidence of Miyazaki's taste for, and in, British children's literature, several caveats should be borne in mind in interpreting it. Some commentators (e.g. Halliday 2017) have glossed the selection as representing simply Miyazaki's favourite children's books, but that is too absolute a claim. The list is drawn, not from all of children's literature but only from the admittedly extensive catalogue of Iwanami Shōnen Bunko. Nothing can therefore be read into the absence of such august figures as Tove Jansson or personal favourites such as Diana Wynne Jones, who were published by other companies. Moreover, the British emphasis in Miyazaki's selection may reflect that of the Iwanami Shōnen Bunko catalogue generally and by extension of the wider tradition of foreign children's literature publishing in Japan. All the same, that tradition did much to shape the taste of Miyazaki, as of many Japanese readers.

Another consideration is that some of Miyazaki's choices were prompted by factors other than his personal taste. This is clear from the recommendations he wrote to accompany his selections, which were later reproduced in his book, *Doorway to Books* (*hon e no tobira*) (2011). In the recommendation for Elizabeth Goudge's *The Little White Horse*, for example, he compliments the book but confesses that he read it only because it was suggested by a 'respected *senpai*' and had been translated by the admired Momoko Ishii (51). The text accompanying Kenneth Grahame's *The Wind in the Willows* ignores the text entirely, reserving its enthusiasm for E. H. Shepard's illustrations, one of which is reproduced: 'What a good picture! Just looking at the picture is enough to satisfy me. If this artist had taken up animation, he would have become a very skilful animator.' Miyazaki's reticence about Grahame's work is explained in the following line: 'And yet, I can't read this book to the end, no matter how many times I try. It's a complete mystery' (Miyazaki 2011: 24).

Doorway to Books consists of two parts: first, the individual book recommendations, then a series of general reflections on children's literature. Miyazaki's reason for including a book that he had not actually finished is revealed in the second section, where he discusses the experience of selecting books for the exhibition:

> In the end, among the fifty books was one that I couldn't read. The recommendation says, 'I can't read this book to the end, no matter how many times I try' [laughs]. I still haven't read it, but everyone who has says it's good, so I couldn't leave it out – there are books like that. (Miyazaki 2011: 77)

As this shows, Miyazaki selected texts partly in accordance with his wider understanding of their canonicity, rather than by personal taste alone. *The Wind in the Willows* was a book that could not be omitted, whether he liked it or not – indeed, whether or not he was able to make it to the final chapter. Other inclusions and omissions may have been influenced by similar considerations.

These caveats notwithstanding, many of Miyazaki's comments on the books in his list demonstrate a close, if idiosyncratic, engagement. Frances Hodgson Burnett's *Little Lord Fauntleroy* reminds him of a boyhood friend who really was as open-hearted and noble as Cedric Errol but who died young (45). He is attracted to K. M. Peyton's *Flambards* because it accurately depicts early aircraft, one of his enthusiasms (27). Rosemary Sutcliff's novel of second-century Britain, *The Eagle of the Ninth*, prompts him to mention a long-standing but unrealized wish to adapt the book, relocating it to Tōhoku (19). At times, he sets books in their broader literary or political contexts. *Treasure Island* is valued as the original of all treasure-hunting adventure stories (39), whereas *The Hobbit* has been 'consumed' (*kuitsukusarete shimatta*) by the many imitations and games based on its ideas (49). The appeal *Robinson Crusoe* had for him as a boy is now tarnished by an awareness of its colonialism: 'The white people who read this book certainly carried their guns to other islands and nations to deprive them of treasure, and took part in slaughter throughout the world. I don't have a gun, nor do I want one' (38).

Miyazaki takes on the role of booklover rather than teacher and does not pretend to speak for anyone but himself. This is not to say, however, that he has not vigorously promoted books and authors he admires. His most sustained efforts in this regard, excluding his film adaptations, have probably been on behalf of the English novelist and short story writer, Robert Westall. Miyazaki's support for Westall is an aspect of his activity that English speakers are generally unaware of, since it has manifested primarily in his promotion of Japanese editions of Westall's work. For example, he illustrated a 2009 translation of Westall's novel *Fathom Five* (*suishin go hiro*, 1979); and in 2014 he drew jackets for two other Westall collections: *Midnight Phone Call* (*mayonaka no denwa*) and *The Call of Distant Days* (*tōi hi no yobigoe*). A wraparound band (*obi*) on the latter book carries a quotation from Miyazaki, declaring simply: 'I like Westall.'

By far the most revealing example of Miyazaki's advocacy, however, is the manga that he created to accompany *Blackham's Bomber* (*burakkamu no bakugekiki*), a volume of Westall's stories published by Iwanami Shoten in 2006, which takes its name from the Japanese title of the longest of the three stories included, 'Blackham's Wimpey'. When Miyazaki first discovered Mizuhito Kanehara's translation of 'Blackham's Wimpey' in a Kichijōji bookshop in 1990, he already knew Westall's work through the Carnegie-winning supernatural thriller, *The Scarecrows* (1981); but it was 'Blackham's Wimpey', with its wartime setting and aeronautical theme, that kindled his enthusiasm. The story, about a Second World War British bomber haunted by the cries of a dying German pilot, was even described in a Japanese documentary as his 'favourite British children's book' (Arakawa 2019). To accompany the 2006 edition, he wrote a twenty-three-page manga or 'illustrated essay' (Miyazaki 2014b: 445) inspired by the story and by Westall's own life, as an *homage* (*omāju*) to the author (Westall 2006: 224). The artwork from 'Westall Fantasy: A Journey to Tynemouth' (*uesutōru gensō: tainmasu e no tabi*) was used by Iwanami Shoten in an exhibition and included as a 'frame' to top and tail the published volume.

'A Journey to Tynemouth' depicts a trip Miyazaki made to England in February 2006 (Miyazaki 2014b: 445). Knowing that 'Blackham's Wimpey' involves a good deal of technical detail about the layout of Wellington bombers, he was keen to make it easier for Japanese readers to understand and uses much of the first part of the manga (which appears in the volume before the story itself) to explain that detail to readers unfamiliar with aircraft terminology or history. In the manga, Miyazaki expresses his admiration for Westall's ability to convey the experience of flying in the noisy, cramped, canvas tube that was a Wellington and clearly wishes readers to share his appreciation: 'What wonderful descriptive power! This was the first novel I'd ever read that caught the interior of a bomber like this' (Miyazaki 2006: 9).[1] In such technical matters, Miyazaki writes from a position of knowledge and passionate interest. His father had been the director of an aviation parts manufacturer, Miyazaki Airplane, so aircraft were an important part of Miyazaki's life from the beginning. Planes and airships had thronged animations such as *Castle in the Sky* (*tenkū no shiro rapyuta*, 1986), *Kiki's Delivery Service* (*majo no takkyūbin*, 1989), *Porco Rosso* (*kurenai no buta*, 1992) and *Howl's Moving Castle* (*hauru no ugoku shiro*, 2004), and would feature even more prominently in his 2013 film, *The Wind Rises* (*kaze tachinu*, 2013), which was partly inspired by the story of the aircraft designer Jirō Horikoshi, whose Mitsubishi A6M Zero fighter was used to devastating effect at Pearl Harbor.

For his technical research, Miyazaki visited Brooklands Museum in Surrey, to see one of the only two remaining Wellingtons. However, as the title of the manga suggests, his primary destination was the town of Tynemouth, on the north-east coast of England. It was in Tynemouth that Westall was born in 1929, it was there he spent his boyhood and it is the setting, explicit or implicit, for much of his fiction. 'A Journey to Tynemouth' is, first and foremost, a fan work: a tribute to an admired writer, an act of empathetic identification and a meditation on an imagined meeting that never happened.

---

1 In fact, Westall made at least one mistake in his story. His narrator, speaking in May 1944, refers to a seabird 'trained by the Japs in kamikaze tactics'; however, the first kamikaze attacks did not take place until the autumn of that year. Miyazaki and Westall briefly discuss kamikaze pilots in the manga, but Miyazaki either did not notice or chose to overlook this error (Westall 1984: 78; 2006: 125).

In the manga, Miyazaki portrays himself as a man (or rather, a whiskery, bespectacled pig) on a literary pilgrimage. We see him wandering along the seafront, seeking out Westall's childhood home and imagining it as it might have been during the Second World War, the setting for many of Westall's stories. Although Westall was Miyazaki's senior by more than a decade, Miyazaki is keen to explore the parallels between their childhoods, recognizing that the war was formative for them both. In particular, both experienced night bombing. Westall lived through the Blitz, an event that would figure repeatedly in his fiction. His home was on the flightpath of Luftwaffe bombers heading for Newcastle upon Tyne, and more than 300 bombs fell on Tynemouth itself. Likewise, in July 1945, the four-year-old Miyazaki was present at the firebombing of Utsunomiya, where his family's company had been evacuated. Miyazaki's manga juxtaposes illustrations of the two towns under night attack, alerting readers to their similarities as well as their differences (Figure 4.1). He recalls the sight being 'like a sunset, only above the city' (18). His comment that 'the experience had a decisive influence on the boy Westall' (18) is, of course, equally applicable to himself. He details how, after the war, he dealt with his experience of the conflict by reading obsessively about its events, coming to hate the Japanese army but also

Figure 4.1 Night raids on Tynemouth and Utsunomiya, from 'A Journey to Tynemouth' (2006: 18). © Hayao Miyazaki/Iwanami Shoten.

shooting down 'thousands of B29 bombers' in his imagination – a recollection he wryly offers as a case study to psychoanalysts (19).

War is a frequent theme in Miyazaki's own work but is generally transferred to fantasy settings, as in *Nausicaä of the Valley of the Wind* (*kaze no tani no naushika*, 1982–94 (manga), 1984 (film)), *Princess Mononoke* (*mononoke hime*, 1997) or *Howl's Moving Castle*. In the historical *The Wind Rises*, the destruction caused by the Second World War is confined to a minute-long series of shots of ruined aircraft towards the end of the film. It fell to Miyazaki's colleague, Isao Takahata, to create the only Ghibli film with a Second World War setting: *Grave of the Fireflies* (*hotaru no haka*, 1988). By contrast, much of Westall's work focused directly on his own wartime experience and that of others. Westall's debut novel, *The Machine Gunners* (1975), had been born of a wish to communicate to his twelve-year-old son what life had been like for him at the same age:

> He had shown me how life was for him at twelve and I suddenly felt the need to show him how life had been for me at twelve. I wanted to invite him back into my world and let the two generations, just for a moment, stand side by side in time. (Northshields173 n.d.)

Westall's writing had a lived quality that appealed to Miyazaki as the mark of an authentic artist: 'I realised when I read Westall's books, *The Machine Gunners* or *The Kingdom by the Sea*, "There is someone walking ahead of me"' (2006: 19).

The first part of the manga concludes with Miyazaki sitting on a bench, where he is joined by Westall himself (depicted as a shaggy dog). In the second part, which is printed after the stories that make up the bulk of the volume, Westall and Miyazaki wander the seafront village of Cullercoats, near Tynemouth. Miyazaki takes the opportunity to praise Westall's work, singling out *Blitzcat* (1989) – the story of a cat travelling through wartime England to find its owner – as a 'masterpiece' (201) and quoting his favourite lines from *The Promise* (1990). The men agree that Japan and Britain share a reluctance to face up to the damage inflicted on, and by, their people. Westall suggests that the British bombardment of Germany was a dreadful thing, 'both for German mothers and children and for the young British men' who carried it out (202). The fictional Westall's breadth of sympathy reflects the thoughts that the real Westall put into the mind of Gary, the young airman who is the narrator of 'Blackham's Wimpey':

> Think about all the English ex-schoolgirls filling bombs till their backs ache, all the German ex-schoolgirls making shells. Think about the guts of German mothers in Hamburg, sheltering their kids with their own bodies from the fire-typhoon we started. Think about the craftsmen's skill in a Rolls-Royce Merlin,

and a German medieval cathedral. All those people with all that guts, and our top brass are just turning them all into one big rubbish tip that's slowly covering Europe. (79)

Miyazaki speculates about the extent to which Westall inserted his own emotions and desires into his fiction, something the manga's Westall acknowledges as a 'weak point' (205) but that Miyazaki identifies as one of the things he admires, adding: 'Mr Westall, your work is filled with the courage to keep struggling with this terrible world and with loving grief for lost things' (206). These words, which were excerpted for use on the volume's wraparound band, can perhaps be taken as a summation of what Miyazaki finds valuable in Westall's writing.

In using Westall as a looking-glass figure in which to see himself, and wartime Britain as an analogue of Japan, Miyazaki is of course making use of one of the pervasive metaphors that underpin the present book. I have gone into some detail in describing 'A Journey to Tynemouth', partly because of its inaccessibility to English-language readers but also because it offers both a penetrating discussion of Westall's work and an even more helpful insight into Miyazaki's own aesthetics, values and way of thinking, to which he was perhaps able to give freer expression here, in a fan work, than he is accustomed to doing in public interviews about his own oeuvre. (In the manga, he expresses relief that Westall has not seen any of his films, and that he therefore need not discuss them (206).)

As Miyazaki prepares to return to Japan, he reflects that Westall was only sixty-three when he died in 1993 – less than Miyazaki's own age (sixty-five) as he writes the manga (208). Here as throughout, Westall's importance to Miyazaki, as artist and as *senpai*, is in part a measure of the extent to which he provides Miyazaki with a refracted image of himself. It is not surprising that Lindy McKinnel, Westall's partner, observes in a quotation that appears on the reverse of the book's wraparound band: 'It's a great shame that Mr Miyazaki and Robert Westall never met. They are clearly much alike' (Westall 2006).

British children's books and adaptation

Fascinating as Miyazaki's views on children's books and authors are, I would not be affording them this much attention were he not also one of the world's foremost filmmakers. To consider his professional engagement with British children's books requires some preliminary acknowledgement of the widely varying nature of that engagement, however. The Studio Ghibli films based on Diana Wynne Jones's *Howl's Moving Castle* and Mary Norton's *The Borrowers*, for all the ways in which they altered and added to the source material, are nevertheless clearly versions of the stories in their British originals and can be uncontroversially termed 'adaptations'. However, Miyazaki's early encounters with British children's books are less predictable, more heterogeneous and generally resistant to satisfactory description in a single word or phrase.

One need not invoke the quasi-ethical discourse of 'fidelity' to wonder at what point a film shades from adaptation to original work, albeit one with identifiable influences or references. Had Miyazaki realized his plan to relocate *The Eagle of the Ninth* to Japan and turned it into a story of, say, Yamato soldiers braving the territory of the Emishi, would it have been the 'same' story, or would the difference in cultural context have been too jarring? How much, and what, would have had to change for the film to move so far from its source material as to escape its orbit altogether and render the word 'adaptation' more misleading than helpful? Again, to what extent is it possible to take an existing character, such as Swift's Lemuel Gulliver, and place him in a story with a different plot and in a different genre, without fundamentally changing his nature? Such questions are not offered here as the prelude to a philosophically rigorous inquiry, although neither are they entirely rhetorical. Rather, they are intended to alert the reader to the limits and ambiguities of the language of adaptation when discussing works that sit in its semantic borderlands, as many of Miyazaki's do.

Miyazaki's output includes both original stories and adaptations, but the distinction has never been very sharp. A case in point is the first animation in which he was involved that drew on a British children's book. This was the Tōei feature, *Gulliver's Travels beyond the Moon* (literally 'Gulliver's Space Journey', *garibā no uchū ryokō*) (1965). The young Miyazaki's role, as a creator of intermediate animation frames, was junior, but the film gives a useful indication of the parameters within which he would later understand the practice of adaptation. Its first two minutes promise a straightforward adaptation of Swift's book. Much as in Max and Dave Fleischer's 1939 cartoon feature of *Gulliver's Travels*, of which Miyazaki had been very fond (Napier 2018: 21), we see Lemuel Gulliver shipwrecked and attempting to make his way to shore; but soon the camera pulls back to reveal the story's true protagonist, a young boy who is merely watching *Gulliver's Travels* in a cinema. Shortly after leaving, the boy is involved in a traffic accident, and there is an implication that the remainder of the plot may be a dream brought on by concussion. He soon encounters Gulliver himself, now much older, who carries him and his companions – a dog and a toy soldier – into space, in a rocket of his own construction. There, they are welcomed by the technocratic inhabitants of the Planet of Blue Hope, who are so advanced as to have created a workforce of robots to enable them to lead a life of leisure. However, the robots have learned to replicate themselves and turned against their masters, and only the intervention of Gulliver and his companions saves the day.

Not much survives of Swift's *Gulliver* here beyond the film poster shown outside the cinema (which depicts the hero in his iconic pose, tied down by Lilliputians), the man himself (who retains his periwig into the twentieth century) and the theme of travel into unknown regions. Possibly the scientific inhabitants of the Planet of Blue Hope are an echo of the aristocratic denizens of the floating island of Laputa in the third book of *Gulliver's Travels*, who are so engrossed in profound mathematical and musical problems that they require the services of a 'flapper' to tap them on the mouth or ear when it is time to speak or listen. But the echo, if present, is faint, and it seems fair to say that *Gulliver's* main role is to provide a general template for the idea of a fantastic voyage to a culturally alien society. That being so, is it helpful to think of this as an adaptation of Swift's book?

The same question could be asked of the film that Miyazaki would make twenty-one years later, as the first production of Studio Ghibli: *Castle in the Sky* (*tenkū no shiro rapyuta*). Here the reference to Laputa is explicit, both in the film's Japanese title (*Laputa: Castle in the Sky*) and within its world. Pazū, a boy from a mining village and one of the film's two child protagonists, explains to his friend Shīta that Laputa is a 'legend' (*densetsu*), adding that, although Swift wrote about Laputa in *Gulliver's Travels*, that was just a 'fantasy' (*kūsō*). However, he possesses a photograph of a real floating island that his father once took from an airship, and Shīta turns out to be a Laputan princess, vindicating Swift's 'fantasy' after all. As in *Gulliver's Travels*, the Laputa of *Castle in the Sky* owes its powers of levitation to a single large stone (a lodestone in Swift, here a 'flying stone' (*hikōseki*)) contained within a large, inverted dome in the middle of the island. The two Laputas also share a history of exercising tyrannical rule over the cities below, but in the film that rule ended several centuries earlier. Laputa still floats, but it is an abandoned, overgrown ruin, home to plants and animals but devoid of human life, tended only by gardening robots left over from its days of technocratic affluence – an echo, perhaps, of the servant robots of *Gulliver's Travels beyond the Moon*.

Deciding whether to understand Miyazaki's story as occupying the same world as Swift's at a point some centuries after Gulliver's voyage or as a separate world entirely – albeit one in which *Gulliver's Travels* exists as a published fiction – is probably not central to most people's experience of *Castle in the Sky*, the focus of which is on adventure: chases, treasure hunting, friendship, airborne pirates and (in terms of cinematography) a spectacular exploration of the vertical, from the dizzying mineshafts of the village to the equally vertiginous galleries and terraces of Laputa itself. To call *Castle in the Sky* either an adaptation of *Gulliver* or an original fiction set in Swift's fictional world may be misleading, but its engagement with *Gulliver's Travels* amounts to considerably more than incidental quotation. This intertextual slipperiness is not atypical of Miyazaki's relationship with literary texts.

Many of Miyazaki's films for Studio Ghibli have some relationship with the work of British children's writers, whether through outright quotation, oblique reference or simply though the fact that Miyazaki's imagination and sense of story were partly shaped by his reading in that literature. At one extreme sits the scene in *Porco Rosso* in which the aviator protagonist tells his friend Fio a war story about a pilot's vision of a procession of dead flyers heading towards the afterlife – a narrative lifted wholesale from Roald Dahl's 1946 short story, 'They Shall Not Grow Old'.[2] On the other hand, the influence of *Alice in Wonderland* on *Spirited Away* (*sen to chihiro no kamikakushi*, 2001), though often suspected, is harder to demonstrate, simply because *Alice*'s presence is so pervasive in Japanese and British culture alike. Satoshi Andō, for instance, has offered a comparison of the two texts in terms of the crisis of identity experienced by both Alice and Chihiro, the ten-year-old protagonist of *Spirited Away*, but, as he acknowledges, this is hardly a feature unique to those two stories; Miyazaki's own films alone furnish several protagonists about whom similar observations might be made (Andō 2008: 23–7). We might point to more specific features, such as the motif of people turning into pigs (as happens to both the Duchess's baby in *Alice* and Chihiro's parents) or the fact that both stories begin with a girl entering a tunnel and emerging into a strange and unfamiliar landscape – but these have too archetypal a significance and too long a literary history to be the basis of a compelling case. Porcine transformations are as old as the *Odyssey*; and why should Chihiro's tunnel not allude rather to the myth of Orpheus, or to the birth canal, or even to the much-quoted opening line of Yasunari Kawabata's 1948 novel, *Snow Country*, in which the narrator emerges from a tunnel into a transformed world?

---

2 'They Shall Not Grow Old' was originally published for adults but is accessible to any child able to enjoy *Going Solo*, Dahl's 1986 book about his days as a pilot.

My purpose here is not to box terminological or intertextual shadows but to highlight some of the complexities involved in deploying such blunt-instrument words as 'influence' and 'adaptation'. Where I use them in the following discussion, they should be understood as being framed by scare quotes, of varying degrees of opacity.

Howl's Moving Castle

Junko Nishimura's translation of Diana Wynne Jones's 1986 novel, *Howl's Moving Castle*, was published in Japanese in 1997 by Tokuma Shoten, which was then Studio Ghibli's parent company. At the time, Jones was not yet well known in Japan. Translations of two of her children's books – *Charmed Life* (1977) and *Wild Robert* (1989), a short book for younger readers – had been published there but were now out of print; two others, *The Time of the Ghost* (1981) and *Fire and Hemlock* (1985), were in print but only in adult editions (Uemura 2021). The situation in some ways resembled that in her home country, where Jones, although recognized by her fans and many of her writing peers as one of the major children's writers of her generation, had never received commensurate critical recognition (Butler 2006: 5–7; Gaiman 2012: viii–x) and where many of her titles had been allowed to languish on various publishers' backlists or to slide out of print entirely. In Britain, that situation would change dramatically around the turn of the millennium, when the Harry Potter boom emboldened HarperCollins to republish almost all of Jones's titles. If Potter was the catalyst for a change in her fortunes in the UK, however, in Japan that role was played by Miyazaki's 2004 adaptation of *Howl*, which prompted a more general Japanese interest in her work.

A medical condition affecting her neck meant that by then Jones could not travel long distances, and she never visited Japan. Nevertheless, the success of her books there pleased her greatly. She was interested in Japanese culture, which she was able to access in part through her daughter-in-law, Noriko Kawabata. However, areas of mutual incomprehension also intrigued and amused her, as was apparent in interview:

> [W]hen my books are translated into Japanese . . . I get terribly formal, serious questions, like 'What are the rules for conkers?' or 'What is the difference between a top hat and a bowler hat?' And you think, I wouldn't have done it like that if I'd known it was going to put them to all this trouble. (Butler 2002: 172)

Howl's Moving Castle is set primarily in Ingary, a fantasy land where fairy-tale conventions are accepted as reality and where eighteen-year-old Sophie Hatter, as the eldest of three sisters, knows that she is fated never to be the heroine of any story. She resigns herself to a life of quotidian dullness in the family hat shop, but this changes one day when the evil Witch of the Waste sweeps in and lays a curse on her that gives her the appearance of a ninety-year-old woman. Unable to face her family or friends in this new guise, Sophie sets off on her own, only to encounter the moving castle of the notorious Wizard Howl, who is well known to make a habit of capturing young women and eating their hearts.

As is often the case in Diana Wynne Jones's books, appearances are deceptive. Howl is vain and irresponsible, but he is not the evil wizard everyone takes him to be. Rather, he is a Welsh ex-doctoral student who has found his way into Ingary through his study of charms and spells and who lives by selling his magical services in various Ingary towns, each of which is connected to his castle by a different portal: one leads to Kingsbury, the capital; one to the seaside town of Porthaven; and a third opens the door of the castle itself, wherever it happens to be. A fourth, secret portal opens onto Howl's home town in Wales, which he visits from time to time, partly to keep a protective eye on his sister and her family. The castle is powered by the magic of a fire demon, Calcifer, whose services Howl rashly obtained in exchange for custody of his own heart and who asks Sophie to find a way to break their contract, which otherwise can end only in the deaths of both parties. The ingenious adventures that follow culminate in the defeat of the Witch, the liberation of Calcifer, the restoration of Sophie and Howl (who gets his heart back) as well as that of several other enchanted characters and the romantic union of the two protagonists.

Studio Ghibli first expressed interest in the rights to *Howl's Moving Castle* in 1999, with the contract being signed the following year. Ghibli was not yet widely known in the West; their Oscar-winning hit, *Spirited Away*, would be released only in 2001, with the English dub following a year later. Jones, however, was already an admirer of both *Castle in the Sky* and *Kiki's Delivery Service*, and she was content to let the rights go to the studio. According to her agent, Laura Cecil, she was well aware that changes to the story were inevitable and, being well disposed to Miyazaki, was prepared to trust him with the project (Cecil 2020). This must have been a relief to Miyazaki, given his previous experiences of attempting to adapt work by living writers. In 1969, Tove Jansson had objected to the inclusion of machinery and themes of fighting in an anime series based on her Moomin books, in one episode of which the 29-year-old Miyazaki had depicted a tank (Greenberg 2018: 32). Two other projects, those to adapt Astrid

Lindgren's *Pippi Longstocking* (1945) and Ursula Le Guin's *Earthsea* books (from 1968), had been rebuffed by the authors entirely, although Le Guin would later relent (Le Guin 2007; Miyazaki 2014b: 439); while Eiko Kadono, the author of *Kiki's Delivery Service* (1985), had reportedly been unhappy with the changes that Miyazaki proposed in order to structure her episodic book as a feature film – changes that included the introduction of an episode featuring an airship. It had required all of Miyazaki's and producer Toshio Suzuki's persuasive skills to secure her acquiescence (MacDonald 2014).

When Cecil visited Studio Ghibli's offices in Tōkyō to discuss terms, she enquired about their intentions for the film. In particular, she was curious about an episode in the novel in which Howl leaves Ingary to visit his sister's family in Wales. Might the Welsh references in that chapter not be too culturally remote for a Japanese audience? At this stage of the project, at least, Cecil was told that Ghibli 'did not have any problem with the episode and . . . were planning to travel to Wales to get first-hand information on the landscape and background' (Cecil 2020). The fact that the chapter in question, 'In which Howl Goes to a Strange Country in Search of a Spell' (Jones 2000a: 145–59), is seen through the eyes of Sophie, from whose Ingarian point of view Wales is at least as baffling as it could be from that of any putative Japanese viewer, may have mitigated the extent to which opaque cultural references were perceived as a problem. The same applies to some of the other Welsh elements that appear throughout the book, such as the Welsh-language anthem of Llanelli RFC, 'Sosban Fach', which Sophie hears simply as 'the saucepan song' (51). However, Howl's Welsh identity is far more than an incidental detail; it is pervasive and signalled in many ways, both subtle and explicit (Hishida 2014). Howl (aka Howell Jenkins, aka Wizard Pendragon) speaks Welsh to his niece, wears a jacket with 'WELSH RUGBY' emblazoned on the back, attends drunken reunions at his university rugby club (265) and maintains a view of his Welsh family home from his bedroom window in the castle. His natural hair colour, though hidden beneath many layers of dye, is implied to be a stereotypically Welsh black (118, 165). At one point he laments that he is 'an unmusical Welshman' (262) and at another complains that 'I love Wales, but it doesn't love me' (208), placing his homeland in the populous ranks of those for whom he feels unrequited desire. Howl's sense of isolation from his country and family offers an important insight into his restless and emotionally insecure character.

The eponymous moving castle is an embodiment of Howl's personality, an impossible creation held together with spells and charms. A castle is an obvious choice of abode not only for a powerful figure in a fantasy kingdom but also for a

Welshman, given that Wales has the greatest concentration of castles in Europe. That Howl, as a Welsh wizard, should conjure a castle is thus no surprise, but its appearance is more specific. Unlike the grey north-Welsh edifices of Caernarfon, Conwy or Harlech, which conform to many people's image of a mediaeval castle, Howl's is constructed from 'huge black blocks, like coal' (40), and its appearance, 'blowing clouds of black smoke from its four tall, thin turrets' (11), is more evocative of a factory with four smokestacks than of a fortification. Indeed, it is possible to read the castle as actually having the appearance of an industrial plant or power station, an appearance interpreted by Sophie and the other Ingary natives in the fantasy terms with which their cultural vocabulary has furnished them. The castle thus reflects Howl's background in the valleys of twentieth-century south Wales, with its heavy industry and the mines that once supplied the world with high-grade coal, as much as it does the country's mediaeval history or Ingary's status as a land of fairy tale.

Jones never lived in Wales, except for a brief period of childhood evacuation at her grandfather's house during the Second World War, but she was of Welsh parentage and Wales was a thirty-minute drive from her home in Bristol. Events beyond the Severn were neither geographically nor emotionally distant. In this context, it is notable that *Howl's Moving Castle* was published in 1986, the same year that *Castle in the Sky* was released. Miyazaki has written that his depiction of the mining village in that film was inspired by a visit to Wales, shortly after the year-long 1984–5 miners' strike, where he was impressed by the miners' resistance to the Thatcher government's destruction of their way of life, feeling 'a real sense of solidarity' with them (Miyazaki 2014a: 339). He reproduced that spirit in the film's depiction of a strong, close-knit mining community. Howl's castle too projects a powerful image of twentieth-century Wales, combining its mediaeval and industrial histories in a form both spectacular and precarious.

Responsibility for directing *Howl's Moving Castle* was initially given by producer Suzuki to Mamoru Hosoda, then in his early thirties (Frank 2018). In November 2000, he and a team from Ghibli, including Suzuki and a scriptwriter, visited Bristol to consult Jones about the film. Jones described the meeting to Laura Cecil shortly afterwards:

We had a rather splendid tea party – in which the official translator and the guide were almost as hard at work as I was, because it turned out that their main reason for coming here was to grill me about the localities that had inspired me to write *Howl's Moving Castle*, which they intended to go and look at. It was surprisingly difficult to dig these out of my head. I realised I don't work at all at the conscious level they do. But by asking astute questions, they got me to admit to Exmoor (where you can look down into chimneys from the moor) and Lyme Regis and Portishead, whereupon even the guide was slightly disconcerted to discover that young Mr Hosoda the Director required an instant change of itinerary and an expedition to Dorset. (Jones 2000b)

Both here and in later conversations, Jones expressed some hesitation about mapping the landscape of Britain directly onto that of Ingary (Butler 2002: 163); but, even allowing for a more oblique relationship, it is easy to see how a view of chimneys from Exmoor might have fed into the scene in which Sophie, having just left Market Chipping, sits on 'a sort of headland, which gave [her] a magnificent view of the way she had come. . . . She could have tossed a stone down the chimney pots of the house next to the hat shop' (Jones 2000a: 38). Easy too to see how Lyme Regis in Dorset, with its famous Cobb, might have contributed Porthaven's curving harbour wall and steep streets and Portishead (a seaside town near Bristol) its marshes and part of its name. Jones was sensitive to the connotations and histories of names more generally and chose them with care. Market Chipping, the 'prosperous town' (9) where Sophie grows up, evokes the Cotswolds region, where the otherwise uncommon 'Chipping' element (which actually means 'market') is found in such placenames as Chipping Campden, Chipping Norton and Chipping Sodbury.

The concentration of the Ghibli team on questions of local influence suggests that at this point the studio's intention was still to create a setting inspired directly by British landscapes. It is intriguing to imagine what a *Howl's Moving Castle* film constructed on these lines might have looked like. A more explicitly Welsh Howl would have produced a very different emotional dynamic. For Hosoda, on the other hand, a film involving portals between real and fantasy worlds would have been quite characteristic. Both before and after his work on *Howl*, he showed a penchant for such stories, as in his earlier feature, *Digimon: The Movie* (2000), and his later *Summer Wars* (2009). Jones's *Howl's Moving Castle* differs from these in that (as is typical of her fiction) it is the fantasy world that it is presented as the norm while the 'real' world is exposed in all its baffling otherness; nevertheless, it seems likely that, under Hosoda's direction, the studio's plan to retain the Welsh elements of the novel would have survived.

That was not how things turned out, however. Following some undisclosed 'trouble' at the studio (Napier 2018: 214), Hosoda left the project shortly after his return from Britain, and Miyazaki took over the film's direction and script personally. Hosoda has since ascribed his departure to creative differences, while remaining vague about their nature: 'I was told to make [the movie] similar to how Miyazaki would have made it, but I wanted to make my own film the way

I wanted to make it . . . The difference . . . was too great, so I had to get off the project' (Frank 2018). Under Miyazaki's guidance, *Howl's Moving Castle* took quite a different direction, veering from both the plot and setting of Jones's book into territory much more recognizably his own.

Many of Miyazaki's changes, such as the amalgamation of various characters and incidents, were of the kind that typically accompany a change of medium from book to film. Rather than being the eldest of three sisters, for example, Sophie was now just the elder of two. The loss of resonance with the common fairy-tale trope of three siblings (and with Jones's own position as the eldest sister of three) was justified by the reduction of the interpretative load on the viewer, who already had a complex plot to get to grips with. A plot point involving the line-by-line co-option of a John Donne poem as a curse was omitted, perhaps for similar reasons. The appearance of the castle, as described in the book, would have been arresting, but arguably less so than the ramshackle, steampunk contraption Miyazaki designed. He was also able to add touches that would have been impossible using the medium of text, such as altering Sophie's appearance so that her apparent age fluctuates according to her state of mind.

Other changes appear to have been differently motivated. Miyazaki's *Howl* is set in a fully immersive fantasy world rather than one accessible from our own. The castle's 'black' portal, which in the book leads to Wales, now opens onto a battlefield in Ingary itself. The book's Welsh scenes were removed entirely, and with them, Howl's Welsh identity – a change with fundamental implications for his motivations and character. Like Hosoda, Miyazaki sought out locations to inspire the towns and landscapes of the film, but he preferred to create a setting evocative of continental Europe, based on the landscape and chocolate-box towns of Alsace (notably Colmar and Riquewihr), rather than the places that Jones had had in mind. As Elyse Martin notes:

> a pan-European [setting], with a vaguely Edwardian aesthetic [is] a common one for anime engaging with fantasy tropes not based in Japanese mythology or storytelling, and a more culturally specific way of signaling what kind of genre the movie is, and what kind of story the audience can expect. (Martin 2020)

Continental Europe at the turn of the twentieth century has indeed been a common setting for anime, in productions as diverse as *Full Metal Alchemist* (2003) and *Violet Evergarden* (2018). In the case of *Howl's Moving Castle*, Miyazaki may also have had a more specific set of associations in mind. The suggestion of *Mitteleuropa* in the uniforms of the Ingary soldiers, the use of a waltz as the film's main musical theme and the appearance of German slogans such as 'Mut und Willenskraft' on the walls of Market Chipping may be intended to evoke Europe's pre–First World War militarization and perhaps even the status of Alsace itself as a contested territory that moved between French and German control four times between 1870 and 1945. For Miyazaki's film, unlike the novel, is about war.

While the removal of the portal between Ingary and Wales might be regarded as a simplification of the plot, the same cannot be said of the introduction of war as a major theme. Although the novel mentions that Ingary will likely soon be at war, this is almost in passing; Howl's only involvement concerns the king's request that he find his missing brother, whose talent as a general will be needed. The actual conflict takes places between the events of *Howl's Moving Castle* and those of its sequel, *Castle in the Air* (1990). As Jones commented, 'I don't really like doing wars' (Mullaney 2003: 36). Miyazaki's Ingary, by contrast, is from the beginning a militarized state, complete with tanks, railways and bombers, as well as nineteenth-century cavalry and uniforms. The war is already raging as the film opens, and Howl is directly involved, entering the battle via the castle's secret portal and, taking the form of a feathered birdman, using his magic to deflect the destruction being wreaked on the country.

We can speculate about the extratextual motivations for this change. According to Miyazaki himself, it was influenced by his anger at the Iraq War, which also led him to boycott the presentation of the 2003 Best Animated Feature Oscar to *Spirited Away* (Gordon 2005). Certainly, the introduction of a war affords Miyazaki scope to air his pacifist views through Howl and Calcifer as well as to include plenty of his beloved flying machines. The consequences for the structure and tone of the film are, however, profound. The defeat of the Witch of the Waste and her fire demon is no longer the story's climax (in Miyazaki's film she is tamed halfway through the action); the major antagonist is now the king's wizard, Suliman, who is intent on prosecuting the war, and the film ends only when Sophie is able to bring about peace. She does this in fairy-tale style, by kissing an enchanted scarecrow who instantly transforms into a prince – not the missing brother of the king, as in the novel, but the prince of a neighbouring kingdom currently fighting Ingary. He immediately announces his intention to return home and bring the war to an end, and the film concludes with Suliman, having been informed of these developments, also deciding to end this 'absurd war' (*bakageta sensō*). The abrupt convenience of this *deus ex machina* ending make the story's resolution feel rather thin, offering no counterweight to the real destruction that has already been shown. On the other hand, the fact that the war – which appears to have had no particular cause or objective in the first place – can be ended in such an offhand way, on the whim of a prince or a wizard, may be Miyazaki's cynical point. Only fairy-tale lands get happy endings.

One of the film's most significant changes is to the presentation of Howl himself, whose motivation and character are no longer informed by his emotional ties to his Welsh family and homeland. Instead, Miyazaki develops a Howl partly defined by his relationship with war. Over the course of the film, Howl's transformations into a feathered and taloned creature of destruction become ever more thoroughgoing and sustained, raising the danger (articulated by both Howl and Calcifer) that he will eventually be unable to return to human form. Jones had developed an analogous theme by emphasizing Howl's need to retain his humanity despite his heart being in Calcifer's keeping, but in Miyazaki's film the ideas are run in tandem, Howl's reversion to human form being a prerequisite for Sophie's eventual return of his heart to his body.

The erasure of Howl's personal history is accompanied by a significant change in his moral character. His first encounter with Sophie at the beginning of the story offers a telling demonstration of the difference made by substituting this self-sacrificing and war-scarred figure for the mercurial hero of the book. The meeting takes place in Market Chipping during the May Day celebrations. In Jones's novel, Howl accosts Sophie, calling her a little mouse and offering to buy her a drink. In the film, the same line is given to two soldiers, and it is Howl who chivalrously steps in to rescue the nervous Sophie from their attentions. This switch from potential villain to hero is indicative of the alteration in his character overall, which is generally in the direction of nobility. Jones's Howl compulsively pursues women, up to (but never beyond) the moment they fall in love with him, at which point he loses interest. His behaviour appears to be driven by insecurity, especially about his appearance. The book makes it clear that, without the aid of assiduously applied magic and cosmetics, Howl is not particularly handsome: he has a 'bony, sophisticated face' (21) or a 'long, angular face' (58) and is even described by Calcifer as 'a plain man' (86). In the film, Howl is a pretty young man, or *bishōnen*, and although his reputation as a lady's man is alluded to, we see little to justify it on screen. He is still vain, and the film retains an episode in which he childishly fills the castle with green slime after Sophie mixes up his hair dyes (perhaps because the episode offers irresistible possibilities for animation), but vanity and romantic pursuit become far less central to his portrayal.

The same applies to other areas of Howl's behaviour. In the book, Howl's obligation to the king of Ingary derives from his having accepted a large cash donation (63), and his attempt to avoid looking for the king's missing brother is motivated both by a dislike of unnecessary danger and a general horror of being pinned down. He is, as Sophie memorably describes him, an inveterate 'slitherer-outer' (78). In the film, Howl has taken an oath to serve the king as a condition of his magical education and tries to avoid doing so only because he disapproves of war on moral grounds.

The removal of the Welsh scenes also has an indirect effect on the ages of the characters. By the time book Howl catches Calcifer on Porthaven Marshes, he is already an adult with a penchant for drunken rugby songs, who has undertaken doctoral research on charms and spells before finding his way into Ingary. By contrast, the Howl who encounters Calcifer in the film (an episode glimpsed by Sophie in flashback) is a fairly young boy. It is for this reason that, when Sophie returns Howl's heart to him at the end of the film and notices it 'fluttering like a small bird' in her hands, Calcifer remarks: 'It's because it's still the same as when he was a child.' At the equivalent moment in the book, when the fire demon Lily Angorian causes Howl to faint by squeezing his heart, Sophie explains that it is because his 'heart's really quite soft' (295) – making Howl's vulnerability an index of his character rather than of his age. There is an even more dramatic reduction in the age of Howl's apprentice, Michael (Markl in the film), who goes from being a teenager in love with Sophie's sister to a child of around ten – a change perhaps made with an eye to the age of Studio Ghibli's primary audience.

Jones saw changes to her story as inevitable and never publicly criticized Miyazaki's film. Indeed, she admired many aspects of it and even kept a large plush toy of the film's version of Calcifer (notably different in appearance from the one she had written) in her fireplace ever after, as I can personally attest. In late 2004, Miyazaki travelled with a team from Ghibli, including Suzuki and his son Gorō, to meet Jones in Bristol. After a private showing of the film at a local arts cinema, the party – which included Jones's family and agent as well as Nick Park and Peter Lord of the Bristol-based studio, Aardman Animations – joined Miyazaki at the Bristol Hotel du Vin for a very convivial dinner. Jones and Miyazaki, speaking through an interpreter, found that they had much in common, from their wartime childhoods to a passionate commitment to cigarettes. Afterwards, Jones remarked, 'It was wonderful . . . I don't think I've ever met anyone before who thinks like I do. He saw my books from the inside out' (Bradshaw 2005).

Rather than comment on additions or omissions, Jones preferred to praise the richness of the film's animation, especially in the sequences where Miyazaki had enhanced scenes already in the text, such as Sophie's laborious ascent of the Kingsbury castle steps ('Interview with Author, Diana Wynne Jones', 2006).

It is therefore difficult to say whether, or how much, she regretted the removal of Howl's Welsh heritage. The only clue to that lies in an interview in which she discussed the casting of a hypothetical live-action version of the story: 'if a real-life actor were to play Howl in *Howl's Moving Castle*, I would not choose someone pretty, like Howl in Miyazaki's animation. I would choose a Welsh actor, with a long, bony face, handsome enough in his way, but not pretty' (Falconer 2013). Miyazaki too appears to have come round to the idea that Howl's appearance did not adequately reflect the character's complexity. According to a 2013 article: 'He wishes he'd drawn the character of Howl in *Howl's Moving Castle*, more "sharp, pointed and devilish," . . . but he wasn't willing to take the artistic risk at the time. "I'm mad at myself," he said' (Keegan 2013).

The Borrowers and *The Borrower Arrietty*: Relocating to Japan and back

In discussing *Howl's Moving Castle*, I spent some time on the question of geographical setting, but since the story is primarily located in a fantasy land, the issue arises in a relatively oblique form. The next two British books to be adapted by Ghibli, Mary Norton's *The Borrowers* (1952) and Joan G. Robinson's *When Marnie Was There* (1967), both have entirely British settings; nevertheless, both were relocated to Japan in the Ghibli adaptations, *The Borrower Arrietty* (2010) and *Memories of Marnie* (2014). In fact, despite being a lifelong lover of British children's books and having visited the country on multiple occasions, Miyazaki has never set an anime feature in Britain.[3] It is worth asking why not.

On occasion he has suggested that, as a Japanese person, it is not his place to do so. Speaking at the 2005 Tōkyō Film Festival alongside Nick Park of Aardman Animations, he recalled his visit to Bristol the previous year:

> I went for a morning walk on the streets of Bristol – without any intention of using the experience in a film – but I suddenly found myself doing some location scouting. I don't consciously think I have to put a particular experience to use. I normally don't go location scouting after we've decided to make a film; I just wind up observing things as I encounter them. It's partly because it's something that doesn't cost any money. But now I have no intention of making a film set

---

3 The only production Miyazaki has worked on with a British setting is *Famous Detective Holmes* (*meitantei hōmuzu*; English-language title, *Sherlock Hound*), a television series about an anthropomorphized canine version of Sherlock Holmes, for which he provided several episodes in 1981 and which was broadcast three years later.

in Britain. Because there's someone perfectly capable of doing that right here. (Miyazaki 2014b: 333)

Whether Miyazaki's eschewal of British settings is primarily a matter of principle – a feeling that such work should be left to 'perfectly capable' natives such as Park – or of doubt in his ability to achieve a satisfactory result is unclear, but it is a position he reiterated with specific reference to *The Borrowers* in *Doorway to Books*. There, he suggests that the cultural and historical milieu of the story would be impossible for a Japanese adaptation to reproduce: '*The Borrowers* is set in England and moreover in the old days, so I understand very well that I can't make it into a movie as it is. If it were done, the British would have to do it, not the Japanese' (Miyazaki 2011: 102).

Despite this assertion, Miyazaki has in fact used European locations on several occasions, notably in the Adriatic setting of *Porco Rosso*. Typically, however, he has constructed films that hint at, rather than reproduce, such locations. His initial proposal for *Castle in the Sky*, for example, stated: 'The setting is vaguely European, but we can't tell exactly what race or nationality its people are' (Miyazaki 2014a: 253). The same degree of calculated vagueness could be claimed for the settings of *Kiki's Delivery Service* and *Howl's Moving Castle*. Of the location for *Kiki*, Miyazaki joked:

> This is how the Japanese imagine an old European city. There are elements of Naples, Lisbon, Stockholm, Paris, and San Francisco, all mixed in, so one side faces the Mediterranean while the other faces the Baltic Sea. (Qtd. *Animage* Editorial Department 2006: 69)

This remark suggests another possible reason for Miyazaki's preference, namely consideration of his home audience. While Miyazaki's name and films are known worldwide, his primary focus has always been on the domestic market:

> I think only about my Japanese audience when I make a film. Of course, I'm delighted that people from other countries also enjoy my films. But I try not to think of this as an international business. (Gordon 2005)

From this point of view, Miyazaki's motive for relocating films to Japan is no different from that which led Hollywood to relocate British stories such as *The War of the Worlds* to the United States – that is, regard for the presumed insular focus of his domestic audience.

The Borrowers, translated by Yōkichi Hayashi in 1956 as *The Little People under the Floor* (*yukashita no kobitotachi*), was already well known in Japan when Studio Ghibli adapted it (Tanaka 2009: 377–405) and would be included by Miyazaki in his selection of fifty children's texts for Iwanami Shōnen Bunko (2011: 32–3). The relocation of the story notwithstanding, its plot was altered far less than had been the case with *Howl*. Nevertheless, the domesticating strategies employed had a profound cumulative effect.

Norton's *The Borrowers* is the story of fourteen-year-old Arrietty Clock and her parents, Pod and Homily, a family of miniature people who live in secret under the floor of a large house and who survive by 'borrowing' necessary items from the humans who live there. The novel describes Arrietty's befriending of a human boy who is staying in the house, the Borrowers' eventual discovery by the housekeeper and their subsequent flight. The book is a skilful blend of adventure story, social satire and *Gulliver*-esque ingenuity in matters of physical scale and is rightly regarded as a classic in Britain. Miyazaki had long harboured the desire to turn it into a film; and, just as he had with *Howl's Moving Castle*, producer Toshio Suzuki invited a young director in his mid-thirties to take on the job of directing. Rather than seek external talent, this time he selected a Ghibli staff member, Hiromasa Yonebayashi. Yonebayashi had been at the company since 1996 and had worked his way up from being a humble in-between animator, much as Miyazaki himself had done thirty years before. This time, Miyazaki was involved from the beginning, collaborating with Keiko Niwa to develop the film's screenplay. The film was eventually released in Japan in 2010, as *The Borrower Arrietty* (*karigurashi no arietti*).

In *The Borrower Arrietty*, the book's original setting – a house near Leighton Buzzard in Bedfordshire at the turn of the twentieth century (Norton 1958: 14) – is transferred to modern Koganei in the suburbs of Tōkyō, not far from Studio Ghibli itself. Although the names Pod, Homily and Arrietty are retained, and with them their English-language origins, the human characters are all given Japanese names. The unnamed boy who befriends Arrietty in the book becomes Shō; his Great-Aunt Sophy becomes Great-Aunt Sadako; and the housekeeper, Mrs Driver, Haru. The only explicit reference to Britain in the film concerns a doll's house belonging to Sadako, originally ordered from Britain by her father as a home for the little people whom he suspected might live in the house. This is a neat acknowledgement of the story's origins but also hints at a broader association of Britain with miniaturization. Mihoko Tanaka has noted, 'even after they grow up, the British people tend to keep their strong fascination for the miniature world' (Tanaka 2009: 348), a thesis spelt out in the 2010 DVD that Studio Ghibli released to coincide with the film, which devotes considerable time to British model villages, doll's houses and miniaturization, describing Britain as a 'land of fairies and fantasy' (*Ghibli's Bookshelf* 2010).

The plot of *The Borrowers* does not depend on a specific landscape or climate to the same extent as some other texts. Its fields, woods and streams are common enough in both Japan and England. Nevertheless, as we saw in the case of *Little Lord Fauntleroy* in Chapter 2, to take a novel set in one country and transfer it to another is never straightforward, for all stories carry the mark of the cultural and aesthetic norms that gave rise to them, not only in their linguistic choices but also in their presentations of characters and relationships and in their exposition and resolution of plots. When a story is moved across cultural borders, some of this information is inevitably lost, even as the specificity of the story's origins becomes more visible, with features that had seemed obvious and natural in its native culture suddenly appearing arbitrary and opaque. Translators and adaptors must find ways to cope with such challenges, a task generally involving complex trade-offs and lateral-thinking solutions. *The Borrowers* is in many ways a distinctively British book. Much of Norton's humour depends on the reader's ability to pick up class-related cues in the various characters' speech patterns and attitudes, and the setting in a large (though not aristocratic) house highlights numerous issues involving the English social system, property rights and the nature of exploitation. Inevitably, many of these nuances are lost with the change of setting.

Things become even more complex when, as in the case of Ghibli's films, a story is subsequently dubbed back into English for cinematic release. This task is usually undertaken by Disney and Pixar studios, whose first goal is to make them comprehensible and appealing to their primary audience in North America. Disney's 2012 English-language version of *The Borrower Arrietty*, titled *The Secret World of Arrietty*, accordingly employed American actors, and Disney tasked screenwriter Karey Kirkpatrick with, in his words, 'making it work for an American audience' (Kirkpatrick 2017). As we will see, the resulting film was Americanized in numerous ways.

Where Ghibli films have been based on British books, Disney has acknowledged their origin to different degrees and in different ways. In the case of *Howl's Moving Castle*, Disney gave a nod to the book's British authorship (and partial setting) by using British actors for some of the main parts: Howl himself was played by Welshman Christian Bale, while the English born actresses Jean Simmons and Emily Mortimer provided the voices of old and young Sophie. However, they were instructed to adopt what screenwriters Cindy and Don Hewitt described as 'a mild "Mid-Atlantic" accent . . . neither American nor British' (Team Ghiblink 2005), a decision suggesting a degree of ambivalence as to the dub's cultural positioning.

The case of *The Borrowers* was rather different. This was a book known in Britain even to many who had not read it, through earlier screen adaptations and an established cultural presence. Even in a version with a non-British setting, the adoption of American accents might have seemed jarring to British viewers. Perhaps for that reason, the unique step was taken of producing not one but two English-language dubs. In 2011, the year before Disney's American-English dub, Studio Canal released a version of the film voiced by a largely British cast, simply titled *Arrietty*.[4]

We thus have five different versions of the story: Norton's original novel; Hayashi's 1956 translation, which Miyazaki and Yonebayashi would have read; Ghibli's anime adaptation; and the American and British English dubs of that adaptation.[5] In their studies of other Ghibli works, Kentarō Yamada and Chihiro Tamura (Yamada 2004, 2005; Tamura 2010) have shown how a comparison of multiple versions can provide valuable insights into the process of adaptation; here, relevant factors include the diverse cultural contexts of the countries involved, the differences between the English and Japanese languages, the change of medium from book to film, the storytelling conventions and preferences of the various directors, writers and studios and their attitudes towards the process and purposes of adaptation itself.

As with *Howl's Moving Castle*, in *The Borrower Arrietty* numerous changes were made to the source material to accommodate the change of medium or to streamline aspects of the story. Norton's novel has a complex frame narrative, in which the narrator, Kate, explains that the story of the Borrowers was told to her as a girl by an old woman, Mrs May, who was told it in turn by her long dead brother, the unnamed boy of the novel. In *The Borrower Arrietty* this device survives only as a brief initial voice-over from Shō, in which he introduces the events from an unspecified point in the future. Again, in the novel the boy initially supplies the Borrowers' home with extra items by stealing from an old (and not especially treasured) doll's house hidden away in a cupboard and only later graduates to pilfering more expensive knick-knacks from the drawing room, where Mrs Driver notices their absence. In Ghibli's film these activities are conflated, with the doll's house itself becoming the focal point of the drawing room, an object with significant monetary and emotional value.

---

4 The part of Arrietty herself was played by the American-Irish actress Saoirse Ronan, although she used an English accent for the role.
5 I shall have little to say here about the Japanese translation, which has already been ably discussed by Mihoko Tanaka (2009: 147–88); nor, for reasons of space, will I discuss the subtitles produced for the English-language versions of the films, which differ in some respects from the dub scripts.

As for characters, sober Great-Aunt Sadako is barely recognizable as a version of bed-ridden Great-Aunt Sophy, who spends each evening getting drunk on Madeira wine, but both serve the function of exercising patrician authority over the house, albeit rather intermittently.

Perhaps the most significant narrative change is the attribution to Shō of a serious heart condition. The boy in Norton's novel is a nine year old convalescing after rheumatic fever and making a good recovery; in the film, Shō appears far closer to Arrietty's age and is staying at Sadako's house prior to dangerous surgery. His conviction that he will soon die informs many of his words and actions in a way that is simply not the case for Norton's boy, who we know from the frame story will grow up to become the colonel of his regiment (Norton 1958: 10).

The ways in which the British and American dubs of Ghibli's film 'returned' the story to the Anglophone sphere, and the changes they made in doing so, are as instructive as the changes made by Ghibli itself. In general, the British dub of *Arrietty* is much closer to being a literal translation of the Japanese script and constitutes (to adopt the terminology of Laurence Venuti (1995)) a far more 'foreignized' version of Ghibli's film than Disney's *The Secret World of Arrietty*, which is heavily domesticated to cater to its American audience. An obvious example of this difference lies in the two adaptations' use of names. The British dub retains the Japanese names used by Ghibli; however, Kirkpatrick's script for Disney domesticates Shō, Sadako and Haru as Shawn, Jessica and Hara, respectively. Neither version reverted to the names used in Norton's novel, perhaps because of the technical constraints imposed by lip-synching.

Both dubs make some effort to remove possible areas of confusion caused by cultural differences. Early the film, for example, Miyazaki's script has Arrietty (already a veteran of garden adventures, unlike the housebound girl of the novel) give her mother a bay leaf and a red *shiso* (perilla) leaf that she has collected on a foraging trip. This prompts the following exchange:

> **Arrietty**: Anyway, that *shiso* leaf has a nice fragrance, doesn't it?
>
> **Homily**: You're right. If I had sugar I could make *shiso* juice. (*The Borrower Arrietty* 2010)

Bay leaves are widely used in Western cuisine, but *shiso* is not, and the custom of using red *shiso* to make a summer drink is unfamiliar to most Western viewers. Accordingly, neither the British nor the American dub uses the word '*shiso*'. The British dub opts for strategic vagueness, making Arrietty remark on the scent of some flowers she is putting into a vase rather than the leaf she has given her mother, while Homily for her part does not name the leaf from which she proposes to make juice.

> **Arrietty**: Oh, don't these flowers just smell lovely?
>
> **Homily**: So they do. With a bit of sugar I could make some juice out of this.
>   (*Arrietty* 2011)

Such substitutions are of course a common feature of translation of any kind. When Hayashi translated *The Borrowers* into Japanese, for example, Norton's references to 'hot-pot' (1958: 151, 152) were replaced with '*nimono*' (Norton 1956: 258, 260), a dashi-based stew with similar connotations of traditional home cooking. The American dub, however, differs more radically:

> **Arrietty**: If you don't like your gift I can put it in my room.
>
> **Homily**: No, no, I shall keep it. I have just the recipe for these. I'll have your
>   father borrow some sugar. (*The Secret World of Arrietty* 2012)

Arrietty's line is changed to a teasing reference to her gift of the leaves as a birthday present. In changing 'juice' to 'recipe', Homily may imply that the leaves will be used to flavour a meal, rather than as the basis of a drink. Small adjustments of this kind occur throughout the film, and the cumulative effect is to decrease the sense of its specifically Japanese setting.

This is a fairly trivial instance, but even small changes can have knock-on effects. Later, as Pod and Arrietty are about to go borrowing, Homily asks them to find a cube of sugar. Clasping her hands in supplication, she adds: 'I could make *shiso* juice – it's delicious in tea.' As she speaks, Homily closes her eyes and looks upward, anticipating the delicious flavour. However, in *The Secret World of Arrietty*, where Homily has not previously spoken of making a drink using sugar, the resemblance of Homily's gesture to Christian prayer (hands clasped, looking upward) evidently struck the screenwriter, and she is given a line to match: 'Oh, please God, please help them.' This device gives Homily a line consistent with her gesture, as interpreted within an American frame of reference, but it also underlines her tendency to worry about her husband and daughter's safety and introduces a Christian inflection to her actions. Overall, it tends to domesticate her as American, vocalized expressions of Christian belief being far more common in the United States than in Japan or, indeed, Britain.

The challenges posed by translation between cultures extend well beyond such relatively discrete examples, into the broader conventions of plotting and characterization. Attitudes to the roles that certain kinds of character may play within a story, strategies for plot exposition, tolerance for digressions and uncertainty, the choice between explicit and implicit methods of conveying information and a sense of what constitutes a satisfactory conclusion are all culturally specific, relying on pre-existing narrative conventions and a shared repertoire of story and character. Part of the adaptor's job may thus involve framing the story to better fit the norms of the target audience, in terms not only of language and material culture but also of interpretative strategies, narrative tropes, character types and so on.

Given that writers of dub scripts need to work within the visual framework provided by the animation, their scope for making changes to the story and characters is limited, but there is still some room for manoeuvre, as we see on several occasions in *The Secret World of Arrietty*. In the Disney film, Arrietty's eagerness to start borrowing spills into a 'sassiness' largely absent from the Japanese script, where she is generally respectful of her parents. Consider this line, in which Arrietty reassures Homily about her forthcoming borrowing expedition:

> **Arrietty**: It's all right, Mother, I'll be very careful. (*The Borrower Arrietty* 2010)
>
> **Arrietty**: Oh, and don't worry Mother, I'll get Papa back safely. (*The Secret World of Arrietty* 2012)

In the Disney version, the straightforward reassurance of Miyazaki's Arrietty becomes a joke, deliberately misconstruing Homily's anxiety. A little later, once they have set off, Disney's Arrietty asks Pod about his lamp: 'Do I get one of those? No? Okay.' These humorous lines are absent from Miyazaki's script, in which Arrietty is attending obediently to Pod's instructions.

One function of such changes is no doubt to set up Arrietty for a fall. She is shown as overconfident and overexcited, and this makes her careless. However, they may also reflect a greater sympathy in American culture for adolescent testing of the boundaries of authority. As a sign of liveliness and independence, they make Arrietty a figure with whom child viewers are invited to empathize. Pod, for his part, is stolid and serious in all three versions, but in the Disney dub he is capable of a humour never displayed by his Japanese counterpart. When Arrietty enquires about his recovery after a leg injury, the Japanese Pod answers factually: 'I'm already almost able to walk' (*The Borrower Arrietty* 2010). In *The Secret World of Arrietty*, he cracks a joke, playing on the fact that Spiller (another Borrower) has just been eating a cricket's leg:

> **Arrietty**: How's your leg?
>
> **Pod**: Better than that cricket's. (*The Secret World of Arrietty* 2012)

A more complex example is that of the mother of Shō/Shawn, a character who does not appear in the film except in the words of others. In Norton's novel, the boy's parents are in India and effectively absent from the story, but in *The Borrower Arrietty* Shō's mother is mentioned at several strategic moments: the opening voice-over identifies the house as the place she grew up; she is said to be the one who first told Shō about the Borrowers; and the doll's house is hers, passed to her by her grandfather, Shō's great-grandfather. Great-Aunt Sadako also suggests that Shō is neglected by his divorced parents, and that his mother is at fault for travelling on business when her son is ill with a heart condition. The situation is, however, left unresolved.

This combination of apparent maternal neglect and narrative inconclusiveness sits uncomfortably in a Disney film. Disney has long maintained a family-friendly image, and a neglectful mother, while possible, is an aberration requiring some explanation. Accordingly, the script of *The Secret World of Arrietty* links the failure of the doll's house to attract any Borrowers during Shawn's mother's childhood to her later neglect of her own child. She is said to have shown great faith in the doll's house project and to have worked hard on it with her father (not her grandfather, as in Miyazaki's script), only to have it end in bitter disappointment. In *The Borrower Arrietty*, Sadako simply tells Shō that he is the fourth generation to inherit the doll's house; but the equivalent line in *The Secret World of Arrietty* has Aunt Jessica explain that the doll's house is the true reason for Shawn's mother's absence: 'I think it's why your mother doesn't like to come here anymore. Too many memories of wishes that never came true' (*The Secret World of Arrietty* 2012). It is implied that something in Shawn's mother was thwarted by this childhood disappointment, which gave rise not only to her reluctance to visit the house but also to a more fundamental disconnection that has made her throw herself into her work, neglect her child and generally behave in a manner coded as unmaternal. By contrast, Shō's mother in *The Borrower Arrietty* is not said to have had any special commitment to or belief in the little people. (In none of the versions is Shō/Shawn's father's equal neglect of his child regarded as requiring comment or explanation.)

I have interpreted this change to the Japanese script in terms of cultural attitudes towards motherhood and family, but this is not the only possible reading. It may also indicate a general reluctance on Disney's part to leave plot points hanging. The indeterminacy of *The Borrower Arrietty*'s references to Shō's mother may have been regarded as a loose thread needing to be tied, rather than appreciated as a realistic reflection of the messiness of life. Toshio Suzuki has noted the American discomfort with unresolved endings (Mishan 2021), and this is evident at other points in the Disney version, where changes have been made that answer questions left open by Ghibli. For example, at the conclusion of *The Borrower Arrietty* we see Arrietty and Shō's farewell, then the credits rolling against a sequence in which Arrietty's family drift downriver in a kettle, a detail borrowed from the third book in Norton's series, *The Borrowers Afloat* (1959). We hear nothing of the Borrowers' subsequent fate, nor of the outcome of Shō's imminent heart operation, although his brief voice-over at the beginning of the film provides implicit assurance of his survival.

By contrast, *The Secret World of Arrietty* not only gives Shawn a more extensive voice-over at the start of the film, explicitly identifying the forthcoming events as ones that will change his life, but it also assuages any anxiety about the Borrowers' fate with the addition of a second voice-over at the story's conclusion:

> **Shawn** (*voiceover*): I never saw [Arrietty] again. But the following summer I returned, and was happy to hear the people in the house down the road talking about how many things in their home had gone . . . missing. (*The Secret World of Arrietty* 2012)

Even Ghibli's ending provides a more certain resolution than that offered by the original novel, which breaks off the main narrative at a point of high excitement, with Mrs Driver having called a rat-catcher to exterminate the Borrowers and the boy's attempt to provide them with an escape route seemingly thwarted. Mrs May declares that she knows nothing more after that point, to which Kate objects that this ending violates the narrative conventions of storytelling:

> 'Kate,' [Mrs May] said after a moment, 'stories never really end. They can go on and on and on. It's just that sometimes, at a certain point, one stops telling them.'
> 'But not at this kind of point,' said Kate. (Norton 1958: 137)

Mrs May then concedes that she found circumstantial evidence of the Borrowers' survival on a subsequent visit to the house, adding with artful ambiguity that the whole story may have been invented by her brother.

One way to appreciate the power of seemingly minor alterations to create substantial changes of tone and meaning is to track a single scene's metamorphoses, from novel to Ghibli film and thence to Disney script. Shortly before the climax of the film, there is a scene in which Arrietty and Shō/Shawn discuss the Borrowers' long-term prospects for survival. It derives from an episode in the novel in which Arrietty and the boy likewise discuss the relationship between humans and Borrowers. In the book, however, rather than coming late in the story, this exchange forms part of the pair's first, wary encounter, with each trying to establish dominance. Norton's Arrietty suggests that humans cannot be very numerous, so profligate is their use of natural resources, and she quotes her father's belief that 'it's a good thing they're dying out . . . [J]ust a few, my father says, that's all we need – to keep us' (69). By 'keep us', Arrietty explains, she means that Borrowers take the things they need from humans. Although she refers to this as 'borrowing', there is no suggestion of repayment, and the boy objects that this amounts to stealing. Arrietty, however, finds the accusation absurd: 'You might as well say that the fire-grate steals the coal from the coal-scuttle . . . human beans are *for* Borrowers – like bread's for butter' (73).

This reversal of human perspective (praised by Miyazaki in *Doorway to Books* as 'a Copernican revolution' (Miyazaki 2011: 101)) is unsettling for the boy and provides a double-edged satire. Arrietty's assumption that Borrowers and their needs are central to the world, and that humans exist for their benefit, parodies human complacency and anthropocentrism. As with Swift's Lilliputians, the parochial nature of her perspective is underlined by the Borrowers' diminutive size. At the same time, the boy's own belief in human pre-eminence is shaken by coming face to face with a way of viewing the world so different from his own, in which humans are farmed by Borrowers for their food and possessions. He sets out to prove, rather aggressively, that humans are far more numerous than Borrowers and to taunt Arrietty about her own species. Norton's boy is young and thoughtlessly cruel, revelling in being more knowledgeable about the world and taking childish revenge for Arrietty's own scorn of humans:

'I believe you're the last three.'

Arrietty dropped her face into the primrose. 'We're not. There's Aunt Lupy and Uncle Hendreary and all the cousins.'

'I bet they're dead,' said the boy. [. . .] 'One day,' he told her, smiling triumphantly, 'you'll be the only Borrower left in the world!' (76)

Miyazaki's script for *The Borrower Arrietty* preserves several aspects of this scene, including its concern with natural resources, but by omitting others it changes its tone considerably. Arrietty still explains to Shō that Borrowers take the things they need from humans, but she does not suggest that humans exist for the benefit of Borrowers, nor that humans will soon die out. On the contrary, Ghibli's Borrowers are aware from the beginning of their own precarious situation. For his part, Shō refrains from accusing Borrowers of theft. The overt causes of conflict within the novel are thus removed. Like Norton's boy, Shō points out the large human population (specifying it at 6.7 billion), and he makes a bleak assessment of the Borrowers' survival prospects, including contemplating a time when Arrietty will be the last survivor of her race. However, where the boy of the novel smiles 'triumphantly', Shō delivers his conclusion with regret. Miyazaki had praised Norton's willingness to show the 'cruelty' (*zankoku*) of the young boy in this scene, highlighting its honesty as a depiction of childhood, but he drew back from following her lead, preferring to endow Shō with a melancholy fatalism (Miyazaki 2011: 101).

Shō's melancholy derives from two sources, one general and one personal. On the one hand, he remembers that many species have died out through being unable to adapt to the changing environment and sees the Borrowers as another in this catalogue of ecological loss. It is to this view that Arrietty takes exception:

> **Shō**: It's cruel, but that's your destiny.
>
> **Arrietty**: 'Destiny,' you say? Don't you see that it's because of *your* needless actions that we're moving away? (*The Borrower Arrietty* 2010)

In Arrietty's view, blaming fate is just a way to evade responsibility. After all, the immediate danger faced by her family was caused by Shō's own interference. Miyazaki's wider point is surely that many other species, too, have become extinct as a result of avoidable human choices.

The second source of Shō's melancholy concerns his own future. He believes he will shortly die from his weak heart, and this naturally influences his thoughts about others. Miyazaki thus substitutes for Norton's boy's childish impulse to hurt Arrietty a scene that combines environmental guilt and personal tragedy, a context that extenuates Shō's insensitivity in predicting the end of Arrietty's race.

In *The Secret World of Arrietty*, this conversation is changed once again. Karey Kirkpatrick reported in interview with me that he felt Miyazaki's environmental focus in this scene would not play well with American audiences:

> If you look at the Japanese dubbed version, and then look at what I did, I was allowed to make substantial changes to what that scene is about. With their blessing, and with respect, but just saying to them, it gets a little environmentally preachy in that scene in a way that I think Americans would have found a bit of a turn-off. Also, it got a little bit off-story. I reworked that scene and tweaked a few others to put greater focus on the differences between the two main characters, as well as the misperceptions between Borrowers and humans. (Kirkpatrick 2017)

Kirkpatrick's script omits any mention of species extinction and environmental change and has Shawn focus entirely on the inevitability of death, which is naturally much on his mind: 'But you know none of us can live for ever, can we?

We all have to die sometime.' It is in this context that Shawn, like Shō, suggests, 'Sometimes you just have to accept the hand of fate.' Arrietty's determined response, rather than pointing out Shawn's responsibility for their situation, constitutes a far more generic assertion of the virtue of self-reliance: 'Oh no you don't. Sometimes you have to stand up and fight for the things that are worth fighting for!' (*The Secret World of Arrietty* 2012).

This robustly American declaration is alien not only to the resigned, Japanese '*shikata ga nai*'[6] attitude to natural disaster but also to the psychological and satirical tenor of Norton's novel. It is one example among many of the ways in which various versions of a story reflect distinctions that go far beyond culturally opaque words and objects.

Much as one might wish to take the next step, and suggest that the differences between the various versions of the story reflect fundamental differences between hypostasized national cultures, this would be a hasty conclusion. Many factors were involved in the creation of the novel, the Ghibli film and its English-language dubs, including personal and commercial priorities. For the American dub, perhaps the most significant is the specific culture of the Walt Disney Company, which has a decades-long tradition of adapting literary texts, often quite freely, in accordance with its own ethos. Disney's greater latitude in making changes to the characterization, dialogue and tone of *The Borrower Arrietty*, in comparison to the more 'faithful' Studio Canal adaptation, reflects its company culture as much as any more general differences between the United States and the United Kingdom. That said, Disney does not exist in a vacuum: it both reflects, and has done much to shape, aesthetic and narrative practice in American popular culture, as well as ideas about desirable family relationships and personal values.

The position of Studio Ghibli within Japan is not quite so dominant, but it too has a mutually influential relationship with the wider culture of which it is a part. Moreover, Miyazaki's personal priorities have repeatedly intersected with those of the texts he has adapted. In both *Howl's Moving Castle* and *The Borrower Arrietty*, he took elements that were present but undeveloped in his source material and made them more central. Just as the King of Ingary's reference to a forthcoming war in Jones's novel was expanded in Ghibli's *Howl's Moving Castle* into a major plot element that could be used as a vehicle for Miyazaki's pacifism, so, in *The Borrowers*, the precarity of Arrietty's people as a race living

6　'It can't be helped.'

in a marginal environment and her remarks about human overuse of resources offered opportunities for an ecological reading that Miyazaki was able to exploit.

Marnie in Norfolk and in Hokkaidō

Unlike *The Borrowers*, which has long enjoyed classic status in the English-speaking world, Joan G. Robinson's *When Marnie Was There* (1967) probably requires some introduction. It is the story of Anna, a child whose parents died in a car crash when she was a baby and whose introversion, asthma and evident unhappiness have prompted her concerned foster mother to send her to stay with her old friends, the Peggs, for sea air and a change of scene. (The story's fictional setting, Little Overton, is based on the village of Burnham Overy Staithe on the north Norfolk coast, where Robinson and her family were regular summer visitors.) The Peggs are welcoming, but Anna finds it difficult to settle or make friends until she encounters the mysterious Marnie, the blonde-haired girl who lives in the Marsh House on the far side of the creek. Over the following days and weeks, Anna and Marnie become intimate friends. They spend most of their time outside, although Anna also surreptitiously attends one of Marnie's wealthy parents' parties, disguised as a flower seller. Despite their closeness, there remains something elusive about Marnie, and the girls agree to keep their friendship a secret. Anna confides to Marnie that she resents her parents for dying, and also her maternal grandmother, who looked after her for a while but also died soon after. More recently, her accidental discovery that her foster mother receives money from the local council for her living expenses has made her mistrust her affection and increased her feelings of isolation.

Anna finds solace in Marnie's friendship, but their relationship starts to deteriorate with the arrival of Edward, Marnie's distant cousin, whose presence means that Anna has to share her friend's time. The crisis comes when Anna discovers Marnie at an old windmill during a storm. Marnie has long been scared of the mill because of the frightening stories told by her parents' maids, and in her terror she appears to abandon Anna there. Anna is angry at first but relents when Marnie later begs her forgiveness, adding that they will not be able to meet any longer.

At this point, Marnie disappears from the story. The book, however, still has more than a third of its length to run. The remainder is taken up with Anna coming to terms with the idea that Marnie was her own invention, an imaginary friend born of loneliness, and then being gradually weaned off that loneliness by a new friendship with the Lindsays, the large, warm and very solid family which has just moved into the Marsh House. The discovery by one of the Lindsay daughters of an old diary shows that Marnie was not, after all, imaginary but a girl who lived in the house fifty years earlier; many of Anna and Marnie's adventures appear to be alluded to in its pages. Eventually, thanks to the expository assistance of a visiting family friend, it is established that Marnie was in fact Anna's grandmother, who looked after her when she was a young child. Anna's feelings of abandonment, isolation and mistrust are thus resolved.

Marnie is a finely written and, in terms its narrative structure and choice of protagonist, quite an unusual book, but it also sits squarely in the literary landscape of its time. The novel's delicate use of ambiguous fantasy in the service of its psychological insights bears comparison with the work of Catherine Storr, but *Marnie's* peculiar strengths have probably been overshadowed, to the detriment of its reputation in its home country, by the palpable influence of Philippa Pearce's *Tom's Midnight Garden* (1958). Indeed, the final paragraph of the novel, in which Mrs Lindsay reports to her husband on Anna's surprisingly familiar way of talking about Marnie (whom she could not have consciously remembered) (278–9), is a striking reprise of the final paragraph of Pearce's book, in which Tom's aunt describes to his uncle how he hugged their elderly landlady (whom he had apparently not met before) 'as if she were a little girl' (Pearce 2008: 227).

When Marnie Was There was critically successful on publication and received a commercial boost from being serialized on the BBC programme *Jackanory* in 1971. However, as noted in the previous chapter, the popularity of time-slip stories was gradually ebbing, and by the time Penelope Lively wrote *A Stitch in Time* in 1976, perhaps the last significant novel of this type, it was already halfway to being a satirical deconstruction of the genre (Butler 2006: 214). By the time Robinson died in 1988, she was remembered more for her self-illustrated series of stories for younger children, *Teddy Robinson* (from 1953), than for *Marnie*. When Ghibli selected it for adaptation, *Marnie* had long been out of print in the UK, and a new edition had to be rushed out in anticipation of the film.

In Japan, however, the book's fortunes had been very different. Having been published in Japanese in 1980 in a translation by Masako Matsuno, it benefitted from the patronage of what Mihoko Tanaka has dubbed the 'two Hayaos' – Hayao Kawai and Hayao Miyazaki (2016: 70). Kawai, the prominent psychologist and critic whose role in the early career of Kaho Nashiki was mentioned in the previous chapter, found *Marnie* appealing as, among other things, a novel demonstrating a strong sense of 'soul' (*tamashii*) and as a penetrating analysis of the process of psychological healing (Sasada 2015b: 204; Tanaka 2016: 60–1). He discussed the book repeatedly, devoting a chapter to it in his psychoanalytically inflected collection, *To Read a Children's Book* (*kodomo no hon o yomu*) (1996), and this may have helped maintain its readership, particularly among adults. For some, indeed, it proved a seminal book. Robinson's daughter, Deborah Sheppard, includes in her 'Postscript' to the 2014 edition an anecdote about a Japanese man on whom *Marnie* had made a great impression as a teenager, who arrived in King's Lynn armed with nothing more than a Japanese translation of the book and the name 'Little Overton' and used that information to track down the setting of the story (Sheppard 2014: 284–5). The man was not (as Nick Bradshaw teasingly speculated) Miyazaki himself (Bradshaw 2018), but the journey he undertook is testament to the novel's power over some Japanese readers, which was enough to keep it continuously in print for more than thirty years prior to its adaptation by Ghibli. Nor was that visit unique; several generations of Japanese fans and academics, from veterans like Masayoshi Ikeda to younger scholars such as Satomi Isobe, have travelled to Norfolk on the same quest and, bypassing the ancient shrine at nearby Walsingham, made their pilgrimage to Burnham Overy Staithe.[7]

Marnie's other powerful advocate was of course Hayao Miyazaki, who included Robinson's novel on his list of fifty favourite children's books and whose enthusiasm led to its being selected for adaptation by Studio Ghibli. Miyazaki's appreciation in *Doorway to Books* speaks eloquently of what he finds valuable in it:

> One landscape will be left in the hearts of the people who read this book: a house standing beside the marsh in the creek, and the windows facing towards them. Even years later, when they have grown up and forgotten this book entirely, the house will remain inside them. And someday they will encounter those windows. They will take a journey and see a house for the first time, but get the feeling that they've seen it before – a nostalgic, longing feeling – and suddenly they will remember Marnie. This is that kind of book. (Miyazaki 2011: 23)

The Japanese title of *When Marnie Was There*, which was also adopted by Ghibli for their adaptation, is *Memories of Marnie* (*omoide no mānī*), and memory

---

7 The Iwanami edition of the novel even includes a detailed map of the village (omitting its name), which pinpoints the locations of Marnie's house and the windmill.

is the aspect that Miyazaki highlights here. He places the putative reader in Anna's position, as someone with a buried childhood memory awakened by an unexpected encounter with a place. The evocation of memory by a powerful emotional trigger is an experience that many will recognize, but its potency depends on a receptive psychological state rather than any obvious external drama. The interiority of the action in *Marnie* raises the question of whether such a book has the cinematic qualities necessary for a successful transfer to the screen. Much of the novel's interest lies in Anna's feelings, thoughts and imagination. To the outside world, by contrast, she habitually shows what she calls her 'ordinary' or 'wooden' face (Robinson 2014: 8) and is seen by others as almost pathologically inexpressive.

According to the film's producer, Yoshiaki Nishimura, despite the book being one of Miyazaki's favourites, this was the first Ghibli film in which neither Miyazaki nor Isao Takahata had any direct involvement ('Extraordinary Thoughts' 2014). Rather, the project was assigned by Toshio Suzuki to Yonebayashi, after Yonebayashi confessed to feeling that he had left something undone in *The Borrower Arrietty* and was determined to make that good ('Extraordinary Thoughts' 2014). At first, Yonebayashi felt that *Marnie* would be too great a challenge, but gradually saw a way to make it work. Anna's lack of expression could be compensated for by making her a talented artist who habitually shields her drawings from others, although they are visible to the viewer ('Director Hiromasa Yonebayashi' 2015). This proved an effective way of indicating the complex inner world behind Anna's passive appearance. Another technical change was to the narrative's proportions: Anna's final encounter with Marnie, which occurs less than two-thirds of the way through the book, is delayed to a point where the film has just 19 of its 143-minute running time remaining, and the appearance of the new family in the Marsh House (now reduced to two rather than five children) slightly overlaps with Anna's time with Marnie, making *Memories of Marnie* less starkly a story of two parts.

Following the example of *The Borrower Arrietty*, the novel's setting was both localized to Japan and brought into the modern era. The modernization arguably presents the more challenging problem in this case. In Robinson's novel, which is set in the 1960s and places Marnie's childhood some fifty years earlier, Marnie's after-story involves her husband Edward being killed in the Second World War and Marnie evacuating their young daughter Esmé to the United States for safety – a separation that Esmé experiences as rejection and that precipitates their estrangement. In the film, the same wartime circumstances cannot be invoked; instead, Marnie's husband Kazuhiko dies young of an illness, and the grief-stricken Marnie dispatches their daughter Emily to boarding school, then checks herself into a sanatorium. The effect is to make Emily's charge that she was rejected by her mother appear more reasonable than the book allows.

Miyazaki reportedly suggested that the Setouchi region near Okayama might be a suitable place to set the action, but Yonebayashi instead selected the northern island of Hokkaidō ('Director Hiromasa Yonebayashi' 2015). Anna's hometown is shown to be Sapporo, Hokkaidō's largest city, from which she travels some 150 miles to stay with the Ōiwas (the equivalent of the Peggs in the book) in the countryside near Kushiro, in the east of the island. This area provides the film with a striking landscape and shares with Norfolk the requisite combination of beaches, wetlands, creeks and samphire beds (the Japanese word for samphire, *akkeshisou*, means 'Akkeshi grass' and is named after a town in the region). However, Yonebayashi is concerned to look beyond such realist details and draw out the psychological and even archetypal potential of the book's landscape, from its ominous dark tower of a windmill (which becomes an even more threatening silo in the film) to the Marsh House itself, which shifts eerily between appearing inhabited and abandoned. At one point, when Anna wakes in the grounds of the Marsh House and realizes she needs to get home, she runs down some stone steps to return across the creek, only to find her way blocked by the high tide. The scene recalls the moment in *Spirited Away* (on which Yonebayashi had worked as a key animator) when the protagonist, Chihiro, attempting to return from the land of the *kami*, likewise runs down stone steps, to discover that the meadow separating her from the human world has become a sea. In both cases, the barring presence of water indicates that the protagonists have entered a realm removed from ordinary life.

The film's Japanese localization promotes the impression of a disconnect between Anna's everyday life and her relationship with Marnie in other ways, too. One early scene is set during the Tanabata festival, which in Japan occurs on 7 July or later. However, when Marnie's diary is discovered, it contains references to events that take place after this in Anna's experience but are dated (as in Robinson's novel) to June. To those familiar with the date of Tanabata this temporal discrepancy may call the reality of Anna's experiences into question, although it is likely to pass unnoticed by most Western viewers.

Just as *The Borrower Arrietty* included a British-made doll's house, *Memories of Marnie* is careful to acknowledge the story's British origins, albeit obliquely. This is achieved primarily through the presentation of the Marsh House and of Marnie herself. The Marsh House in Robinson's novel was inspired by a building

Figure 4.2 The Granary, Burnham Overy Staithe, 2021 (photograph by the author).

in Burnham Overy Staithe known as the Granary, which sits on the creek where the River Burn flows into the North Sea (Figure 4.2). Its appearance is by no means luxurious; its two storeys are squat and its windows small, probably to provide protection from winter storms and floods. Illustrator Peggy Fortnum's line drawing renders it fairly accurately, although it makes the ground floor windows larger and more welcoming (Figure 4.3).

Yonebayashi's Marsh House, by contrast, is a full-scale Western-style villa (Figure 4.4). Like the villa in Kaho Nashiki's *Back Garden*, discussed in the previous chapter, it is said by Mrs Ōiwa to have been used by 'foreigners' for a long time, and Marnie's name (which is written in *katakana*)[8] and her appearance (with striking blue eyes and blonde hair) underline this foreign origin. Anna herself is more ambiguous. While 'Anna' is of course an English name, it is also quite common in Japan and can be written, as in this case, using *kanji*: 杏奈. Anna's not-quite-black hair and her eyes that have a touch of blue mark her, too, as having foreign ancestry, a sensitive point with her. When another child, Nobuko, points out her unusual eye colour ('just like a foreigner's') Anna responds aggressively, calling her a fat pig. Nobuko's response – 'It's no use pretending to

---

8 *Katakana* is a Japanese script used (among other things) for writing foreign words and names.

Figures 4.3–4.4 (*Top*) 'The house . . . was large and old and square, its many small windows framed in faded blue woodwork' (Robinson 2014: 25). Illus. Peggy Fortnum. (*Bottom*) The Marsh House from *Memories of Marnie*. Studio Ghibli, 2014.

be normal, because you look like just what you are' (*futsū no furi shite mo muda date anta wa anta no tōri ni mieterunda kara*) – incorporates an exact translation of the gnomic retort used by Sandra, her equivalent in the novel: 'You look like – just what you are' (Robinson 2014: 55). However, in the film's Japanese setting this sentence inevitably takes on a racial component absent from the book.

Miyazaki disapproved of the depiction of Marnie as blonde, calling it 'outdated and cheesy' ('Poster for Ghibli's new movie' 2014). It seems that he saw the character design as an attempt to gain attention by highlighting the film's exotic elements, and a remark Yonebayashi made in an interview suggests the charge was not unfounded: 'It would be easier for the story if Marnie was also Japanese, but I decided to make her blond-haired and blue-eyed. It creates more mystery that way, and I figured it would draw the viewer's eye more' (Giardina 2015). Nevertheless, utilizing Anna's un-Japanese appearance as a cause and symbol of her isolation also adds a plausible new element to her character. Moreover, the physical contrast between Marnie and Anna is an important element of the book, not least in Anna's own mind, and their differing hair colour is its most obvious aspect:

[Anna] thought [Marnie] was the prettiest girl she had ever seen, and hated her own dark hair and sunburnt skin. I look like a witch compared with her, she thought. (Robinson 2014: 121).

The contrast is reflected in Fortnum's illustrations, notably in a drawing subsequently used as the basis of the jacket of the 2003 Iwanami Shōnen Bunko edition of the novel. It depicts Anna and Marnie standing together, one in shorts with dishevelled dark hair, the other blonde and serene in a white nightdress (Figure 4.5). The difference was highlighted in the colouring added by Iwanami, which made Marnie's hair a startling straw yellow – a shade considerably moderated for her appearance in Yonebayashi's film. The contrast between Anna and Marnie, as written by Robinson and illustrated by Fortnum, reflects their characters and to some extent their respective social situations, Marnie being a well-off girl whose long hair is regularly brushed by her nurse, Anna an orphan left largely to her own devices, but it has no obvious racial component except in the form of a late hint that Anna's father was Spanish, which may be an element in her darker colouring (Robinson 2014: 265). In the film's Hokkaidō landscape, however, the same contrast inevitably highlights Marnie's position as a foreigner, whose romance is accentuated by her foreignness.

Figure 4.5 Marnie and Anna, from *When Marnie Was There* (Robinson 2014: 64). Illus. Peggy Fortnum.

After Miyazaki? *Mary and the Witch's Flower* and *Āya and the Witch*

In September 2013 Miyazaki announced his retirement, an event that seemed tantamount to announcing the end of Studio Ghibli itself. (Ultimately reports both of Miyazaki's retirement and of the studio's demise proved premature.) The announcement, while not unexpected, naturally caused some consternation among the studio's younger staff, who wondered where their own futures might lie. Yonebayashi, whose *Memories of Marnie* would not be released until the following July, was among these, as was producer Nishimura, who had just finished shepherding Takahata's *The Tale of the Princess Kaguya* (2013) to the screen, as well as producing *Marnie*. The result was that Nishimura, Yonebayashi and several other Studio Ghibli staff left the company in 2014 to found their own studio. Studio Ponoc was officially established in April 2015, the name being taken from the Croatian word for 'midnight'.

The question naturally arose of what the studio's first production should be. Nishimura suggested that Yonebayashi make a film about a witch, feeling that a lively story about an energetic girl might suit the director's talents better than another meditative, relationship-centred work such as *Marnie*. They were aware that the theme of a girl witch would inevitably invite comparison with Studio Ghibli's early success, *Kiki's Delivery Service* (1989), but at the press conference announcing the project in December 2016 Nishimura embraced the comparison, adding that Studio Ponoc's film would be aimed at a new generation of children:

> We enjoyed watching *Kiki's Delivery Service* when we were kids. Now we want to make a new witch movie for our own children. We should have what it takes! The creators at Studio Ponoc inherit the blood of Miyazaki, Takahata, and Suzuki. Director Yonebayashi made movies with those three for 20 years, and I think he wants to instil all that he has learned and cultivated from them during his life at Ghibli into this. ('Director Hayao Miyazaki' 2016)

One significant departure from Ghibli's practice lay in the new studio's choice of setting. The story of *Kiki* had been Japanese in origin, being based on Eiko Kadono's 1985 novel, but its presentation of witches, complete with brooms and black cats, was inspired by popular images of European witchcraft. Miyazaki had thus turned to Europe for his setting, adapting the buildings of Stockholm and Gotland, among other places, and drawing eclectically on the continent's architectural and climactic possibilities.

Thirty years later, with Harry Potter at the height of its popularity in Japan, a British setting was the obvious choice for a witch story aimed at the next generation of children. Yonebayashi, who had just directed films based on two of Miyazaki's favourite British children's fantasies, had also clearly developed an affinity with the material. The book he and Nishimura selected was *The Little Broomstick* (1971), by the English writer Mary Stewart. This had been Stewart's first children's novel, although by the time she wrote it she was already a successful author for adults in multiple genres, including historical fantasy. *The Little Broomstick* had enabled her to stay in the realm of magic, this time with a contemporary setting.

Stewart was a well-known writer, but by 2015 *The Little Broomstick* was not a well-known book. If *When Marnie Was There* had been less celebrated in Britain than *The Borrowers*, *The Little Broomstick* was more obscure still. Unlike *Marnie*, it also lacked any significant fan base in Japan. Although it had been translated into Japanese in 1975 by Yasuko Kakegawa as *The Little Magic Broomstick* (*chīsana mahō no hōki*), it was by now unknown except to those who had read it as children. There was thus little existing enthusiasm for the text that could be exploited to create traction for Ponoc's project, the success of which would rely on the qualities of the film itself and on the reputation of its makers.

The story of *The Little Broomstick* concerns ten-year-old Mary Smith, a girl who, like Marnie before her and Tom Long earlier still, has been sent to stay for an extended period in a childless home. Red Manor is a substantial house in the Shropshire countryside, but Great-Aunt Charlotte, her companion Miss Marjoribanks, the housekeeper Mrs McCleod and Zebedee the gardener are all middle-aged or elderly and, although not unkind, have little time to spare for Mary. Left to her own devices, Mary wanders into the nearby woods, where she discovers an unusual flower known as fly-by-night – a plant associated with witches. Using the magic power of the flower, Mary accidentally enchants a small broomstick, which promptly carries her and a black cat she has befriended to Endor College, a school for witches. There she is mistaken for a new pupil and given a tour by the headmistress, Madam Mumblechook, who is impressed with her potential. However, it becomes apparent that Madam Mumblechook and her associate, Doctor Dee, are engaged in Moreau-esque animal experimentation, and Mary (with some help from a local boy, Peter) successfully undertakes to release their captives.

In some ways *The Little Broomstick* is a traditional domestic fantasy, of the type that Nina Beachcroft's novels would exemplify a little later in the 1970s. As in much post-war British children's fiction, the protagonist is firmly middle class – Mary Smith's father is a Cambridge professor (52), while Peter is the local vicar's son (94) – and the existence of a servant class, albeit part-time, is taken for granted. The appeal of the book may have been limited by Stewart's use of nursery rhymes as the basis of the spells at Endor College, which makes those passages seem suited to a younger readership than the overall narrative, a tonal error all the more jarring when combined with the book's parodies of Senior Common Room chatter. Neither of these shortcomings would have been especially evident to the book's Japanese readers, however, and in compensation Stewart's story boasted features that may have enhanced its appeal to Nishimura and Yonebayashi.

One was the theme of animal welfare, which constituted a significant area of continuity with the work of Miyazaki, whose films had always been marked by a strong ecological focus. Still more significant was the book's inclusion of a magic school. Endor College was one of the first such establishments in British children's literature and can be seen as a precursor of the blend of witchcraft and boarding-school fiction later popularized by the Harry Potter series.

The staff at Studio Ponoc were very conscious of their inheritance from Ghibli. They were under conflicting obligations; on the one hand, to do justice to that prestigious provenance and, on the other, to create something distinct from it. Accordingly, *Mary and the Witch's Flower* was framed both as a continuation of and a departure from *The Borrower Arrietty* and *Memories of Marnie*. Like those films, it was based on a British children's book and featured the kind of isolated-but-feisty female protagonist familiar from Miyazaki's films. Mary's picture was even adopted as the studio's logo, in an echo of Ghibli's similar use of Totoro. In terms of animation style and colour palate, there is much about the film that feels 'Ghibli-esque', which is unsurprising, considering how many Ponoc staff were Ghibli veterans, including the animation director, Takeshi Inamura.

In contrast to his earlier adaptations of British children's literature, however, Yonebayashi retained the book's setting in rural Shropshire rather than moving the story to Japan. In one sense, this marked a sharp departure from Ghibli's practice, but in travelling to Europe for location research he and Nishimura were also consciously following in the footsteps of Miyazaki and Takahata. Miyazaki had pioneered the use of location hunting for anime when he visited Sweden in 1971, in preparation for his projected anime of *Pippi Longstocking*; and, although that project had foundered, in July 1973 he, Takahata and others had visited Switzerland to seek locations for *Heidi, Girl of the Alps* (1974), instituting a practice that continues to this day. Nishimura paid tribute to Miyazaki's example in an interview recorded for the DVD of *Mary and the Witch's Flower*, noting that 'to go there and breathe the air and see the country is very important' ('Interview with the Filmmakers' 2018). Accordingly, in August 2015 Yonebayashi and a group of Ponoc staff visited Britain, on what was the director's first visit to the country. Having been proud of creating in Hokkaidō a cloudscape previously unseen in Ghibli films (Giardina 2015), he declared himself equally inspired by English clouds:

> They seemed very close and they went on forever. They really stirred the imagination. I felt like those clouds had been an inspiration for British writers to create lots of fantasy works. It looked as if some hidden castle were about to emerge from them. (Rose 2018)

For all the inspirational importance of being on the spot, a degree of distance was also regarded as necessary to allow space for imagination, and the Ponoc artists 'were encouraged to draw from what they remembered rather than direct references like photos, [so that] they would capture the personality and impression of the place' (Stogdon 2018). Here too the filmmakers were adopting Miyazaki's practice on that *Heidi* expedition forty-two years earlier. Of that trip, the character designer and animation director Yōichi Kotabe later recalled:

> Miyazaki never sketched on site. [The director, Junzō] Nakajima took photos, I sketched, but Miyazaki was just looking. However, after returning to Japan, Miyazaki started to draw what he had seen in Switzerland. I was really surprised to see it. (Qtd. Yamamura 2020: 70)

The Ponoc team focused their location hunting on Shropshire. The National Trust property Sunnycroft, in Wellington, was one model for Great-Aunt Charlotte's house, but the primary site was the farmhouse where Ponoc based their operations, Lower Buckton House near Leintwardine, on the border with Herefordshire. The owners, Carolyn and Henry Chesshire, were accustomed to Japanese guests, and the warm, red-brick, nineteenth-century farmhouse offered many of the qualities that the filmmakers were looking for, both internally and externally. Ornaments and items of furniture present in various rooms found their way into the film, and Coxall Knoll, about a mile away, was cast as the hill where Mary finds the magic flower.

For all Studio Ponoc's on-the-spot research, *Mary and the Witch's Flower*'s evocation of Britain has a few discordant notes. Early in the film, Mary is seen practising her class self-introduction, a staple for any anime transfer student but not a custom in British schools; and the housekeeper wraps her packed lunch neatly in a very Japanese-looking *furoshiki*.[9] More surprisingly, her friend Peter, in his backward baseball cap and jacket, appears to have wandered in from the United States. However, the filmmakers undoubtedly produced a highly attractive, not to say lush, rendition of the English countryside.

Neither *Memories of Marnie* nor *Mary and the Witch's Flower* achieved the commercial success of *The Borrower Arrietty*. Although a film crew from the Japanese morning television programme *Zip!* visited Lower Buckton in May 2017 in anticipation of the film's Japanese release, and presenter Miku Sakakibara was filmed (little broomstick in hand) exploring the house and its environs, *Mary and the Witch's Flower* has yet to produce a surge of tourists coming to visit the film's setting, whether from Japan or Britain. Nevertheless, Nishimura has continued in his focus on British children's books. For some time, he considered making Studio Ponoc's next feature an adaptation of a book by the Scottish author, Alex Shearer (Rose 2018), well known in Japan from his comic dystopian novel, *Bootleg* (2003), which became a manga and anime in 2008 under the title *Chocolate Underground* (*chokorēto andāguraundo*). In the end, however, Nishimura selected A. F. Harrold's 2014 fantasy about a girl with an imaginary friend, *The Imaginary*, which he commissioned from director Yoshiyuki Momose and retitled *Rudger's Attic* (*yaneura no raja*) ('The Imaginary' 2023). It seems that the Japanese practice of turning British children's books into feature-length anime still has some momentum.

Advocates of fidelity in adaptation may wish to ponder the relationship between various trends observable over the series of films discussed in this chapter. Firstly, they have become more faithful to the source material; the plots, characterization and settings of *Howl's Moving Castle*, *The Borrower Arrietty*, *Memories of Marnie* and *Mary and the Witch's Flower* have converged ever more closely with those of the books on which they are based. Secondly, and probably not coincidentally, the personal involvement of Hayao Miyazaki has become steadily more attenuated: he was the director of *Howl's Moving Castle*, a writer for *The Borrower Arrietty*, just a senior colleague for *Memories of Marnie* and with *Mary and the Witch's Flower* had no connection at all except as a source of professional inspiration. Thirdly, each successive film has grossed less money at the Japanese box office than its predecessor. These trends no doubt reflect a complex set of factors, but taken together they suggest the need for a change

---

9 A *furoshiki* is a cloth, normally patterned, used to wrap and transport light packages of various kinds.

of direction. In the case of Studio Ghibli, that change came with *Āya and the Witch* (2020).

At the dinner with Diana Wynne Jones held after the private showing of *Howl's Moving Castle* in 2004, Miyazaki had mentioned how much he admired her Dalemark quartet (1975–93), the only book series that Jones had set wholly in a fantasy world (Cecil 2020). Miyazaki expressed a particular wish to adapt the second book, *Drowned Ammet* (1977). With its freedom fighters against high-handed oppression, moral quandaries, sea voyages, foes who become friends and mystical encounters with nature gods, *Drowned Ammet* has many of the ingredients that have proved to be strengths for Miyazaki. However, the project was never pursued. One factor may have been the relative failure of *Tales from Earthsea* (*gedo senki*), the 2006 debut by Miyazaki's son Gorō, which was based on the Earthsea fictions of Ursula Le Guin and contained a number of similar elements; although Jones's agent, Laura Cecil, was also told that Ghibli had an informal policy of never adapting more than one book by the same author (Cecil 2020).

Nevertheless, Ghibli did, uniquely, adapt a second book by Jones. It was not *Drowned Ammet* but her late novella, *Earwig and the Witch*, published in 2011, the year of her death. A Japanese translation appeared in 2012, with lively illustrations by Miho Satake, depicting the protagonist Earwig (Āya in the Japanese edition) as a bold and energetic girl with spiky pigtails, who stares confidently out from the book's cover. This was a marked contrast to Marion Lindsay's illustrations for the British edition, where Earwig is a buck-toothed child with limp bunches, generally depicted looking at another character or out of frame in various degrees of anxiety or despondency. The story and Satake's illustrations strongly appealed to Hayao Miyazaki, who wrote in a puff quote for the Japanese edition that he had read the book five times from cover to cover, and when Studio Ghibli bought the film rights early in 2017, Satake's work was used as the basis of the character designs. The film was released at the end of 2020.

The plot of *Earwig and the Witch* is straightforward. Earwig is a young girl living in a children's home somewhere in England, having been left there by her mother as a baby. She has proved herself a skilled manipulator of children and adults alike and lives a contented life, having arranged her environment to her liking. However, one day she is chosen for adoption by a witch called Bella Yaga and her companion, the taciturn and perhaps demonic Mandrake. Once in their house she is set to work as a dogsbody, cleaning the filthy rooms and collecting and preparing the ingredients needed for Bella Yaga's spells. However, Earwig is undaunted and, having made an ally of the witch's cat, steadily sets about gaining the upper hand over her captors, using a combination of magic, resourcefulness and charisma. By the end of the book she has succeeded triumphantly: 'Everyone in her new home now did exactly what she told them to do' (Jones 2011: 138).

In *Āya and the Witch*, Studio Ghibli stuck closely to this plot. The film's main change was the addition of a backstory for Bella Yaga and the Mandrake, who turn out to have been in a rock band with Āya's mother (another witch) in their younger days. The device humanizes Āya's antagonists, resembling in this respect an analogous backstory added to *Mary and the Witch's Flower* that showed a youthful Madam Mumblechook and Doctor Dee in a more sympathetic light. Just as importantly, it allowed the film to have a rock soundtrack very different from that normally associated with the studio.

Āya and the Witch was a departure for Ghibli in numerous respects. Unlike previous Ghibli adaptations, it retained its British setting. The studio sent the film's background designer, Yūki Takeuchi, to Britain to find locations, and she took advantage of Jones's lack of specificity, combining aspects of the Cotswold countryside with the English Channel coast ('The Setting of *Āya and the Witch*' 2020). *Āya* was also the first of the studio's films to be initially released, not in cinemas but on Japan's national television broadcaster, NHK, with a (slightly modified) worldwide theatrical release following some months later. This strategy was initially producer Suzuki's response to the long-term decline in cinema audiences, although the coincidence of the film's completion with the Covid-19 epidemic made the strategy seem especially judicious in retrospect. A third innovation was that the film was made entirely in CGI, rather than the hand-drawn animation with which Studio Ghibli had made its name. Responsibility for its production was accordingly handed to Gorō Miyazaki, as the director with the most experience of CGI techniques. He in turn recruited numerous non-Japanese staff for their expertise. This was a change from Ghibli's previous practice but, according to Suzuki, had the effect of achieving a return to the collegiality and give and take that had characterized the studio's early days. The new colleagues, not being steeped in Japanese company culture, with its strict hierarchies and taboo on challenging seniors, felt freer to contribute creatively, to the benefit of the film (Suzuki 2021).

The most significant of *Āya and the Witch*'s innovations, however, is the character of Āya herself. Jones's Earwig is a very different female protagonist from those associated with Ghibli. From one point of view, admittedly, the premise of the story – a ten-year-old girl[10] who finds herself in the house of a

---

10 Āya's age is given on the official film site ('Characters' 2020).

witch and is forced to do manual labour before eventually winning her freedom – echoes that of a previous Ghibli film, *Spirited Away*, in which the protagonist Chihiro is forced to work for the bathhouse witch, Yubāba. It also echoes an older stock of stories, notably those involving the Slavic goddess-cum-witch Baba Yaga (to whose name Bella Yaga's clearly alludes). In the Russian folktale, 'Vasilisa the Beautiful', for example, a girl's cruel stepmother sends her to Baba Yaga's hut to fetch fire, in the hope that she will be killed; but, with the advice and aid of a magical doll given her by her dying birth mother, Vasilisa is able to complete the seemingly impossible tasks set by Baba Yaga and is even rewarded.

Although these parallels are striking and highlight all three protagonists' resilience and capacity for hard work, the comparison also underscores their differences. Vasilisa is a brave but largely passive figure, who survives only by obeying the instructions of the doll who is her mother's representative, while Chihiro's success derives largely from her open-hearted kindness. Earwig, by contrast, is a strong-willed and emotionally independent child who consciously manipulates people and situations, having no further end in view than her own comfort and convenience. Diana Wynne Jones had long been a specialist in creating manipulative female characters, from Gwendolen Chant in *Charmed Life* to Laurel in *Fire and Hemlock*, Maria in *Black Maria* (1991) and Gammer Pinhoe in *The Pinhoe Egg* (2006) – but these were all cast as antagonists. Although positive portrayals of 'badly behaved' young girls are also to be found, such as Awful in *Archer's Goon* (1984), Earwig was the first such character to take on the role of protagonist.

The challenge, for Jones and later for Gorō Miyazaki, was to render such a character sympathetic, but to the Ghibli staff it was Earwig/Āya's unwavering focus on her own interests that made her a suitable protagonist for a film aimed at contemporary children. Suzuki, calling Āya 'bratty yet somehow cute' (*nikutarashii kedo, nazeka kawaii*), compared her to Astrid Lindgren's Pippi Longstocking, as a girl who achieves through intelligence what Pippi achieves through physical strength – that is, the ability to live as she pleases ('Plan: Hayao Miyazaki' 2020). Gorō Miyazaki has pointed out in interview that modern children, being more isolated than those in the past (especially in Japan, with its low birth rate), are subject to unprecedented levels of monitoring by adults, and that Āya can serve as a model for resistance: 'You have to manoeuvre a little differently, or you won't be able to do the things your group wants to do. I think it's probably better that they do manipulate adults now, in these times' ('Creating *Earwig and the Witch*' 2020). The tagline used on the film's advertising posters, provided by Suzuki, is defiant: 'I'm not under anyone's thumb!'

The end credits of *Āya and the Witch* contain callbacks to several previous Studio Ghibli films. We see one of the Mandrake's small demon servants sheltering beneath a leaf, much like Totoro in *My Neighbour Totoro* (*tonari no totoro*, 1988), and Āya herself is glimpsed watching the film of *Howl's Moving Castle* – a knowing piece of product placement for both Studio Ghibli and Jones. Such touches amount to an assertion of continuity, but they also highlight the stylistic contrast between the films produced by 'classic' Ghibli and its modern and likely future productions. The 'long, withdrawing roar' of Hayao Miyazaki's personal and creative influence has been a protracted phenomenon, but it seems that the days of the full-scale adaptation of British children's novels in the traditional Ghibli style may be over, at Ghibli if not at Studio Ponoc.

Throughout his sixty-year career, Hayao Miyazaki's work has been marked by contradictions, some even dating from his post-war childhood, when he hated the Japanese army and shot down imaginary American bombers with equal vehemence. As a pacificist and environmentalist who is nevertheless besotted with the machinery of war, as a luminary in an industry rooted in American culture who remains deeply ambivalent about that culture's hegemonic influence, as a pioneer of international anime locations who habitually creates non-specific evocations of place and as a devotee of British children's literature who has consistently shunned British settings in his films, Miyazaki is an artist whose instincts, fantasies and desires pull strongly in contrary directions. These oppositions have never been entirely resolved; however, much of his power as a filmmaker lies in his ability to harness their tensions productively. He remains a formidable figure within Japanese culture, not least in influencing the reception of British children's books and in positioning Britain itself, culturally and in literary terms, as a land of fantasy. It is to that wider perception of Britain, and to the role of children's books in sustaining it, that I turn in the next chapter.

5

Children's literature, tourism and the Japanese imagination

In the hot spring town of Yufuin, on Japan's southern island of Kyūshū, there is a small 'British-style theme park' (*Yufuin*). Yufuin Floral Village, which opened for business in 2012, comprises a collection of shops, food stalls and small-animal enclosures, each themed around a different text from children's literature, film and television (Figure 5.1). Some of these are Japanese in origin, such as *My Neighbour Totoro* and *Kiki's Delivery Service*; others, like *Heidi* and Tove Jansson's Moomin books, are European but known in Japan largely through successful anime adaptations; *Curious George* (1939) and a Disney Princess shop constitute the American contribution. Despite this being a 'British-style theme park', only a few of the shops are themed around British texts or characters, these being *Alice's Adventures in Wonderland*, *The Tale of Peter Rabbit* and Aardman Animations's *Shaun the Sheep* (2007–18), a more recent hit in Japan. Nevertheless, Yufuin Floral Village is self-consciously Anglocentric in its presentation. A Mini with a Union-Jack motif is proudly displayed, there are cream teas for sale and the main gift shop specializes in British-themed goods. Moreover, the Village's buildings, small and rustic in appearance, are modelled on those of the Cotswold hills in southern England, as the resort's website explains:

> Yufuin Floral Village in Ōita Prefecture is just like the world of Harry Potter. Yufuin Floral Village is a new amusement facility that recreates the townscape of the Cotswold region of Britain, which was also used as a location for *Harry Potter*. (*Yufuin*)

The double reference to Harry Potter might lead one to expect a Harry Potter attraction or merchandise. In fact, Yufuin Floral Village boasts neither, although the website goes on to claim a resemblance between Harry Potter's owl, Hedwig, and the snowy owl pictured at the entrance to its 'Owl Forest'. The Cotswold connection is equally striking, and again the website doubles down on it,

Figure 5.1 'The Rabbit', Yufuin Floral Village, Ōita Prefecture, 2018 (photograph by the author).

suggesting that Yufuin Floral Village is modelled on 'what is called the world's most beautiful village, in the Cotswold region of the United Kingdom' (*Yufuin*).

Yufuin Floral Village conveniently combines a number of the tropes and striking juxtapositions with which this chapter will be concerned. In particular, it illustrates the Japanese association of children's literature (of whatever provenance) with Britain, and specifically with the Cotswolds. That association is a complex one, the history and nature of which it is one of my purposes to describe; but it also exemplifies a type of diffuse cultural interaction not easily captured by conventional critical approaches to the relationship of literature and place.

Those approaches are by now well-established. Critics working on literary tourism typically combine cultural geography with reception analysis, examining the interaction of readers and tourists with places seen as significant for specific authors and texts and discussing the ways in which their activities inflect literary experience (Watson 2006; Booth 2016). Literary tourism studies are strong on the emotional connections that attach to tourist sites, but they are limited by their focus on specific texts and places. By contrast, topoanalysis, a term proposed by Gaston Bachelard to denote the psychological study of 'the sites of our intimate lives' (2014: 30), allows for the exploration of places and their affective qualities at a more general and archetypal level, as for example in Jane Suzanne Carroll's work on Susan Cooper and J. R. R. Tolkien (Carroll 2012, 2013). Yet other critics (e.g. Nikolajeva 1996: 121–52) have made productive use of the Bakhtinian concept of the chronotope as a tool with which to investigate the indissoluble connection of space and time in the construction of fictional settings. Topoanalytical and chronotopical approaches, with their respective archetypal and intertextual emphases, escape some of the restrictions of literary tourism studies, although their capacity to articulate the relationships of texts and readers to physical places is correspondingly weaker.

These methodologies cover a good deal of territory but are in only intermittent conversation with each other. In this chapter, I aim to establish a more flexible, syncretic mode of analysis, capable of doing justice to the complex interactions of reading, tourism and imagination. I will use the Cotswolds as an example of a place where the insufficiency of conventional approaches to children's literature tourism is especially apparent and show that such an analysis illuminates aspects of Japanese experience otherwise difficult to capture.

'Literary tourism' is a well-established term in Anglophone countries, but I will generally prefer the Japanese-English phrase, 'contents tourism' (*kontentsu tsūrizumu*), which has been current since the early years of this century. In the words of a 2005 report from Japan's Ministry of Land, Infrastructure, Transport and Tourism, contents tourism involves:

> the addition of a 'narrative quality' or 'theme' to a region – namely an atmosphere or image particular to the region generated by the contents – and the use of that narrative quality as a tourism resource. (Qtd. Seaton et al. 2017: 2)

'Contents tourism' offers a less restrictive arena for analysis than 'literary tourism', accommodating the fact that tourists may be engaged with multiple media, and that their journeys are often not to the settings of literary texts or to places supposed to have inspired authors but to film or television locations. Many contents tourists, indeed, may not consider literary texts to be the primary form of a narrative, even where they have chronological priority. Young Japanese visitors to Yufuin Floral Village are likely to encounter the anime versions of *Heidi*, the Moomin books and *Kiki's Delivery Service* long before the novels on which they are based. Similarly, Harry Potter fans (whether Japanese or Anglophone) may regard the films rather than the books as the stories' primary instantiation. Contents tourism acknowledges this complex and fluid combination of experiences, motivations and associations without automatically privileging its literary aspects. More importantly for my current purpose, in its focus on 'narrative' rather than on specific texts, contents tourism allows for a flexible articulation of the relationships of story and place, mediated by the imaginative interpretations and interventions of tourists themselves. Flexible as contents tourism is, however, it too has its limitations, as we shall see.

The Cotswolds as *Genfūkei*: Or, Harry Potter and the limits of contents tourism

We can establish some of these ideas more concretely by accompanying two figures prominent in previous chapters as they explore the English landscape with children's literature in mind. First, here is Momoko Ishii at Beatrix Potter's home in Near Sawrey in the Lake District, a visit she made in 1972 (Nakagawa et al. 2014):

> Every room and every staircase prompted a memory. This is because they are faithfully reproduced in [Potter's] books. On the display shelf, even the handkerchief that Miss Moppet uses to wrap up the mouse in *The Story of Miss Moppet* was preserved, in different dimensions, with the pattern just the same. However, what most surprised the visitors was an original picture by Potter displayed in *emaki*[1] style in the room on the first floor. Its delicacy and beauty of colour were such that it would not have seemed surprising to hear that the young Potter had painted it yesterday. (Ishii 2014: 41)

And here is Hayao Miyazaki, recalling a visit to a stately home in the context of discussing Frances Hodgson Burnett's *The Secret Garden* (1911):

> What I couldn't really understand about *The Secret Garden* (*himitsu no hanazono*) was why the mansion had a garden with a wall. I couldn't make it out.
> By chance, I had the opportunity to see a large manor house in England, and – ah, there really were farms and vegetable gardens set in huge grounds, and there was a greenhouse just for growing cut flowers to decorate the mansion. Then I understood. It was surrounded by a proper stone wall, and apples were trained along the wall, which was quite a sight. Many expert gardeners live on the castle grounds. The houses of the people who work in the castle are dotted about the estate. Everyone commutes from there. I realised that the people who work on the gardens tend them all year round – the vegetable gardeners grow

---

1 *Emaki* are narrative scrolls, usually including both illustrations and calligraphy.

the vegetables, the flower gardeners grow the flowers, and so on. This was how I first came to understand the world of *The Secret Garden*.

It's a hard world for Japanese people to imagine. (Miyazaki 2011: 113–14)

Ishii's visit is very specific, both in its destination and in the quality of attention it pays to that destination. Hill Top Farm is Beatrix Potter's home and thus a suitable place for a pilgrimage; the sense that Potter might walk through the door at any moment naturally lends a sense of intimacy. But Ishii is just as interested in using the experience as a way into Potter's books. To see the very handkerchief that the kitten Miss Moppet used to wrap up the mouse in *The Story of Miss Moppet* (1906) – or rather, to see the handkerchief that Potter used as a model, or perhaps just one of the same type – appears to offer access to the fiction as well as to the author. However, the handkerchief is significant to Ishii only because she already has the knowledge to recognize and interpret it. This is the kind of informed touristic pleasure offered by books such as Yumiko Sakuma's *A Journey through Seven British Fantasies* (2000), Chiba Kaori's *Journeys to World Masterpiece Theatre* (2015), Satoshi Andō's *The Landscapes of British Fantasy* (2019) or Masayoshi Ikeda's *A Journey through World Children's Literature* (2020), which visit places where children's books are set or that were important to their authors. Sites such as Hill Top, or the Ashdown Forest in East Sussex (where A. A. Milne, in a stylized sense, 'set' the *Pooh* books), are highly popular with Japanese tourists undertaking this sort of visit, to the extent that both have bilingual English/Japanese signs (Figures 5.2 and 5.3).

In Miyazaki's case, by contrast, there is no suggestion that the unnamed mansion was the model for Burnett's Misselthwaite Manor, or that Burnett

Figures 5.2–5.3 (*Left*) Bilingual sign, Hill Top, 2021. Photograph courtesy of Ayako Katsube. (*Right*) Bilingual sign, *en route* to the Pooh Sticks bridge, Ashdown forest, 2021. Photograph courtesy of Ayako Katsube.

herself had ever been there. Any of the numerous stately homes in Britain with the features he mentions might have provided him with a similar experience. Indeed, the garden he describes appears to be a walled kitchen garden with espalier fruit trees, not a flower garden like that discovered by Mary Lennox in Burnett's novel. Nevertheless, his experience not only gives him contextual information about working practices on large British estates, thus helping him to build an imaginative model of the kinds of relationships described in the book, but also solidifies his sense of such places as having physical reality. His experience therefore still functions as contents tourism, even though it lacks the purposive and destination-focused qualities conventionally seen as constituting that activity.

Which comes first, the contents or the tourism? The intuitive answer is that the contents precede the tourism that they inspire. Lovers of children's literature would not be visiting Near Sawrey in large numbers had Beatrix Potter not lived and written there. Even in that case, however, the contents have been modified to reflect the existence of touristic interest and even to provide a pre-emptive response to it. From the gift shop and the display cases to the careful preservation of objects that would otherwise be treated as ephemeral and the presentation of the interior so that one might believe Potter had just stepped out of the room, this is a place that comes to meet tourists' imaginations halfway. In a paradox that will recur throughout this discussion, the very attempt to offer an authentic Beatrix Potter experience inevitably involves a degree of artificial construction. In Chapter 3, I discussed the case of the city of Antwerp, which felt obliged to commission a statue of *A Dog of Flanders*'s Nello and Patrasche (in other words, to create contents) to cater to a touristic interest that already existed but lacked a satisfactory focus. Such a situation may seem exceptional but, as I will show, in many ways it is the norm.

Miyazaki, in the passage I have quoted, is clearly not engaged in contents tourism in quite the same way as Ishii. The estate he is visiting may, like Hill Top, be in the care of the National Trust or a similar heritage organization charged with preserving the past and making it legible; it may try to secure that legibility by utilizing visitors' prior experience of stately homes, of which an encounter with Burnett's novel will in some cases be one element. However, it is unlikely to be trading explicitly on its (non-existent) direct connections with *The Secret Garden*. That Miyazaki can nonetheless use his visit 'to understand the world of *The Secret Garden*' tells us something about contents tourism's relative independence of literary or authorial provenance. In this chapter, I pay particular attention to such indirect forms of touristic activity because, although they have been given little weight in critical discussion, they account for a great deal of Japanese children's-literature-related tourism. Rather than pilgrimages to authors' homes or to the settings of books, activities that confine inquiry within an established contents tourism paradigm, I will focus on a destination that is hugely popular with Japanese visitors but lacks the same contents tourism credentials: the Cotswolds.

Unlike the Lake District, the Cotswolds boast no one place – town, house, landmark – with a famous children's literature connection comparable to Hill Top. The remark in the Wikipedia entry on the Cotswold village of Bibury, that it is 'famous as Emperor Hirohito's favourite place in England and as the home of no-one famous or remarkable', might, with due allowance for self-deprecation, stand for the region as a whole ('Bibury' n.d.). For my purposes, the lack of iconic children's literature sites is precisely where the interest of the Cotswolds lies, for in the absence of such sites other features and processes become more easily visible.

While it is not impossible to read the Cotswolds in conventional contents tourism terms, the limitations of this approach quickly become apparent. The example of J. K. Rowling's Harry Potter series, which (as we saw in the publicity for Yufuin Floral Village) has been claimed for the Cotswolds, is a case in point. How far can a contents tourism approach carry us towards understanding that association? My contention is that it largely eludes such analysis, exemplifying the diffuse and tangential qualities in play in tourist activity and demonstrating the extent to which an area's narrative potential is realized through the imaginative labour of visitors.

Rowling's series has been by far the most popular example of British children's literature of the last generation, and the appetite for associated contents tourism is correspondingly high. However, not only do the plots of the books largely take place in fictional locations, but the most important of these – Hogwarts and its neighbouring village, Hogsmeade – are invisible to ordinary humans, factors that appear to limit touristic potential. Relatively few visible (and hence visitable) places feature in the series, the most famous probably being King's Cross station in London, where a luggage trolley has been duly sunk into the wall for fans to pose with. Otherwise, would-be contents tourists must make do with visiting the Warner Bros. Studios at Leavesden in Hertfordshire, film locations and inspirations for studio sets, or places thought to have inspired Rowling herself. These are the conventional fare of contents tourism.

The case for regarding the Cotswolds as a site of Potter contents tourism on grounds such as these is not entirely void. Rowling spent her childhood nearby, first in the small town of Yate, northeast of Bristol, and later in Tutshill on the River Severn, and must have known the area well. The unusual surname Dursley, which she gave to Harry Potter's foster family, is found in its greatest concentration near the Cotswold town of the same name, from which it derives, some twenty miles from both these childhood homes (PublicProfiler 2016). The appearance in *Harry Potter and the Deathly Hallows* (2007) of Gloucestershire's Forest of Dean and the attribution of a Wiltshire location to Malfoy Manor are suggestive of the wider area's presence in Rowling's imagination, though tantalizing for those who might wish to secure for the Cotswolds an unambiguous foothold in the Potter canon.

As for film locations, the claim of the Yufuin Floral Village website that the Cotswolds were 'used as a location for "Harry Potter"' relies on a rather generous definition of the region's boundaries. Gloucester Cathedral provided one of the sets for Hogwarts, while the grounds of Blenheim Palace were the stage for James Potter's bullying of Severus Snape in *The Order of the Phoenix* (2007), but both lie just outside the Cotswolds region, one a little to the west, the other to the east. A few miles south-east of the Cotswolds, the Wiltshire village of Lacock is one of the most filmed small settlements in Britain, having provided sets for many historical dramas, including *Pride and Prejudice* (1995) and *Downton Abbey* (2010–15). Lacock contributed James and Lily Potter's house to the film of *Harry Potter and the Philosopher's Stone* (2001) and Horace Slughorn's house and the Babberton Arms to *Harry Potter and the Half-Blood Prince* (2009), while the cloisters of Lacock Abbey were yet another contributor to the Hogwarts architecture. According to Abbey staff, the Harry Potter connection is the main attraction for many of their Japanese visitors, but neither they nor any of the retailers to whom I spoke in the village considered Lacock to be in the Cotswolds: responses to the question included 'No, it's in Wiltshire', 'It's very close', 'It depends how you define "Cotswolds"' and so on.

Lacock is on the itinerary of many Japanese coach tours, which may take it in, along with Bath and one or two Cotswold villages, as part of a day excursion from London. Readers of some Japanese Cotswold guidebooks will find Lacock included (e.g. Kobayashi 2015: 128–33), and tote bags sold by the National Trust shop on the High Street are branded with a map of the Cotswolds that has been expanded to include the village. From a Japanese perspective, then, while it may not be accurate to claim the Cotswolds as a location for Harry Potter, neither is it entirely unreasonable. Nevertheless, the Cotswolds proper offer only very limited scope for contents tourism, whether for Harry Potter or for other British children's texts well known in Japan. In order to understand the Japanese association of the Cotswolds with children's literature, and the reasons why an attraction such as Yufuin Floral Village might emphasize its debt to the region's architecture, we must broaden our focus to consider the wider position of the Cotswolds as a Japanese tourist destination.

The Cotswold hills lie some 100 miles west of London, occupying about 800 square miles of Oxfordshire, Gloucestershire, Wiltshire, Warwickshire and Worcestershire. In this chapter, the phrase 'the Cotswolds' generally refers to the Cotswolds Area of Outstanding Natural Beauty (AONB), as designated by Natural England, along with the smaller but overlapping area administered by the Cotswold District Council.[2] At times, however, 'the Cotswolds' can also denote a more loosely defined imaginative concept, clustered around such features as a pastoral landscape of hills and sheep, market towns and villages, cottages of honey-coloured limestone and an ethos of rural craftsmanship. Like Arcadia, the Cotswolds function both as a geographical place and as an idealized *topos*. The exact borders of such an area must remain fuzzy; indeed, that fuzziness helps make it adaptable to new cultural and geographical contexts.

It is to the latter version of the Cotswolds that Japanese visitors are generally attracted, and it has brought them in such numbers that, like Hill Top and the Ashdown Forest, the railway station at Moreton-in-Marsh (where passengers arrive from London) has signage in Japanese as well as English for their benefit. No official figures are kept, but anecdotal evidence from retailers and Tourist Office staff across the region, whom I interviewed over the summer of 2018, suggests that in some popular spots, notably Bibury, Bourton-on-the-Water and Castle Combe,[3] a large proportion (perhaps the majority) of foreign visitors are from Japan.

The historical origins of the Cotswolds's popularity in Japan are unclear. As hinted in the Wikipedia entry quoted earlier, one possible cause was the enthusiasm of the future Emperor Shōwa, who is said to have stayed in Bibury as part of his six-month tour of Europe in 1921. Another was the praise of the poet and designer, William Morris, a respected figure in Japan (Nakayama 1996), who remarked in a letter of August 1890 that Bibury was 'surely the most beautiful village in England' (Morris 2014: 188). Since the Edo era, Japanese tourist culture has set great store by ranked lists and places authoritatively deemed superlative, and Morris's phrase has been widely quoted, although the referent and scope of his words have sometimes changed in the telling. They

2 The area controlled by Cotswold District Council does not cover the southern part of the AONB, which includes Castle Combe, but stretches further east to encompass the town of Lechlade.
3 For more on Castle Combe and contents tourism, see Butler (2020).

almost certainly lie behind the otherwise cryptic reference on the Yufuin Floral Village website to 'what is called the world's most beautiful village', for example, and probably inform the title of Shabako Kobayashi's Globetrotter guidebook, *England's Most Beautiful Place: The Cotswolds* (*ingurando de ichiban utsukushī basho: kottsūoruzu*, 2015). The website of the Hotel Monterey Grasmere in Ōsaka, where the twenty-second and twenty-third floors are occupied by a three-quarter replica of All Saint's Church in Brockhampton, Herefordshire, claims it for the Cotswolds via a mangled version of William Morris's remark: 'The design imitates the churches of the Cotswolds, described by the renowned designer William Morris as the most beautiful in England' (Hotel Monterey Grasmere). Even a group of Japanese schoolchildren, whom I encountered in Bourton-on-the-Water in July 2018, engaged on a two-week cultural exchange, carried a single-sheet itinerary that promised an imminent visit to 'Bibury, praised by the artist William Morris as "the most beautiful village in England"'.

One attraction of the Cotswolds, particularly for adult visitors, appears to lie in the contrast the area offers with urban Japanese life, as a place where 'people live together with nature in a peaceful atmosphere' (*Yufuin*). David Strachan of Totteoki Cotswolds Tours, who has been giving private tours of the Cotswolds to Japanese visitors since 2004, reported in interview that his clients are not generally interested in the public events of British history, but that they value the Cotswolds as a retreat from the pressures of modernity:

> There was a couple and their teenage daughter. We met them at the station. They'd come from Japan to London, London to Moreton, then into our vehicle. We took them to a little village. She got out and burst into tears, because, she said, she didn't realise anywhere could be so beautiful. She was like that the rest of the day, overwhelmed by everything. . . .
>
> Another mother and daughter, at the end of the tour I asked them what they thought of it, and the mother said, 'I feel like I've been cured'. And then she went all wet-eyed, and her daughter said she'd been under a lot of stress; she lived in Tokyo, and her job and family situation was really stressful, and spending the day just chilling out in the Cotswolds just made it all go away . . .
>
> A lot of people, they just want to sit and relax, and when they go to Sudeley Castle, I always say to them, just sit on the bench. Then they sit down, look round, and lean back, and then their eyes close and all the stress just disappears from them. (Strachan 2017)

One Japanese guidebook introduces the Cotswolds under the heading, 'England's Primary Landscape that Heals the Heart', emphasizing this restorative function (Ōhashi 2013: 8–9). To value the Cotswolds as an escape from modern life and its stresses is, almost by definition, to view them in opposition to those things, as belonging to the past or to a realm removed from historical change altogether – a place of story. The term I have translated above as 'primary landscape' is *genfūkei*, which refers both to a nostalgically remembered scene from early childhood and to an archetypal landscape evocative of a place's past. Such topoanalytical landscapes powerfully combine personal and public geography, anchoring both in the past and using generic cues to evoke emotional reactions and memories, even of places only ever visited in imagination or play.

Children's literature offers one potent way of framing the Cotswolds so as to fulfil this function, and the language of children's stories is accordingly common in Japanese accounts of the region. The same guidebook's entry on Bibury, for example, is titled 'Beloved Cotswold Village That Appears to Be from the World of Fairy Tale' (Ōhashi 2013: 18), while *England's Most Beautiful Place*, similarly, asserts that Castle Combe seems 'to have been taken from a nursery tale' (Kobayashi 2015: 124). Such places evoke a generalized, 'Once upon a time' past rather than one linked to historical dates or events. Such 'occidentalist' uses of the Cotswolds suggest one possible reason why a children's-literature-themed site such as Yufuin Floral Village might claim the area as an inspiration. Its cultural or historical importance, and even its status as a setting or inspiration for children's texts, may count for less than its capacity to be imaginatively reframed by Japanese tourists, writers and readers.

The association of the Cotswolds with children's literature is no less powerful for being diffuse rather than specific. On the contrary, that quality lends the Cotswolds region greater flexibility than would be the case if its towns and landscapes were bound to a particular contents-tourism site or narrative context. The area's rustic cottages, kitchen gardens, ancient churches, winding lanes and narrow stone bridges recall both the texts and the illustrations of many children's books, especially for younger readers. Castle Combe and Bibury are not alone in appearing to have been 'taken from a nursery tale'; the Japanese tourists to whom I spoke in Bourton-on-the-Water were reminded of a picture book (*ehon*), a fairy tale (*otogibanashi*), of *Harry Potter*, *Alice's Adventures in Wonderland* and *The Tale of Peter Rabbit*. The Cotswolds may not be their setting, but these texts provide a frame of reference through which the area can be readily interpreted. Indeed, classic children's stories have long provided a template for Japanese understanding and perception of the English countryside, one that has been constantly renewed both within and beyond literature. Studio Ghibli designer Yūki Takeuchi, recalling her time exploring Cotswold locations for *Āya and the Witch*, records her strong experience of this sense:

> I spent that day strolling around. I could see where sheep and horses were grazing, where the rows of hills continued into the distance, unlike Japan; I could see low clouds drifting like slices of bread, and so on. It was like being in a picture book. It was difficult to convey even through photos, so I was glad that I could actually see it. ('The Setting of *Āya and the Witch*' 2020)

In 1985, the Japanese toy company Epoch set the world of their popular Sylvanian Families toys in a place that, although officially unidentified, seems 'quintessentially English . . . pastoral and blissfully low-tech (all lacy aprons, mob-caps, Morris Minors and caravans)' (Clark 2012) – an image that might have been calculated to stir a sense of familiarity in a subsequent visitor to the Cotswolds. With their cast of woodland creatures, Sylvanian Families emphasize the qualities of 'smallness' and 'snugness' that Jerry Griswold has identified as characteristic of children's literature (Griswold 2006). Similarly, the Cotswolds Tourism Officer, Chris Jackson pointed out in our interview that one of the area's primary attractions is that its settlements are all small, with populations running at most into a few tens of thousands (Jackson 2018). Among the towns and villages most visited by the Japanese, Bourton-on-the-Water has a population of 3,300, Bibury 700 and Castle Combe fewer than 400. Individual houses and shops, too, are generally modest in scale, with low beams and lintels, having been built at a time when people were generally smaller in frame.

The importance of scale is brought most vividly to bear in Bourton-on-the-Water's model village, an attraction built from Cotswold stone over four years from 1936 and reproducing the village of that time at a scale of one to nine. In a playful use of *mise en abyme*, the model village contains a small replica of itself, which in turn contains an even smaller replica, while in a life-size picture at its entrance Lemuel Gulliver can be seen wandering among Bourton's diminutive houses (Figure 5.4). The presence of *Gulliver's Travels* was already implicit in a 1938 Pathé News film about the attraction, *Lilliput Village*, but was reinforced throughout the 1950s and 1960s through a self-published booklet sold at the site, *Gulliver in the Cotswolds*, which offered an admiring account of the model village written as if by Gulliver himself. In it, 'Gulliver' takes the opportunity to meditate on the imaginative effect of such sudden changes of scale:

> I tried to project myself into the mind of [a model maker] and thought how he must be always living in two worlds at once – the actual and the miniature. How he must subconsciously be changing from the powerful Brobdingnagian when in his own workshop to the apprehensive Lilliputian when he battles in the vast world of reality. (*Gulliver in the Cotswolds* 1955: n.p.)

Figure 5.4 Gulliver wanders through a Lilliputian Bourton-on-the-Water, 2018 (photograph by the author).

As this suggests, the model village is offered not just as an exercise in craftsmanship but also as an affective prompt, one that has primed visitors ever since to experience it in narrative terms. Mary Norton was sufficiently inspired by seeing a model village that she used it to house her Borrower family in *The Borrowers Afloat* (1959) and *The Borrowers Aloft* (1961). Her fictional model village, Little Fordham, was probably based on Bekonscot in Buckinghamshire, which is situated less than 30 miles from Leighton Buzzard, the approximate setting of *The Borrowers*. However, when Studio Ghibli released its 2010 documentary, *Ghibli's Bookshelf (jiburi no hondana)*, to coincide with *The Borrower Arrietty*, it was to Bourton-on-the-Water that the studio sent its cameras – such is the pull of the Cotswolds. As for Japanese tourists, several of their TripAdvisor reviews mention the ways in which the village plays with perception, often making reference to Gulliver. A typical comment reads: 'It feels just like being Gulliver. When you arrive in the town, first come here, then stroll around the town and its river, and then come back to this place to double the fun' (ichan0108 2015) (Figure 5.5). The model village is a convenient metaphor for, but also a tangible example of, the ways in which the Cotswolds accommodate fantasy, evoking fairy tales and children's stories about beings large and small.

It is a commonplace of reader response theory that readers approach texts with a pre-existing set of genre scripts and expectations; likewise, John Urry has described the 'particular filter of ideas, skills, desires and expectations' that constitutes the so-called tourist gaze, ensuring, for example, that 'when a small village in England is seen, what [tourists] gaze upon is the "real olde England"' (Urry 2011: 5). These are probably variant forms of the same activity, in which prior knowledge and desire mediate present experience in ways that can be anticipated and exploited. Japanese visitors to the Cotswolds (along with the area's inhabitants and custodians) adopt and actively maintain a Cotswold 'filter', selecting certain qualities as valuable and visible and setting parameters for their reception and reuse. That filter determines which views and buildings will feature in brochures or Instagram feeds, which metaphors will offer themselves for use and which aesthetic and emotional responses will arise as if unbidden. The relationships between places, visitors, texts and readers, and their ability to anticipate and modify each other, create a complex semantic space potentially generative not just of literary experience but also of new texts, whether in the form of physical sites such as Yufuin Floral Village and other Cotswold-inspired tourism centres in Japan or of fictions that (as we shall see) draw or build on the Cotswolds for their atmosphere and aesthetics.

Rowling too, in writing her Harry Potter series, made extensive use of long-established *topoi* to establish her world's appearance and atmosphere. Many of these involved the evocation of antiquity. For example, her school is located in a castle rather than a modern building; the pupils travel there by steam train; they wear academic gowns and use quills rather than ballpoint pens. These features partly echo the sartorial and other eccentricities of British public schools, but

Figure 5.5 'It feels just like being Gulliver'. The model village at Bourton-on-the-Water, 2018 (photograph by the author).

(while not magical in themselves) they also utilize the chronotope of witchcraft and wizardry in their many prior representations in literature and art, where they are typically associated with ancient buildings and a generic past. That chronotope was powerful enough to influence both Rowling's portrayal of Hogwarts and her readers' reception of it; but it also extends into the reception of physical experience. For someone already steeped in the world of Harry Potter, as represented in the books, films and tourist sites such as Universal Studios Japan's Harry Potter attraction in Ōsaka, a townscape of ancient stone cottages of the kind for which the Cotswolds are famed inevitably conjures the wizarding world – especially if, for reasons of tradition and practicality (frequent earthquakes, lack of building stone), similar buildings are rare in one's own country. In this respect, the Cotswolds do not provide a point of origin; rather, they exemplify an established archetype.[4]

The Cotswolds in Japan

One way to understand how Japanese people interpret the Cotswolds is to consider the features they select and emphasize when they set up British-themed attractions in Japan itself. Besides Yufuin Floral Village, there are numerous establishments that make reference to British children's literature and culture. These include Shuzenji Niji no Sato in Shizuoka Prefecture, where visitors to the 'British Village' can see a toy museum and ride a replica of a British miniature steam railway; the eclectic attractions at Lockheart Castle[5] in Gunma Prefecture (transported stone by stone from the Scottish borders in the 1980s), with its teddy bear and Santa Claus collections; and the meticulous reconstruction of Beatrix Potter's house and garden at Saitama Children's Zoo, home to Daitō Bunka University's Beatrix Potter Reference Library. Manipulation of scale and a degree of visitor participation are particularly frequent elements. The centrepiece of the short-lived Gulliver's Kingdom theme park, which operated near Mount Fuji for four years from 1997, was a 45-metre model of Gulliver, pegged down by Lilliputians. In the *Alice in Wonderland*-themed shop, 'Alice on Wednesday', the entrance is made deliberately small so that adult customers

---

4　The Cotswolds are not unique in this respect. A comparable example is the popular association of Studio Ghibli's *Kiki's Delivery Service* with Ross Village Bakery in Tasmania, which has become a centre for contents tourism despite not having been used as a source by the studio itself (Norris 2013, 2018: 115–22).
5　The spelling of the original owner's name ('Lockhart') was changed after its relocation, to enhance the destination's credentials as a wedding venue.

are forced to stoop as they enter, sharing Alice's discomfort. Shinjuku's 'Alice in Picture Book Land' (*ehon no kuni no arisu*) restaurant not only boasts staff dressed as Alice and the Mad Hatter, with décor to match, but also serves food and drink with 'Eat Me' and 'Drink Me' labels, chosen from a menu that (thanks to ingenious paper engineering) takes the form of a scattered deck of playing cards when opened.[6] Other establishments trade on broader cultural tropes of Britishness. In Ikebukuro's Swallowtail 'butler café', the (predominantly female) customers are escorted to their seats by staff in tailcoats, through a room featuring chandeliers, swag curtains, pastoral art and alcoves with books such as *Peter Rabbit* on display. A butler, summoned with a small handbell, will produce tiered plates of crustless sandwiches and cakes served with Earl Grey tea and bid goodbye to his 'mistress' (*ojōsama*) by announcing that her 'carriage' (*basha*) is waiting. For all their diversity, such establishments share an emphasis on providing customers with an immersive experience, in which they are the main characters in an English fantasy – and a fantasy of Englishness.

That fantasy tends to concentrate on a relatively narrow set of traits. There is little here of urban, or indeed of modern, Britain. Rather, the vision is of a rural, hierarchical society, set somewhat back in time – a vision, in fact, rather like that of the Cotswolds. In Japan, this vision finds its purest incarnation in the village of Dreamton (*dōrimuton*), situated in the hills outside Kameoka, in Kyōto Prefecture. The brainchild of an Anglophile native of Kyōto, Mayumi ('Marie') Haruyama, Dreamton opened in 2011 as an attempt to create a Cotswold village in the very different landscape and climate of Japan. Cotswold stone being hard to source, its cottages were constructed using British sand and cement, but the interiors are carefully furnished from Haruyama's regular visits to the UK as an antique dealer. At the Pont-Oak restaurant, diners can eat a full English breakfast or fish and chips to the accompaniment of Elizabethan airs and be served by waitresses in the mobcaps and aprons of a traditional English tearoom (Figure 5.6). Other features include an antique shop, a pub, a chapel and a row of bed-and-breakfast cottages with whitewashed interiors reminiscent of Cotswold cottages a century or more ago.

The attention to detail is impressive (Haruyama's company was later hired to create the buildings in Yufuin Floral Village), but in our interview Haruyama was keen to stress that Dreamton is no theme park. Rather, it is an attempt to recreate in Japan the atmosphere and spirit that she found when visiting the

---

6 See Jaques and Giddens (2016: 226–7) for a fuller description of a sister restaurant in the Ginza district.

Figure 5.6 Interior of the Pont-Oak Restaurant, Dreamton, near Kameoka, Kyōto Prefecture, 2018 (photograph by the author).

Cotswolds, a place she considers more faithful to its traditional identity than her native Kyōto:

> I was born in the 'most historic town' in Japan, and I hate that it is getting more and more Americanised; it feels like a show. But people who just get on with their lives in the Cotswolds are cool. . . . People who have their own style are very cool. (Haruyama 2018)

Dreamton village is intended to provide not entertainment but something akin to the experience of actually being in the Cotswolds; not settings yoked to particular texts, like the *Snow White* or *Winnie-the-Pooh* attractions to be found at Tōkyō Disneyland, but an environment where such narratives might occur almost spontaneously and where the 'narrative qualities' characteristic of contents tourism can be developed through visitors' imaginative participation. Dreamton is an oneiric space, as its name implies, and children's literature can be an important catalyst in activating its topoanalytical potential. Describing a forthcoming enterprise to build a traditional Italian village on similar lines to Dreamton, Haruyama described it as the kind of place one might encounter 'an old man carving Pinocchio' (Haruyama 2018). Another plan was to create a Muromachi-era village, where (as her architect put it to me) you might stand beside a stream and find a Peach Boy floating towards you. In these references to Carlo Collodi's classic Italian story and one of Japan's most iconic folktales, the collaboration between immersive tourism and children's literature is foregrounded, but it is implicit in Dreamton too, in its evocation of the narrative qualities of the Cotswolds.

British Hills (*buritisshu hiruzu*) in Fukushima Prefecture is an even more elaborate attempt to create an authentic experience of Britain (especially, in practice, of England), in this case specifically with children and young adults in mind. This educational centre and resort includes half-timbered guest houses with names such as Drake and Chaucer, the Ascot tearooms, the Falstaff Arms pub, 'Ye Shoppe' and, at its heart, a full-scale manor house (Figure 5.7). Built in 1994, British Hills – 'the Britain that anybody can visit without a passport' (*British Hills* 2019) – was intended to provide an immersive British environment for university and school pupils learning English, with Kanda Institute of Foreign Languages being instrumental in its establishment. School and university groups make up around 80 per cent of visitors, with private and business guests accounting for the remainder (Dhebar 2018). As far as possible, within its ample grounds only

Figure 5.7 Statue of Shakespeare in front of the Manor House, British Hills, Fukushima Prefecture, 2018 (photograph by the author).

English is spoken, British food is served in the dining hall and British sports and games such as cricket and snooker are taught. British and Commonwealth citizens are recruited as customer-facing staff, and until 2010 there was even a trained British butler, John Stanbury, to underline both the resort's British credentials and its aristocratic representation of the country. British furniture and bathroom fittings were imported for the guest houses, which were constructed by Border Oak, a Leominster company specializing in oak-framed buildings. For Ryūji Sano, the founding president of British Hills, authenticity was crucial. He wanted to avoid the kind of discomfort he often felt on encountering inaccurate representations of Japan in Western films: 'I did not want to create something that British people would feel uncomfortable seeing' (Sano 2011).

The quest for authenticity was a matter not only of sparing hypothetical British visitors' sensibilities but also of providing Japanese guests with accurate understanding, which Sano saw as most effectively achieved through experience: 'the real thing is not understood by appearance, it is first understood by touch' (Sano 2011). The result is certainly impressive: if British Hills betrays its recent construction, it is primarily in its relatively pristine appearance (notwithstanding the carefully constructed church 'ruins' in its grounds). In practice, however, that educational strategy runs in tandem, and to an extent in competition, with the fiction-making of the students who are British Hills's primary customers. As former butler John Stanbury noted in interview:

> British Hills is a fairyland (*otogi no kuni*). It is England in Japan, without having to worry about getting on a plane. You can get on the Shinkansen or a school bus and come. As soon as you arrive at the gates of British Hills, it is like a door to another world. (Stanbury 2011)

The language of 'fairyland' is familiar from reactions to the Cotswolds, but the custodians of British Hills have found that children's literature plays a more specific role in making the place legible to visitors. For example, when guests who have stepped through this 'door to another world' discover a large wardrobe in one of the manor house bedrooms, they may exclaim: 'Narnia!' (Dhebar 2018).[7] Similarly, Yūki Kawada, former director of British Hills, explained that in its early days students were unfamiliar with the traditions followed in the manor house's refectory, an imposing room hung with coats of arms and chandeliers, based architecturally on the dining hall of Christ Church, Oxford (Figure 5.8): 'I

---

7 Wardrobes are not traditional items of Japanese furniture – to the extent that when C. S. Lewis's *The Lion, the Witch and the Wardrobe* (1950) was translated into Japanese in 1966, its title was shortened to *The Lion and the Witch* (*raion to majo*).

Figure 5.8 The 'Hogwarts' refectory, British Hills, Fukushima Prefecture, 2018 (photograph by the author).

explained that a refectory is a meeting place in a British public school . . . but after the *Harry Potter* movie was released, there was no need for explanation' (Kawada 2011). Exposure to the Great Hall of Hogwarts (also modelled on the Christ Church dining hall) provided students not only with 'historical' information but also with a narrative context for their own experience. The staff whom I interviewed in 2018 told me that students and teachers alike now invariably read the building in these terms. In the words of British Hills employee, Luke Houghton:

> The teachers of the schoolchildren almost uniformly introduce [the refectory] as 'Hogwarts'. The teachers are telling the kids before they arrive, or as they're getting off the bus, 'This is the Harry Potter wing'. . . . These are the people that are framing the kids' worldview, so they're not going to question that. (Hashimoto and Houghton 2018)

As in the Cotswolds themselves, Harry Potter has become part of the repertoire of imagery through which experience is interpreted. The same is true of the cloaks with which British Hills guest rooms are provided, originally in the interests of historical accuracy (because 'there were no umbrellas in the eighteenth century' (Kawada 2011)). Kawada again initially found this a difficult concept to convey to young visitors, but that problem disappeared with the advent of Harry Potter. Although predating the first Potter film, the British Hills cloaks strongly resemble the gowns worn by Harry and his friends, even to the placement of their heraldic crests. This should come as no surprise, since both draw on common historical models, but history is routinely bypassed by British Hills's visitors in favour of literary identification.

The automatic 'Potterization' of sites such as British Hills is partly indicative of the narrowness of the palette many Japanese people work with when seeking to understand British culture – a less toxic version of Chimamanda Ngozi Adichie's 'danger of a single story' (Adichie 2009). Distinctions of period, location, purpose, class and occasion, which may be grasped intuitively by someone steeped in British culture and history, are liable to be missed by those from a very different cultural context. The process is, however, often more dynamic and bidirectional than this suggests. Lawrence Venuti has noted that the demand in the post-war United States for a certain kind of Japanese literature (emphasizing aestheticism, transience, wistfulness and other stereotypically 'Japanese' qualities) led to Japanese publishers and writers catering to that taste in order to secure translation and foreign sales (Venuti 1998: 71–5). There is a similar circularity in tourist locations' presentation of themselves in ways calculated to meet visitors' expectations, from the careful curation of sites such as Hill Top to show-villages such as Lacock and Castle Combe making themselves 'film-set ready' by banning television antennae and satellite dishes.

Social pressure to conform to such requirements can be intense. In 2015, for example, Peter Maddox, a resident of Bibury's famous Arlington Row (a street so iconic that its picture used to appear in British passports), became the centre of a regional cause célèbre when he had the temerity to spoil tourists' photographs by keeping a bright yellow car in front of his picturesque mediaeval cottage, a practice that led eventually to the car being vandalized and a convoy of outraged yellow car drivers processing through the village in his support ('Yellow Car Owners' 2017). Walking through Castle Combe with a young Japanese friend in 2017, I was not surprised to hear her ask, 'Do people really live here?' (Figure 5.9). The village does indeed look as if it might be a film set, not only when being temporarily dressed for location shooting in features such as *Doctor Dolittle* (1967) and *War Horse* (2011) but as if it were built specifically for the purpose, in Kameoka or perhaps Hollywood.

It is in this respect that the Cotswolds make their closest approach to Baudrillardian hyperreality, of being a copy without an original. Ironically, while the curators of Dreamton and British Hills strive for authenticity, the pressure on

Figure 5.9 'Do people really live here?' – Castle Combe, Wiltshire, 2018 (photograph by the author).

residents of villages such as Castle Combe and Bibury is to suppress authentic aspects of contemporary village life (such as the possession of modern technology) in favour of a fantasy construct, tailored to tourist desires. Although the staff at British Hills ruefully recounted how their attempts at historical education had been short-circuited by their guests' habit of reading what they saw through the filter of Harry Potter, in this respect British Hills is no different from historical sites in Britain itself. York's most famous mediaeval street, The Shambles, is now home to several Potter-themed shops, inevitably framing it in terms of its resemblance to Diagon Alley rather than its own long history; and my last visit to Christ Church's Tom Quad was enlivened by a group of Chinese children, wearing Gryffindor robes and waving wands, for whom Cardinal Wolsey, or even Alice Liddell, might as well not have existed. They were in Hogwarts.

Japanese manga and anime in the Cotswolds

The 'consumption' of the Cotswolds by Japanese visitors, whether in the Cotswolds themselves or in the region's various Japan-based avatars, is far from being a passive activity; rather, it is characterized by the creative adaptation and reframing of Cotswold-related imagery, often in combination with *topoi* characteristic of children's literature texts and genres. It is time to complete the circle of cultural production by considering two Japanese children's texts formed in significant part through this kind of activity, each using a Cotswold setting and each being in conversation with established British children's texts and genres. Kore Yamazaki's manga, *The Ancient Magus' Bride (mahōtsukai no yome)* (2014–present), bears witness to the influence of both British children's fantasy literature and British folklore; while the four-panel manga *Kin-iro Mosaic (kiniro mozaiku)* (2010–21), by Yui Hara, draws on *Alice's Adventures in Wonderland* as well as exploiting the 'Arcadian' image associated with Cotswold life. Both have been adapted into anime that confirm and extend the original texts' use of the Cotswolds, although largely as a 'stealth' setting rather than an explicit one.

Yamazaki's *The Ancient Magus' Bride* concerns a teenage girl, Chise Hatori, whose lifelong ability to perceive and attract supernatural creatures has brought her only misery in her native Japan. Sick of life, Chise puts herself up for auction and is bought by a British mage named Elias Ainsworth – an ancient creature with an animal skull for a head – who uses magic to transport her to his home in the English countryside, where he proposes to make her first his apprentice and later his bride. The 'beauty and the beast' element of the story is obvious, but a large part of the manga's appeal lies in the richness and generosity of its depiction of a world peopled with many kinds of supernatural creature, drawn from the folklore of Britain, Ireland and mainland Europe.

Yamazaki was eleven years old when the first Harry Potter book was translated into Japanese. She quickly became devoted both to that series and to others in the wave of British fantasy that followed. (More recently, she has graduated to the work of Diana Wynne Jones, citing *Dogsbody* (1975) and *Fire and Hemlock* (1985) among her favourites (Yamazaki 2022).) The cumulative effect was to reinforce the association of Britain with magic and fantasy, making it the natural setting for her own story. As Elias puts it in *The Ancient Magus' Bride*, Britain is 'a land of ancient magic, where witches and mages are deeply rooted in the way of life' (Yamazaki 2014: 97). While Western children's books were important to Yamazaki's development, they also provided her with an introduction to the folklore of the British Isles: 'I've been studying the original material since I was a child, and I gradually got drawn to the folklore of Britain and Ireland' ('250,000 copies' 2014). That interest shows in the multifarious magical traditions and creatures encountered by Chise over the course of the manga. In plundering books such as Katharine Briggs's *Dictionary of Fairies (yōsei jiten)* (Briggs 1976;

trans. 1992) to populate her supernatural landscape, Yamazaki was following in the footsteps of many British fantasy authors before her.

As a young *mangaka* living in rural Hokkaidō, Yamazaki had limited opportunities for first-hand research, and she began her British-set series without having visited the UK, which thus remained something of a country of the imagination: 'I grew up reading a lot of fantasy books about fairies. A lot of them took place in England. It was a place that was very close to my heart' (Orsini 2017). *The Ancient Magus' Bride* uses various locations, including several episodes in London, and in recent volumes a magic school located under the British Library has entered the story, but the main setting is Elias's house and its immediate surroundings, in what he calls 'the countryside west of London, on the edge of England' (Yamazaki 2014: 18). Yamazaki has stated in interview that the primary inspiration for Elias's home is Bibury, adding however, that 'it is more mysterious to keep it a little ambiguous' (*chotto bokashiteita*) (Yamazaki 2022). Elias's words are accordingly vague, at most gesturing towards the Cotswolds as a liminal zone on England's 'edge' (*hashikko*). Yamazaki's illustrations are often more precise, however. Working from photographs taken by a friend, she created numerous scenes with identifiable locations. An illustration of Chise and her friend Angelica sitting outside a pub near Elias's house in Volume 3, for example, is modelled on the Horse and Hound in the north Cotswolds village of Broadway (Yamazaki 2015: 81; Figures 5.10 and 5.11). On the following page

Figures 5.10–5.11 (*Top*) Chise and Angelica's pub, Broadway version. *The Ancient Magus' Bride*. © Kore Yamazaki/MAG Garden. (*Bottom*) The Horse and Hound, Broadway, Worcestershire, 2018 (photograph by the author).

Figures 5.12–5.13 (*Left*) Chise and Angelica's pub, Burford version. *The Ancient Magus' Bride.* © Kore Yamazaki/MAG Garden. (*Right*) The Mermaid, Burford, Oxfordshire, 2018 (photograph by the author).

the same establishment, viewed from a different angle, becomes the Mermaid Inn in Burford, some 20 miles away (Yamazaki 2015: 82; Figures 5.12 and 5.13), while in the 2017–18 anime adaptation the scene was relocated to yet a third Cotswold town, Bourton-on-the-Water ('None So Deaf' 2017). None of these places is named in either the manga or the anime; such details simultaneously confirm the story's Cotswold setting and frustrate any impulse to map its events to a coherent physical geography. Sometimes Yamazaki even laterally inverts research photographs in order to create a looking-glass effect, combining both familiarity and strangeness (Yamazaki 2022). An example is the Frontispiece to Volume 7 of the manga, which shows Elias and Chise on a 'reversed' version of the footbridge that crosses the River Coln to Arlington Row (Yamazaki 2017a: 3; Figures 5.14 and 5.15).

Although Yamazaki did not visit the UK until several volumes of her manga had already been published, another form of research was open to her, as she describes in the Author's Note to Volume 7. This was a field trip to British Hills, 'the astonishingly wonderful establishment in Fukushima Prefecture' (Yamazaki 2017a: 175). There, as she explains, she was able to wander round the manor house, browse the library, bathe in a lion's-paw bath and enjoy all the amenities described earlier in this chapter. The highly mediated environment of British Hills thus became one of the sources for Yamazaki's even more mediated version of the Cotswolds and ultimately part of the filter through which future readers

Figures 5.14–5.15 'Looking glass' Britain. (*Left*) Frontispiece, Volume 7, *The Ancient Magus' Bride*. © Kore Yamazaki/MAG Garden. (*Right*) The footbridge to Arlington Row, Bibury, 2022 (photograph by the author).

of her manga would experience the Cotswolds themselves. Yamazaki finally visited Britain in 2016, in the company of staff working on the anime adaptation (Yamazaki 2017b: 177), and has since returned on several occasions. Even without such direct experience, however, it was possible for the Cotswolds to be a potent presence in her story, arguably the more so for being uncredited and for being at first a fantasy construction, comprised of children's literature, carefully curated images and desire.

Yui Hara's four-panel manga, *Kin-iro Mosaic*, relates the light-hearted adventures of a group of five high school girls in Japan. At first glance, its connection with the Cotswolds may appear slight, but two of its cast, Alice Cartelet and her half-Japanese friend Karen, have moved to Japan from England, and the manga includes numerous flashbacks to their former Cotswold lives. Again, British children's literature – specifically *Alice's Adventures in Wonderland* – forms a significant part of the way in which England, and Alice Cartelet in particular, are read. Alice shares both her name and her hair colour with Lewis Carroll's heroine, as depicted by Tenniel. Indeed, her blonde, or *kinpatsu*, hair, which causes her Britain-obsessed friend Shinobu great excitement, gives the manga part of its name. Carroll's *Alice* is explicitly invoked early on, when Shinobu receives an airmail letter announcing Alice's imminent arrival in Japan. On hearing that the letter is from Alice, another friend exclaims, 'Wow! From Wonderland!' (Hara 2011: 10). Although this is a joke, it has some weight, because in Shinobu's imagination Britain really is a kind of wonderland. To drive the point home, the cover of the manga's first volume shows Shinobu, dressed

Figures 5.16–5.17 (*Left*) Shinobu's arrival at Alice's Cotswold home, *Kin-iro Mosaic*. © Yui Hara/Hōbunsha. (*Right*) Shinobu's departure from Alice's Cotswold home, *Kin-iro Mosaic*. © Yui Hara/Hōbunsha.

as Tenniel's Alice, asking a bemused Alice Cartelet whether she has seen a white rabbit, above a caption reading, 'Shinobu in Wonderland' (*fushigi no kuni no shinobusan*) (Hara 2011).

Like Yamazaki, Hara (another young Hokkaidō author) began her manga without having ever been to the UK. The brief depiction of Alice's house in the first volume of *Kin-iro Mosaic* reflects this: it is shown with wooden walls and a background of snow-capped mountains and forests more evocative of the Japanese countryside than anything to be found in southern England (Hara 2011: 13; Figures 5.16 and 5.17). When an anime adaptation was made in 2012, however, the production company, Studio Gokumi, resolved to pursue greater realism and fixed on Fosse Farmhouse, a guesthouse near Castle Combe, as the model for Alice's home (Figure 5.18). Their choice was not random. Caron Cooper, Fosse Farmhouse's owner, already had Japanese connections through the hotel and antiques trades, including a close friendship with Dreamton's Marie Haruyama. In the 1990s, she had collaborated with the academic and cultural commentator Nozomu Hayashi[8] to create a book on British food and in 2009 had even welcomed NHK viewers to a cookery lesson in her home, in a Cotswold-based episode of the long-running travel series, *Somewhere Street* (*sekai fureai machi aruki*). Cooper still gives lessons in English cookery to Japanese people, both in Japan and in her farmhouse kitchen, and that activity was duly replicated in the *Kin-iro Mosaic* anime, with Alice's mother teaching Alice and Shinobu to bake their names in pastry letters. The three panels originally devoted to Alice's home in the first volume of the manga were expanded to almost the entire

---

8 Coincidentally, Hayashi had also been Lucy Boston's lodger at Hemingford Grey Manor in the 1980s, when he was cataloguing a collection of mediaeval Japanese manuscripts held at the University of Cambridge.

Figure 5.18 Fosse Farmhouse, 2019 (photograph by the author).

opening episode of the anime (significantly titled 'In Wonderland' (2013)), and the charm of Fosse Farmhouse's Cotswold setting was emphasized in a montage of location shots including Cirencester High Street, Arlington Row and Bibury Court, the Jacobean manor house on the edge of Bibury. Fosse Farmhouse itself was reproduced in detail, down to the pattern on the bedspreads and the collection of rocking horses in the front garden. In later episodes, several other Cotswold views were added, readily recognizable to anyone familiar with the area.

As with *The Ancient Magus' Bride*, however, none of these places is named. When Shinobu arrives in England for her homestay, she boards the train at Paddington, the London station that serves the west of the country, and Cotswold aficionados may even recognize the station where she alights as Kemble near Cirencester, but it is not until Episode 11 that the word 'Cotswolds' is mentioned ('Try and Guess' 2013). Despite the near-photographic realism of the depictions of individual locations, the geography of the Cotswolds undergoes considerable contortions in *Kin-iro Mosaic*, just as in *The Ancient Magus' Bride*. For example, in Episode 7 of the anime's second season ('My Dear Hero' 2015), Karen leaves her house (represented as Bibury Court) on foot to visit Alice (in Fosse Farmhouse), continues on to the canal bridge at Bathampton and finally returns home via Arlington Row – a round trip of some 80 miles, if one were to make it in reality rather than using the non-Euclidean cartography of anime. Such license is indicative of the arm's-length relationship of the fiction to the physical Cotswolds and the extent to which it represents a dream country – a wonderland.

Despite this, the 'secret' of Alice's house's location was not well kept. Sharp-eyed viewers might have spied the address of Fosse Farmhouse written in English on a jar of homemade jam visible on Shinobu's breakfast table in Episode 2 of the anime ('Although I'm Small' 2013), and many devotees of *Kin-iro Mosaic* have made Cooper's home a pilgrimage site. Since the anime's broadcast in 2013, most of her guests have been Japanese enthusiasts, coming to pay homage and take selfies in the places habituated by their favourite characters. The farmhouse, having been the model *for* the anime, has thus come in turn to model itself *on* the anime. Cooper is well aware that she changes her furnishings (or even the bedspreads) at her peril, lest she disappoint her guests' expectations. Jean Baudrillard described the postmodern erasure of the distinction between reality and its simulacra in terms of loss – '[b]ecause it is difference that constitutes the poetry of the map and the charm of the territory, the magic of the concept and the charm of the real' (Baudrillard 1994: 2) – but the collapsing of such distinctions also creates a new kind of experience, and, as is attested in Cooper's guest book, many Japanese fans of *Kin-iro Mosaic* have found visiting Fosse Farmhouse deeply moving.

Kin-iro Mosaic is widely considered a 'healing' (*iyashikei*) story (see e.g. Saeki 2012), a genre characterized by heart-warming incident and innocent humour, and offering its readers and viewers respite from the pressures of daily life. As noted earlier, these qualities are also an important aspect of the way that the Cotswolds themselves are marketed and experienced in Japan. The client of Totteoki Cotswolds Tours who declares herself 'cured' on seeing a beautiful Cotswold village and the viewer of *Kin-iro Mosaic* who finds comfort in following the light-hearted adventures of Alice and her friends have much in common, and for many visitors a pilgrimage to Fosse Farmhouse effectively allows these activities to be combined. Some bring figurines of Alice or Shinobu with them, to stand in for the characters when they take photographs. Sony Corporation has also included *Kin-iro Mosaic* in its *Butai Meguri* phone app (2015), which uses GPS-driven augmented reality to allow fans to pose with anime characters in situ. Thus equipped, guests are able to create memories not only of the anime's setting but also of its characters' presence and company. Such technological aids exploit the potential of contents tourism to confer an ontologically ambiguous status, making Alice's house, and by extension the Cotswolds as a whole, both a location that can be physically visited and somewhere 'taken from a fairy-tale', a pastoral chronotope of quintessential Englishness, set back a little from the present day and at a slight remove from ordinary life. It is a place where, as Mikhail Bakhtin puts it, '[t]ime . . . thickens, takes on flesh, becomes artistically visible; likewise, space becomes charged and responsive to the movements of time, plot and history' (Bakhtin 1981: 84).

In Japan, the creation of anime with built-in contents tourism appeal is now common. Studios and local governments frequently join forces to co-promote anime with local settings. Anime tourism is supported and publicized by initiatives such as the annual eighty-eight-stop anime pilgrimage ('Anime Pilgrimage Sites' 2019), a name echoing traditional Buddhist pilgrimage routes such as the eighty-eight-temple path in Shikoku. No such initiative exists in the Cotswolds; *The Ancient Magus' Bride* and *Kin-iro Mosaic* are both notably shy about advertising their precise settings. The contrast naturally reflects the relative inaccessibility of the UK to Japanese manga and anime fans but also suggests a difference in the type of imaginative work these settings are being asked to do.

The relationship of the Cotswolds to Japan is unusual in its complexity and in the striking contrast between the area's high cultural profile and its relatively modest claims as a destination for contents tourism in terms of literary settings, film locations and authorial associations. To the extent that it inhibits premature recourse to such conventional modes of understanding, the area is a particularly illuminating example of some of the more diffuse and multifaceted ways in which contents tourism operates, which are more easily visible there than in places where they are occluded by obvious associations with famous names or texts.

'At times when we believe we are studying something, we are only being receptive to a kind of daydreaming', wrote Bachelard (2014: 21). The distinction is not a hard one, however; much engagement with literature takes place in the aftermath of reading rather than during it, in daydream, speculation, tourism and various forms of participatory culture (Butler 2018: 42–71). These activities extend well beyond the moment of reading, constituting a complex but far from chaotic system, an appreciation of which is vital to understanding literature's interactions with its readers and with the world. Investigating literary sources and seeking out locations and inspirations in the physical landscape are useful scholarly (and fan) endeavours that anchor places to texts in demonstrable and direct ways, but they do not provide a full picture. By combining and extending established critical approaches, we can begin to map a multidimensional territory where physical, affective and cultural geographies are all in dynamic play. Because readers and tourists bring their own desires and interpretative templates with them, even places with few conventional contents tourism credentials may have the power to evoke 'narrative qualities' and to occasion further creative activity in the form of published work, fan fiction or private fantasy. In this sense, the Cotswolds are significant as a paradigmatic example of a far more widespread phenomenon rather than as a special case; however, they are exceptional in the extent of the complex fascination they have engendered in their Japanese visitors, whose sense of Britain and its narrative potential they have done so much to shape.

Postscript

Reading from the inside out

Edmund Blunden – poet, veteran of the trenches, cricket enthusiast – was still in his twenties when, in 1924, he took up the position of Professor of English at Tōkyō Imperial University, where he would remain for the next four years. On his return to Britain, his home became a natural port of call for Japanese friends visiting the country. Blunden found, however, that their visits occasioned a degree of apprehension:

> The Japanese colour-print, which has delighted myriads of us, is not a product of fantasy. It is merely a summary of the real. So, I have felt a little anxious when I had the chance to act as host and companion to Japanese travellers who had resolved to see something of the territory known to them in the prose of Gilbert White, the poetry of Shakespeare and Meredith, the paintings of Constable and Gainsborough. It seemed to me, while they were looking forth from a hillside over orchards in bloom, and silvering intervals of rivers, and grey towers and brown roofs, that they did not feel a serious inferiority in the picture to the topographical truths of Hiroshige and Hokusai and Toyonobu. If their accomplished taste in sheer prospects and panoramas and vignettes was not unsatisfied, why should their guide dissimulate a certain satisfaction? (Blunden 1942: 9–10)

This passage comes from *English Villages*, Blunden's 1941 contribution to William Collins's 'Britain in Pictures' book series, which was published throughout the 1940s as a means of boosting patriotic feeling and morale at a time of national crisis. Blunden's description is thus already framed by a context of expectation that the English countryside will not be found wanting, either by his guests or by his readers. Nevertheless, his anxiety lest the 'truths' of Japanese artists show up the works of Gainsborough, Constable and even Shakespeare as 'the products of fantasy', is familiar. I too have been in Blunden's position. Indeed, I acquired my own copy of *English Villages* (reduced to £1 because of scuffing on the jacket) while showing two Japanese postgraduates around the second-hand bookshops of Hay-on-Wye, and the consciousness of involuntarily second-guessing what impression the prospect of the Welsh Marches might be making on my companions brought Blunden's words home vividly.

All the same, the opposition of truth and fantasy that underpins his anecdote is not one to which I can subscribe, for reasons I have explored throughout this book. In my opening chapter, for example, the 1877 reaction of Annie Brassey, catching her first glimpses of the Japanese landscape and people and being struck by 'the truthfulness of the representations of native artists, with which the fans, screens, and vases one sees in England are ornamented' (Brassey 1984: 306), was informed by her experience of imported goods consciously adapted to Western expectations of Japan. In my final chapter, the reactions of Japanese tourists to the villages of Bourton-on-the-Water and Castle Combe were informed no less by those villages' efforts to cater to Japanese fantasies of Britain, fantasies shaped in no small part by children's literature. I do not see the element of fantasy in these experiences as a matter of regret, however, still less as one requiring correction. Fantasy draws on reality for its raw material, but the reverse is also true.

What holds in the domain of tourism holds no less in other areas of cultural interaction. At times, in reading of Japan, of Japanese views of Britain, and of British views of those views, one seems to be in a Hall of Looking-Glasses, a *mise en abyme* of anticipation and deferral in which the roles of viewer and viewee are constantly exchanged and confused and where (as Roland Barthes put it in *Empire of Signs*) 'the mirror intercepts only other mirrors' (1982: 78). But this is also a Wonderland, giving a definite shape to unfamiliar concepts and images that would otherwise elude us and (in a photographic sense) 'fixing' them. Blunden continues:

> We were following the path across the hayfields and the old cricket-ground . . . when my friend the Tokyo professor, noticing a stately house encircled with a moat and fringed with tufted trees, asked what it was. 'The Vicarage – the parson's house.' He repeated with a smile of wonder, 'The parson's house!' I fancy it was the first time that he, a studious admirer of England for almost half a century, had truly envisaged the solidity and dignity of each small world which acknowledges itself to be an English village. (1942: 10)

The Tōkyō professor's realization, as perceived by Blunden, of the 'solidity and dignity' of the parson's house and of the village beyond is characteristic of those moments when geographical and imaginary places combine – whether during physical travel, in fictional encounters or through the kind of imaginative labour that enabled Kenji Miyazawa to discover the White Cliffs of Dover in Iwate Prefecture. Such moments have made my own labour in writing this book truly pleasurable. If reading it occasions similar experiences in others, or the desire to seek them out, then the labour was not wasted.

References

'250,000 Copies Sold in First Three Months – Breakout Success!' (*hatsubai 3-kagetsu de 25 manbutoppa!*) (2014), *Da Vinci News*. 1 August. Available online: ddnavi.com/news/202121/a (accessed 18 December 2021).

A Dog of Flanders (*furandāsu no inu*) (1975), [TV series] Dir. Yoshio Kuroda, Japan: Nippon Animation.

Adichie, Chimamanda Ngozi (2009), 'The Danger of a Single Story', *TED*, 7 October. Available online: youtu.be/D9Ihs241zeg (accessed 20 December 2021).

Alcock, Sir Rutherford (1863), *The Capital of the Tycoon: A Narrative of a Three Years' Residence in Japan*, London: Longman.

Alcott, Louisa May ([1868] 2014), *Little Women*, New York: Puffin.

'Although I'm Small' (*chicchaku tatte*) (2013), *Kin-iro Mosaic*, Season1 Ep. 2, [TV programme] AT-X, 13 July.

Andō, Satoshi (2008), 'Regaining Continuity with the Past: *Spirited Away* and *Alice's Adventures in Wonderland*', *Bookbird*, 46 (1): 23–9.

Andō, Satoshi (2019), *The Landscapes of British Fantasy* (*igirisu fantajī no fūkei*), Tōkyō: Nihonkeizai Hyōronsha.

Angus, D. C. ([1882] 1890), *The Eastern Wonderland: Pictures of Japanese Life*, London: Cassell & Co.

Angus, D. C. ([1882] c.1906), *Japan: The Eastern Wonderland*, London: Cassell & Co.

Animage Editorial Department ([1989] 2006), *The Art of Kiki's Delivery Service*, Tōkyō: Tokuma Shoten.

Anime Tourism Association (2019), 'Anime Pilgrimage Sites', *88 Anime Tourism*. Available online: animetourism88.com/ja (accessed 4 April 2019).

Anon (1885), 'An English Village from a Japanese Point of View', *Punch*, 24 January: 47.

Arakawa, Kaku (2019), 'Ponyo is Here', *10 Years with Hayao Miyazaki*, Ep. 1 [TV programme] NHK World TV, 23 February. Available online: https://www3.nhk.or.jp/nhkworld/en/ondemand/video/3004569/ (accessed 23 December 2021).

Arrietty (2011), Dir. Hiromasa Yonebayashi, screenplay Hayao Miyazaki and Keiko Niwa, [DVD], France: Studio Canal.

Āya and the Witch (*āya to majo*) [*Earwig and the Witch*] (2020), Dir. Gorō Miyazaki, [DVD], Japan: Studio Ghibli.

Bachelard, Gaston ([1958] 2014), *The Poetics of Space*, trans. Maria Jolas, New York: Penguin.

Bakhtin, Mikhail (1981), 'Forms of Time and of the Chronotope in the Novel', in Michael Holquist (ed), *The Dialogic Imagination: Four Essays*, trans. Caryl Emerson and Michael Holquist, 84–258, Austin, TX: University of Texas Press.

Barrie, J. M. ([1906/1911] 1999), *Peter Pan in Kensington Gardens/Peter and Wendy*, ed. Peter Hollindale, Oxford: Oxford University Press.

Barthes, Roland (1982), *Empire of Signs*, trans. Richard Howard, New York: The Noonday Press.

Baudrillard, Jean ([1994] 1981), *Simulacra and Simulation*, trans. Sheila Faria Glaser, Ann Arbor, MI: University of Michigan Press

Beauvoir, Ludovic de (1874), *Voyage autour du monde: Pékin, Yeddo, San Francisco*, Vol. 3, Paris: E. Plon et Cie.

'Bibury' (n.d.), *Wikipedia*. Available online: en.wikipedia.org/wiki/Bibury (accessed 10 April 2019).

Bird, Isabella ([1880] 1984), *Unbeaten Tracks in Japan*, intro. Pat Barr, London: Virago.

Blunden, Edmund (1942), *English Villages*, London: William Collins.

Booth, Alison (2016), *Homes and Haunts: Touring Writers' Shrines and Countries*, Oxford: Oxford University Press.

Bradshaw, Nick (2005), 'He Saw My Books from the Inside Out', *The Telegraph*, 23 September. Available online: https://www.telegraph.co.uk/culture/film/3646735/He-saw-my-books-from-the-inside-out.html (accessed 23 December 2021).

Bradshaw, Nick (2018), '*When Marnie Was There* – House of the Sprits', *Scraps from the Loft*, 4 February. Available online: https://scrapsfromtheloft.com/movies/when-marnie-was-there-house-of-the-spirits-nick-bradshaw/ (accessed 12 September 2021).

Brassey, Lady Annie ([1878] 1984), *A Voyage in the Sunbeam: Our Home on the Ocean for Eleven Months*, London: Century Publishing.

Briggs, Katharine ([1976] 1977), *Dictionary of Fairies*, Harmondsworth: Penguin.

Briggs, Katharine (1992), *Dictionary of Fairies* (*yōsei jiten*), trans. Keiichi Hirano, Tōkyō: Fuzanbō.

British Hills (2019), British Hills Corporation, Available online: www.british-hills.co.jp/ (accessed 23 December 2021).

Brooke, James (2003), 'Japanese Hail *The Mikado*, Long-Banned Imperial Spoof', *New York Times*, 3 April. Available online: https://www.nytimes.com/2003/04/03/world/japanese-hail-the-mikado-long-banned-imperial-spoof.html (accessed 3 August 2021).

Bunyan, John ([1684] 1996), *The Pilgrim's Progress from this World to That Which is to Come, Delivered Under the Similitude of a Dream*, introd. Stuart Sim, Ware: Wordsworth.

Butler, Annie R. (1888), *Stories About Japan*, London: The Religious Tract Society.

Butler, Catherine (2002), 'Interview with Diana Wynne Jones', in Teya Rosenberg, Martha P. Hixon, Sharon M. Scapple, and Donna R. White (eds), *Diana Wynne Jones: An Exciting and Exacting Wisdom*, 163–73, New York: Peter Lang.

Butler, Catherine (2006), *Four British Fantasists: Place and Culture in the Children's Fantasies of Penelope Lively, Alan Garner, Diana Wynne Jones and Susan Cooper*, Lanham, MD: Scarecrow.

Butler, Catherine (2018), *Literary Studies Deconstructed: A Polemic*, Cham: Palgrave.

Butler, Catherine (2020), 'The Cotswolds and Children's Literature in Japanese Fantasy: The Case of Castle Combe', in Takayoshi Yamamura and Philip Seaton (eds), *Contents Tourism and Pop Culture Fandom: Transnational Tourist Experiences*, 85–97, Bristol: Channel View.

Butler, Catherine (2021), 'The Green Knowe Books – A Patchwork of Genres', in Victor Watson, Mihoko Tanaka, and Catherine Butler (eds), *Lucy M. Boston: An Artist in Everything She Did*, 37–52, Hemingford Grey, Cambs.: Oldknow Books.

Carroll, Jane Suzanne (2012), *Landscape in Children's Literature*, London: Routledge.

Carroll, Jane Suzanne (2013), 'A Topoanalytical Reading of Landscapes in *The Lord of the Rings* and *The Hobbit*', in Peter Hunt (ed), *J. R. R. Tolkien: A New Casebook*, 121–38, Houndmills: Palgrave.

Carroll, Lewis ([1865/1871] 1962), *Alice's Adventures in Wonderland/Through the Looking Glass*, London: Penguin.

Castle in the Sky (tenkū no shiro raputa) (1986), [Film] Dir. Hayao Miyazaki, Japan: Studio Ghibli.

Cecil, Laura (2020), Private correspondence with Catherine Butler, 10 August.

Chamberlain, Basil Hall ([1890] 1905), *Things Japanese*, London: John Murray.

'Characters' (2020). *Āya and the Witch* [official site], NHK/NEP/Studio Ghibli. Available online: https://www.aya-and-the-witch.jp/about/characters.html (accessed 18 October 2022).

Checkland, Olive (1989), *Britain's Encounter with Meiji Japan, 1868–1912*, Houndmills: Macmillan.

Chiba, Kaori (2015), *Journeys to World Masterpiece Theatre (sekai meisaku gekijō e no tabi)*, Tōkyō: Shinkigensha.

Chimori, Mikiko (2005), *Alice in the Orient*, London: Anthem.

Clark, Eric (2012), 'Model Society: At the Sylvanian Families Toy Convention', *Daily Telegraph*, 19 October. Available online: www.telegraph.co.uk/finance/newsbysector /retailandconsumer/9617865/Model-society-at-the-Sylvanian-Families-toy -convention.html (accessed 18 December 2021).

Coles, Diana (1983), *The Clever Princess*, illus. Ros Asquith, London: Sheba Feminist Publishers.

Copeland, Rebecca L. (2000), *Lost Leaves: Women Writers of Meiji Japan*, Honolulu: University of Hawaii Press.

'Creating *Earwig and the Witch*' (2021), *Earwig and the Witch*. [DVD] Dir. Gorō Miyazaki, Japan: Studio Ghibli.

Dhebar, Dharmesh (2018), Interview with Catherine Butler, 13 May.

Dilke, Sir Charles Wentworth (1876), 'English Influence in Japan', *The Fortnightly Review*, 20 (1 July–1 December): 424–43.

'Director Hayao Miyazaki Encouraged him by Saying, "Be Prepared!" Hiromasa Yonebayashi's *Mary and the Witch's Flower* Production Announcement Press Conference' (*miyazaki hayao kantoku ga kakugo o motte yare to shitta gekirei yonebayashi hiromasa kantoku meari to majo no hana seisaku happyō kaiken*) (2016), *Cinema Ranking Communication*, 15 December. Available online: http://www .kogyotsushin.com/archives/topics/t7/201612/15202400.php (accessed 23 September 2021).

'Director Hiromasa Yonebayashi Tells the Truth about the New Concept and the "No Face" Model Theory!' (*jiburi yonebayashi hiromasa kantoku, shinsaku kōsō to "kaonashi" moderu-setsu no shinsō o kataru*) (2015), *CinemaCafe*, 8 March. Available online: https://www.cinemacafe.net/article/2015/03/08/29878.html (accessed 30 September 2021).

Downer, Lesley (2018), '*The Mikado* and the Japanese Village in Victorian Knightsbridge', *The History Girls*, 14 March. Available online: http://the-history-girls.blogspot.com /2018/03/the-mikado-and-japanese-village-in.html (accessed 2 August 2021).

'Extraordinary Thoughts on *Memories of Marnie*, from Director Hiromasa Yonebayashi' (*yonebayashi hiromasa kantoku omoide no mānī ni kakeru naminaminaranu omoi*) (2014), *Eiga.com*, 16 April. Available online: https://eiga.com/news/20140416/2/ (accessed 30 September 2021).

Falconer, Emma (2013), 'Diana Wynne Jones Interview: January 2009', *A Note on a Rainy Night*, 4 June. Available online: http://www.anoteonarainynight.com/diana -wynne-jones-interview/ (accessed 3 September 2021).

Fan Circle International (n.d.), 'Japanese Fans', Available online: https://www.fancirclein ternational.org/history/japanese-fans/ (accessed 21 July 2021).

Forster, E. M. ([1924] 2005), *A Passage to India*, ed. Oliver Stallybrass, intro. Pankaj Mishra, London: Penguin.

Foxwell, Chelsea (2009), 'Japan as Museum? Encapsulating Change and Loss in Late-Nineteenth-Century Japan', *Getty Research Journal*, 1: 39–52.

Frank, Allegra (2018), 'Getting Fired from a Miyazaki Movie was "A Good Thing" for this Anime Director', *Polygon*, 20 October. Available online: https://www.polygon .com/2018/10/20/18001588/mamoru-hosoda-fired-howls-moving-castle-interview (accessed 4 September 2021).

Fraser, Mary Crawford [Mrs. Hugh] ([1898] 1904), *A Diplomatist's Wife in Japan: Letters from Home to Home*, London: Hutchinson & Co.

Gaiman, Neil (2012), 'Foreword', in Diana Wynne Jones, *Reflections on the Magic of Writing*, vii–x, London: David Fickling.

Gay, John ([1726] 1801), 'From Mr. Gay', in Thomas Sheridan (ed), *The Works of Rev. Jonathan Swift*, Vol. 12, 214, London: J. Johnson.

Geerts, Sylvie and Sara Van den Bossche (2014), 'Never-Ending Stories: How Canonical Works Live on in Children's Literature', in Sylvie Geerts and Sara Van den Bossche (eds), *Never-Ending Stories: Adaptation, Canonisation and Ideology in Children's Stories*, 5–19, Ghent: Academia Press.

Ghibli's Bookshelf (*jiburi no hondana*) (2010), [DVD] Japan: TV Man Union Inc.

Giardina, Carolyn (2015). '*When Marnie Was There* Director Talks "Mysterious Tone" of New Studio Ghibli Film', *The Hollywood Reporter*, 21 May. Available online:

https://www.hollywoodreporter.com/movies/movie-news/marnie-was-director-talks
-mysterious-797114/ (accessed 11 September 2021).

Gibson, Charlotte Chaffee (1908), *In Eastern Wonderlands*, Boston: Little, Brown, & Co.

Gilbert, Pamela (2010), 'Ouida and the Other New Woman', in Nicola Diane Thompson (eds), *Victorian Women Writers and the Woman Question*, 170–88, Cambridge: Cambridge University Press.

Gilbert, W. S. (1874), *Topsyturveydom: An Entirely Original Musical Extravaganza*, The Gilbert and Sullivan Archive. Available online: https://www.gsarchive.net/gilbert/ plays/topsyturvy/topsy.pdf (accessed 3 August 2021).

Gilbert, W. S. (1885), 'The Story of a Stage Play', *New-York Daily Tribune*, 9 August, The Gilbert and Sullivan Archive. Available online: https://www.gsarchive.net/gilbert/ interviews/stage_play.html (accessed 3 August 2021).

Gilbert, W. S. (1921), *The Story of the Mikado*, Illus. Alice B. Woodward, London: Daniel O'Connor.

Gilbert, W. S. and Arthur Sullivan (2006), *The Mikado: Or, the Town of Tititpu – Vocal Score*, London: Faber Music.

Gombrich, Ernst (1960), *Art and Illusion: A Study in the Psychology of Pictorial Representation*, London: Phaidon Press.

Gordon, Devin (2005), 'A "Positive Pessimist"', *Newsweek*, 19 June. Available online: https://www.newsweek.com/positive-pessimist-119801 (accessed 12 September 2021).

Gordon Ginzburg, Etti (2018), 'Queering the Victorian Nursery: Laura Richards's "My Japanese Fan"', *Children s Literature in Education*, 49 (2): 379–95.

Greenberg, Raz (2018), *Hayao Miyazaki: Exploring the Early Work of Japan's Greatest Animator*, New York: Bloomsbury.

Griswold, Jerry (2006), *Feeling Like a Kid: Childhood and Children's Literature*, Baltimore, MD: Johns Hopkins University Press.

Grobar, Matt (2018), 'Mourning Loss of Paint-And-Paper Anime, *Mirai* Director Attempts Animated First With Four-Year-Old Protagonist', *Deadline*, 12 November. Available online: https://deadline.com/2018/11/mirai-mamoru-hosoda-cannes-film -festival-interview-1202494128/ (accessed 23 December 2021).

Gulliver in the Cotswolds (c.1955), Bourton-on-the-Water: Old New Inn.

Hall, Linda (2003), 'Ancestral Voices – "Since Time Everlasting and Beyond": Kipling and the Invention of the Time-Slip Story', *Children's Literature in Education*, 34 (December): 305–21.

Halliday, Ayun, (2017), 'Hayao Miyazaki Picks His 50 Favorite Children's Books', *Open Culture*, 29 May. Available online: http://www.openculture.com/2017/05/hayao -miyazaki-picks-his-50-favorite-childrens-books.html (accessed 23 December 2021).

Hara, Yui (2011), *Kin-iro Mosaic (kiniro mozaiku)*, Vol. 1, Tōkyō: Hōbunsha.

Haruyama, Mayumi ('Marie') (2018), Interview with Catherine Butler, 18 May.

Hashimoto, Masaki and Luke Houghton (2018), Interview with Catherine Butler, 14 May.

Hendry, Joy (2000), *The Orient Strikes Back: A Global View of Cultural Display*, Oxford and New York: Berg.

Hennessey, John L. (2018), 'Moving up in the World: Japan's Manipulation of Colonial Imagery at the 1910 Japan–British Exhibition', *Museum History Journal*, 11 (1): 24–41.

Hinton, Perry R. (2013), 'Returning in a Different Fashion: Culture, Communication, and Changing Representations of Lolita in Japan and the West', *International Journal of Communication*, 7: 1582–602.

Hishida, Nobuhiko (2014), 'Welshness and Class Identity in Diana W. Jones' *Howl's Moving Castle*', *Kawamura Gakuen Woman's University Research Bulletin*, 25 (1): 17–28.

Holt, Jenny (2017), 'Distressed Micropsia: Size Distortion and Psychological Disturbance in Isabella Bird's *Unbeaten Tracks* and in Subsequent Travel Writing on Japan, 1880–1900', *Studies in Travel Writing*, 21 (1): 47–62.

Horie, Tamaki (1999), 'Kenji Miyazawa and *Alice's Adventures in Wonderland*' (*kenji miyazawa to fushigi no kuni no arisu*). *British & American Language and Culture*, 47: 73–85.

Hotel Monterey Grasmere Ōsaka (n.d.), 'Facilities', *Hotel Monterey*. Available online: www.hotelmonterey.co.jp/en/grasmere_osaka/facilities/ (accessed 1 August 2018).

Howl's Moving Castle (*hauru no ugoku shiro*) (2004), [Film] Dir. Hayao Miyazaki, Japan: Studio Ghibli.

Humbert, Aimé (1874), *Japan and the Japanese*, trans. Cashel Hoey, London: Richard Bentley. Available online: https://openlibrary.org/books/OL14015963M/Japan_and _the_Japanese_illustrated (accessed 16 August 2021).

Hur, Hyungju (2012), 'Staging Modern Statehood: World Exhibitions and the Rhetoric of Publishing in Late Qing China, 1851–1910', PhD diss., University of Illinois at Urbana-Champaign.

Ichan0108 (2015), 'I Feel Just as if I've Become Gulliver' (*sukkari garibā ni natta kibun da*), *TripAdvisor*, 28 June. Available online: www.tripadvisor.jp/Attraction_Review -g186283-d218206-Reviews-or10-The_Model_Village-Bourton_on_the_Water _Cotswolds_England.html (accessed 16 October 2019).

Ichikawa, Jun (2016), '"Alice" in Japanese Pop Culture: Transformation through Translation', *Bulletin of Nippon Science University*, 46 (1): 27–38.

Ikeda, Masayoshi (2020), *A Journey Through World Children's Literature* (*sekai no jidō bungaku o meguru tabi*), Tōkyō: X-Knowledge.

'In Wonderland' (*fushigi no kuni no*) (2013), *Kin-iro Mosaic*, Season 1, Ep. 1, [TV programme] AT-X, 6 July.

'Interview with Author, Diana Wynne Jones' (2006), *Howl's Moving Castle*, [DVD] Dir. Hayao Miyazaki, Japan: Studio Ghibli.

'Interview with the Filmmakers' (2018), *Mary and the Witch's Flower*, [DVD] Dir. Hiromasa Yonebayashi, Japan: Studio Ponoc.

Ishii, Momoko (2014), *Pooh and I* (*pū to watashi*), Tōkyō: Kawade Shobō Shinsha.

Isobe, Satomi (2018), 'How Nashiki Met the "West": The Influence of British Children's Literature in Kaho Nashiki's Works', [paper] IBBY Congress, Athens.

Iwaya, Sazanami (1891), *Kogane-maru*, Tōkyō: Hakubunkan. Available online: https://www.aozora.gr.jp/cards/000981/files/3646_12287.html (accessed 3 December 2021).

Iyer, Pico (2019), *A Beginner's Guide to Japan: Observations and Provocations*, London: Bloomsbury.

Jackson, Chris (2018), Interview with Catherine Butler, 13 April.

Jaques, Zoe and Eugene Giddens ([2013] 2016), *Lewis Carroll's* Alice's Adventures in Wonderland *and* Through the Looking-Glass: *A Publishing History*, London and New York: Routledge.

Jagusch, Sybille A. (2021), *Japan and American Children's Books: A Journey*, New Brunswick, NJ: Rutgers University Press.

Jenkins, Alice (2013), 'Getting to Utopia: Railways and Heterotopia in Children's Literature', in Carrie Hintz and Elaine Ostry (eds), *Utopian and Dystopian Writing for Children and Young Adults*, 23–37, London: Routledge.

Jinnō, Yuki (2017), 'Consumer Consumption for Children: Conceptions of Childhood in the Work of Taishō-Period Designers', trans. and adapted by Emily B. Simpson. In Sabine Frühstück and Anne Walthall (eds), *Child's Play: Multi-Sensory Histories of Children and Childhood in Japan*, 83–101, Oakland, CA: University of California Press.

Jones, Diana Wynne ([1986] 2000a), *Howl's Moving Castle*, London: Collins.

Jones, Diana Wynne (2000b), Letter to Laura Cecil, 14 November, Seven Stories Archive: LC-01-01-39-01.

Jones, Diana Wynne (2011), *Earwig and the Witch*, illus. Marion Lindsay, London: HarperCollins.

Jones, Diana Wynne (2012), *Reflections on the Magic of Writing*, London: David Fickling.

Kawada, Yūki (2011), 'Interview', *Kanda Gaigo Alumni Association*. Available online: www.kandagaigo.ac.jp/memorial/interview/06/interview_06_1.html (accessed 18 December, 2021).

Kawai, Hayao (1996), *To Read a Children's Book* (*kodomo no hon o yomu*), Tōkyō: Kōdansha.

Kawanishi, Eriko (2015), *The Goddesses of Glastonbury* (*gurasutonberī no megamitachi*), Tōkyō: Hōzōkan.

Kawano, Yoshihide (2007), 'Early Japanese Translations', *The Beatrix Potter Society Newsletter*, 106 (October): 16–17.

Keegan, Rebecca (2013), 'An Unusual Departure for Beloved Japanese Animator Hayao Miyazaki', *Los Angeles Times*, 13 November. Available online: https://www.latimes.com/entertainment/movies/moviesnow/la-et-mn-miyazaki-20131113-story.html (accessed 5 September 2021).

Kennell, Amanda (2017), 'Alice in Evasion: Adapting Lewis Carroll in Japan', PhD diss., University of Southern California.

Kiritani, Elizabeth (1995), *Vanishing Japan: Traditions, Crafts and Culture*, Rutland VT and Tōkyō: Charles Tuttle.

Kirkpatrick, Karey (2017), Interview with Catherine Butler, 18 June.

Kobayashi, Shabako (2015), *England's Most Beautiful Place: The Cotswolds* (*ingurando de ichiban utsukushī basho: kottsūoruzu*), Tōkyō: Diamond.

Labbe, Jacqueline (2003), 'Illustrating Alice: Gender, Image, Artifice', in Morag Styles and Eve Bearne (eds), *Art, Narrative and Childhood*, 21–36, Stoke on Trent: Trentham Books

Lawrence, E. P. (1974), 'The Banned *Mikado*: A Topsy-Turvey Incident', *The Centennial Review*, 18 (2): 151–69.

Le Guin, Ursula K. (2007), 'Gedo Senki', *Ursula K. Le Guin*. Available online: https://www.ursulakleguin.com/gedo-senki-1 (accessed 5 November 2021).

Lilliput Village (1938), *Pathé News*, [Film]. Available online: www.britishpathe.com/video/lilliput-village (accessed 19 December 2021).

Lindseth, Jon A. and Alan Tannenbaum, eds (2015), *Alice in a World of Wonderlands: The Translations of Lewis Carroll's Masterpiece*, 3 Vols., New Castle DE: Oak Knoll Press.

Lockley, Thomas (2019), 'English Dreams and Japanese Realities: Anglo-Japanese Encounters Around the Globe, 1587–673', *Revista de Cultura/Review of Culture*, 60: 124–39.

Lu, Amy Shirong (2008), 'The Many Faces of Internationalization in Japanese Anime' (*nihon anime ni okeru kokusaika no sho sokumen*), *Animation: An Interdisciplinary Journal*, 3 (2): 169–87.

M., Allison (2016), 'More about *The Little Broomstick*', *Mary Queen of Plots*. October 29. Available online: https://marystewartreading.wordpress.com/2016/10/29/more-about-the-little-broomstick/ (accessed 28 August 2021).

Macdonald, Christopher (2014), 'Today in History: *Kiki's Delivery Service*', *Anime News Network*, 29 July. Available online: https://www.animenewsnetwork.com/interest/2014-07-29/today-in-history-kiki-delivery-service/.77109 (accessed 25 September 2021).

Markley, Robert (2004), 'Gulliver and the Japanese: The Limits of the Postcolonial Past', *Modern Language Quarterly*, 65 (3): 457–79.

Martin, Elyse (2020), 'Howl-ever It Moves You: Diana Wynne Jones and Hayao Miyazaki Do the Same Work With Different Stories', *Tor.com*, 5 May. Available online: https://www.tor.com/2020/05/05/howl-ever-it-moves-you-jones-and-miyazaki-do-the-same-work-with-different-stories/ (accessed 23 December 2021).

Mary and the Witch's Flower (*meari to majo no hana*) (2017), [Film] Dir. Hiromasa Yonebayashi, Japan: Studio Ponoc.

Memories of Marnie (*omoide no mānī*) [*When Marnie Was There*] (2014), [Film] Dir. Hiromasa Yonebayashi, Japan: Studio Ghibli.

Milward, Peter (1980), *Oddities in Modern Japan: Observations of an Outsider*, Tokyo: Hokuseido Press.

Mishan, Ligaya (2021), 'Hayao Miyazaki Prepares to Cast One Last Spell', *New York Times*, 3 November. Available online: https://www.nytimes.com/2021/11/23/t-magazine/hayao-miyazaki-studio-ghibli.html (accessed 1 December 2021).

Miyazaki, Hayao (2006), 'Westall Fantasy: A Journey to Tynemouth' (*uesutōru gensō: tainmasu e no tabi*), in Robert Westall (ed), *Blackham's Bomber* (*burakkamu no bakugekiki*), 5–21, 201–8, Tōkyō: Iwanami Shoten.

Miyazaki, Hayao (2011), *Doorway to Books* (*hon e no tobira*), Tōkyō: Iwanami Shoten.

Miyazaki, Hayao (2014a), *Starting Point: 1979–1996*, trans. Beth Cary and Frederik L. Schodt, San Francisco: VIZ Media.

Miyazaki, Hayao (2014b), *Turning Point: 1997–2008*, trans. Beth Cary and Frederik L. Schodt, San Francisco: VIZ Media.

Miyazawa, Kenji ([1923] 2003), 'The English Shore' (*igirisu kaigan*). Available online: https://www.aozora.gr.jp/cards/000081/files/4417_9667.html (accessed 20 November 2021).

Miyazawa, Kenji (1925), 'Advertisement for *The Restaurant of Many Orders*'. Available online: https://www.aozora.gr.jp/cards/000081/files/43733_17907.html (accessed 29 December 2021).

Miyazawa, Kenji (2020), *Night on the Milky Way Train*, trans. Roger Pulvers, London: Balestier Press.

Monden, Masafumi (2014), 'Being Alice in Japan: Performing a Cute, "Girlish" Revolt', *Japan Forum*, 26 (2): 265–85.

Mori, Hideo (2017), 'Record of a Lecture on a Film Looking Back on the Life of Momoko Ishii' (*eizō de furikaeru ishii momokosan no shōgai kōen-roku*), *Saitama Public Library*. Available online: https://www.lib.city.saitama.jp/images/upload/講演録（中央図書館開館10周年記念）. pdf (accessed 2 December 2021).

Morris, William (2014), *The Collected Letters of William Morris (1889–92)*, Vol. 3, ed. Norman Kelvin, Princeton, NJ: Princeton University Press.

Mullaney, Andrea (2003), 'Diana Wynne Jones', *SFX* (November): 36.

'My Dear Hero' (*mai dia hīrō*) (2015), *Kin-iro Mosaic*, Season 2, Ep. 7, [TV programme] AT-X, 17 May.

Nakagawa, Rieko, et al. (2014), *The Words of Momoko Ishii* (*ishii momoko no kotoba*), Tōkyō: Shinchōsha.

Nakata, Yasuko, et al. (2000). *A History of Japanese Translations of Children's Books from Abroad* (*kodomo no hon honyaku ayumiten tenjikaime roku*), Tōkyō: National Diet Library.

Nakayama, Shuichi (1996), 'The Impact of William Morris in Japan, 1904 to the Present', *Journal of Design History*, 9 (4): 273–83.

Napier, Susan (2018), *Miyazakiworld: A Life in Art*, New Haven: Yale University Press.

Nashiki, Kaho (1994), *The Witch of the West is Dead* (*nishi no majo ga shinda*), Tōkyō: Shinchōsha.

Nashiki, Kaho ([1995] 2016), *Back Garden* (*uraniwa*), Tōkyō: Rironsha.

Nasuno, Ayako (2020), 'Lewis Carroll's Influence on Lafcadio Hearn's Works' (*hān bungaku ni okeru ruisu kyaroru no eikyō*), *Studies in International Relations*, 40 (2): 37–44.

Natsume, Sōseki (2016), *Natsume Sōseki's 'Study in London' and 'Introduction to Literature': Letters from London to Kyōko and Terada Torahiko and Masaoka Shiki* (*natsume sōseki gendaigoyaku watashi no igirisu ryūgaku to bungaku-ron bungaku-ron joron tsuki rondon kara tsuma kyōko, terada torahiko, masaoka shiki e no tegami*), Kindle.

'Nello and Patrasche' (n.d.), *Welcome to Antwerp*. Available online: https://www .visitantwerpen.be/en/events-exhibitions/winter-in-antwerp-en/nello-patrasche (accessed 15 January 2022).

Nesbit, E. ([1904] 1959), *The Phoenix and the Carpet*. Harmondsworth: Puffin.

Nikolajeva, Maria (1996), *Children's Literature Comes of Age: Toward a New Aesthetic*, New York: Garland.

Niwa, Gorō (1911), *A Long Fairy-Tale: A Child's Dream* (*chōhen otogi banashi: kodomo no yume*), Tōkyō: Momiyama Shoten. Available online: https://dl.ndl.go.jp/info:ndljp /pid/1919744 (accessed 9 November 2021).

'None So Deaf as Those Who Will Not Hear' (2017), *The Ancient Magus' Bride* (*mahōtsukai no yome*), Ep. 9, [TV programme] MBS, 1 December.

Norris, Craig (2013), 'A Japanese Media Pilgrimage to a Tasmanian Bakery', *Transformative Works and Cultures*, 14. Available online: https://doi.org/10.3983/twc .2013.0470 (accessed 18 December 2021).

Norris, Craig (2018), 'Studio Ghibli Media Tourism', in Alisa Freedman and Toby Slade (eds), *Introducing Japanese Popular Culture*, 114–22, Abingdon: Routledge.

North, Marianne (1894), *Recollections of a Happy Life: Being the Autobiography of Marianne North*, New York and London: Macmillan & Co.

Northshields173 (n.d.), 'Robert Westall: Biography'. Available online: https:// northshields173.org/blog/2005/02/21/robert_westall_biography_1/ (accessed 27 July 2020).

Norton, Mary (1956), *The Borrowers* (*yukashita no kobitotachi*), trans. Yōkichi Hayashi, Tōkyō: Iwanami Shoten.

Norton, Mary ([1952] 1958), *The Borrowers*. Harmondsworth: Puffin.

Numabe, Shinichi ([2007] 2014), 'Revealed at Last, the "Secret" of Momoko Ishii's Life' (*tsuini akasa reta ishii momoko, sono shōgai no 'himitsu'*), *Chiba Beach Diary* (*chiba kaihin nikki*). Available online: https://numabe.exblog.jp/19983666/ (accessed 26 November 2021).

Ogawa, Kazuki (2009), 'From the Neverland to the Midnight Garden: The Changing Representation of Boys in Children's Literature', *Language and Cultural Theory* (*gengo to bunka ronshū*), 15: 53–94.

Ogiwara, Noriko (2006), *Another Way to Fly* (*mō hitotsu no sora no tobikata*), Tōkyō: Kadokawa.

Oguma, Keiji (2002). *A Genealogy of 'Japanese' Self-Images*, trans. David Askew, Melbourne: Trans Pacific Press.

Ōhashi, Keiko, ed. (2013) *The United Kingdom: Britain's Genfūkei* (*igirisu: eikoku no genfūkei*), Tōkyō: Rurubu.

Orsini, Lauren (2017), 'An Interview with *The Ancient Magus' Bride* Creator Kore Yamazaki', *Forbes*, 11 September. Available online: www.forbes.com/sites/ laurenorsini/2017/09/11/an-interview-with-the-ancient-magus-bride-creator-kore -yamazaki/ (accessed 18 December 2021).

Ortabasi, Melek (2008), 'Brave Dogs and Little Lords: Some Thoughts on Translation, Gender, and the Debate on Childhood in Mid Meiji', *Review of Japanese Culture and Society*, 20: 178–205.

Ōsaka International Institute for Children's Literature (1993), *Japanese Children's Literature Encyclopaedia* (*nihon jidō bungaku dai jiten*), 3 Vols., Tōkyō: Dainippon Tosho.

Ouida (1872), *A Dog of Flanders, and Other Stories*, London: Chapman & Hall. Available online: http://webapp1.dlib.indiana.edu/vwwp/view?docId=VAB7049 (accessed 1 December 2021).

Ouida (1908), *A Dog of Flanders* (*furandāsu no inu*), trans. Hiyoshi Hidaka, Tōkyō: Naigaishuppan. Available online: https://dl.ndl.go.jp/info:ndljp/pid/875928 (accessed 4 December 2021).

Ouida ([1894] 1987), 'The New Woman', *The North American Review*, Special Heritage Issue: The Woman Question, 1849–1987, 272 (3): 61–5.

Park, Mee Ryoung (2018), 'A Case Study of Russification in Two Translations of *Alice's Adventures in Wonderland* by Vladimir Nabokov and Boris Zakhoder', *Children's Literature in Education*, 49 (June): 140–60.

Pearce, Philippa ([1958] 2008), *Tom's Midnight Garden*, Oxford: Oxford University Press.

Pinsent, Pat (2002), 'The Education of a Wizard', in Lana Whited (ed), *The Ivory Tower and Harry Potter: Perspectives on a Literary Phenomenon*, 27–50, Columbia, MI and London: University of Missouri Press.

'Plan: Hayao Miyazaki & Director Goro Miyazaki's *Āya and the Witch* Will be Broadcast on NHK General TV in the Winter of 2020!!' (*kikaku: miyazaki hayao to kantoku miyazaki gorō āya to majo 2020 nen fuyu sōgōterebi de hōsō yotei*) (2020), *NHK*, 3 June. Available online: http://www6.nhk.or.jp/anime/topics/detail.html (accessed 22 October 2021).

'Poster for Ghibli's new Movie Under Fire . . . From the Big Guru Himself' (2014), *Japan Today*, 23 April. Available online: https://japantoday.com/category/entertainment/ poster-for-ghiblis-new-movie-under-fire-from-the-big-guru-himself (accessed 11 September 2021).

Proceedings of the General Conference of Protestant Missionaries in Japan Held in Tokyo October 24–31, 1900 (1901), Tōkyō: Methodist Publishing House. Available online: https://archive.org/details/proceedingsgene01unkngoog/page/n8/mode/2up (accessed 27 June 2021).

PublicProfiler (2016), 'Named: Predicting Places from Names in the UK', *PublicProfiler*. Available online: named.publicprofiler.org/ (accessed 19 December 2021).

Robinson, Joan G. ([1967] 2014), *When Marnie Was There*, illus. Peggy Fortnum, London: HarperCollins.

Rodman, Tara (2015), 'A More Humane *Mikado*: Re-envisioning the Nation Through Occupation-Era Productions of *The Mikado* in Japan', *Theatre Research International*, 40 (3): 288–302.

Rohe, Gregory (2015), 'Travel Guides, Travelers and Guides: Meiji Period Globetrotters and the Visualization of Japan', *Interpreting and Translation Studies*, 15: 75–90.

Rose, Steve (2018), '"A Full English Every Morning": How UK Food and Weather Inspires Japanese Anime Directors', *Guardian*, 4 May. Available online: https://www .theguardian.com/film/2018/may/04/hiromasa-yonebayashi-interview-studio-ghibli -mary-and-the-witchs-flower (accessed 23 September 2021).

Rubin, Julia (2014), 'Forty Years Young: Hello Kitty and the Power of Cute', 18 November. Available online: https://www.racked.com/2014/11/18/7568323/hello -kitty-sanrio (accessed 4 November 2021).

Saeki (2012), 'Long-awaited Anime Decision for Healing Four-panel Manga, *Kin-iro Mosaic*!!' (*iyashikei yonkoma manga kin iro mozaiku taibō no anime-ka kettei! !*). *Repotama*, 19 December. Available online: repotama.com/2012/12/41863/ (accessed 18 December 2021).

Saitō, Tamaki (2011), *Beautiful Fighting Girl*, trans. J. Keith Vincent and Dawn Lawson, Minneapolis, MN: Minnesota University Press.

Sakuma, Yumiko (2000), *A Journey Through Seven British Fantasies* (igisiru 7tsu no fantajī o meguru tabi), Tōkyō: Media Factory.

Sano, Ryūji (2011), 'Interview', *Kanda Gaigo Alumni Association*. Available online: www.kandagaigo.ac.jp/memorial/interview_bh/01/interview_01_1.html (accessed 18 December 2021).

Sasa, Taiga (2015-present), *Bird in Wonderland (fushigi no kuni no bādo)*, Tōkyō: Kadokawa.

Sasa, Taiga (2021), 'Although I was Born and Brought up in Tōkyō, I had a Sense of Being Rootless' (*umare sodachi wa tōkyō dakedo nenashigusa no kankaku ga atta*), *Bunshun Online*, 28 June. Available online: https://bunshun.jp/articles/-/46181 (accessed 29 July 2021).

Sasada, Hiroko (2015a), 'The Wish-granters in Children's Fiction: Comparison Between the Psammead and Doraemon', *Bulletin of Seisen University*, 63 (December): 53–62.

Sasada, Hiroko (2015b), 'Encounter and Self-Development of the Girl Protagonist in Joan G. Robinson's *When Marnie was There*' (Joan G. Robinson *no* When Marnie Was There *ni okeru deai to shōjo no seichō*), *Bulletin of Seisen University Research Institute for Cultural Science*, 36 (March): 204–14.

Seaton, Philip, Takayoshi Yamamura, Akiko Sugawa-Shimada, and Kyungjae Jang (2017), *Contents Tourism in Japan: Pilgrimages to 'Sacred Sites' of Popular Culture*, Amherst, NY: Cambria Press.

Seeley, Paul (1985), 'The Japanese March in *The Mikado*', *The Musical Times* (August): 454–6.

Sheppard, Deborah (2014), 'Postscript', in Joan G. Robinson (ed), *When Marnie Was There*, 281–5, London: HarperCollins.

Shimizu, Yuri (2019), 'Significance and Methodology of Research on *World Masterpiece Theatre*: Children's Literature Across Borders' (*sekai meisaku gekijō: kenkyū no igi to hōhō — kokkyō o koeru jidō bungaku*), *Glocal Studies*, 6: 181–8.

'*Signor Topsy-Turvy's Wonderful Magic Lantern; or, The World Turned Upside Down*' ([1810] 1898–9), in Andrew W. Tuer (ed), *Forgotten Children's Books*, 217–21, London: The Leadenhall Press.

Sinclair, Catherine ([1839] 1856), *Holiday House*. Edinburgh: William Whyte & Co.

Sladen, Douglas Brooke Wheelton (1895), *A Japanese Marriage*, London and Bombay: George Bell.

Spiker, Christina M. (2018), '"Civilized" Men and "Superstitious" Women: Visualizing the Hokkaido Ainu in Isabella Bird's *Unbeaten Tracks in Japan*, 1880', in Kristen L. Chiem and Lara C. W. Blanchard (eds), *Gender, Continuity, and the Shaping of Modernity in the Arts of East Asia, 16th–20th Centuries*, 287–315, Leiden and Boston: Brill.

St Vincent, Anne (1886), 'A Little Bird Sings from Over the Sea', *St Nicholas*: 948.

Stanbury, John (2011), 'Interview', *Kanda Gaigo Alumni Association*. Available online: www.kandagaigo.ac.jp/memorial/interview_bh/04/interview_04_6.html (accessed 18 December 2021).

'Starting Over' (2017), *Little Witch Academia* (*ritoru uitchi akademia*), Ep. 1, [TV programme] Netflix, 9 January.

Stein, Sadie (2015), 'Nonsense Verse', *The Paris Review*, 5 October. Available online: https://www.theparisreview.org/blog/2015/10/05/nonsense-verse/ (accessed 5 November 2021).

Stewart, Mary ([1971] 1973), *The Little Broomstick*, London: Hodder and Stoughton.

Stoddart, Anna M. (1906), *The Life of Isabella Bird (Mrs. Bishop)*, London: John Murray.

Stogdon, Matthew (2018), '*Mary and the Witch's Flower*', *The Red Right Hand Movie Reviews*, 10 April. Available online: http://reviews.theredrighthand.co.uk/2018/04/10/598mary/ (accessed 23 September 2021).

Stopes, Marie (1910), *A Journal from Japan: A Daily Record of Life as Seen by a Scientist*, London: Blackie & Son.

Strachan, David (2017), Interview with Catherine Butler, 16 October.

Strang, Herbert (1905), *Kobo: A Story of the Russo-Japanese War*, London: Blackie & Son.

Suzuki, Miekichi (1918), *Red Bird Manifesto* (*akai tori hyōbōgo*), 1. Available online: https://www.library.city.hiroshima.jp/akaitori/webdeyomu/pdf/oth02.pdf (accessed 18 November 2021).

Suzuki, Miekichi (1921), 'Strawberry Country', *Red Bird* (*akai tori*) 4. Available online: https://dl.ndl.go.jp/info:ndljp/pid/962796 (accessed 16 November 2021).

Suzuki, Toshio (2021), *Toshio Suzuki's Sweaty Ghibli* (*suzuki toshio no jiburi ase mamire*), [podcast], 29 August. Available online: https://www.tfm.co.jp/asemamire/index.php?itemid=180562&catid=168 (accessed 24 October, 2021).

Swift, Jonathan ([1728] 1801), 'An Account of the Court and Empire of Japan', in Thomas Sheridan (ed), *The Works of Rev. Jonathan Swift*, Vol. 10, 267–79, London: J. Johnson.

Tagore, Rabindranath ([1913] 2012), *The Crescent Moon*, New Delhi: Niyogi Books.

Takano, Hisa (2019–2022). *Professor Amemiya's 3pm Teatime* (*gogo sanji amemiya kyōju no ocha no jikan*), 4 Vols., Tōkyō: Bunch Comics/Shinchōsha.

Takano, Michiyo (2020), 'John Bunyan's *The Pilgrim's Progress* in Japan: Early Translations', *Yamanashi International Research* (*yamanashi kokusai kenkyū*), 15: 37–44. Available online: https://www.yamanashi-ken.ac.jp/media/kgk2020004.pdf (accessed 26 July 2021).

Tamura, Chihiro (2010), 'A Study on the Addition of Lines in the English Dubbed Version of Japanese Animated Films – From an Analysis of Studio Ghibli's Anime Works' (*nihon no animēshon eiga no eigo fukikaeban ni okeru serifu no tsukekuwae ni kansuru kenkyū sutajio jiburi no anime sakuhin no bunseki kara*), *Invitation to Interpretation and Translation Studies* (*tsūyaku honyaku kenkyū e no shōtai*), 4 (May): 87–105.

Tanaka, Mihoko (2009), *Aspects of the Translation and Reception of British Children's Fantasy Literature in Postwar Japan: With Special Emphasis on* The Borrowers *and* Tom's Midnight Garden, Tōkyō: Otowa-Shobō Tsurumi-Shoten.

Tanaka, Mihoko (2016), 'The Japanese Reception of *When Marnie Was There*' (*omoide no mānī nihon ni okeru honyaku juyō*), *Tinker Bell: Studies in Children's Literature in English*, 61 (March): 57–71.

Taniguchi, Hideko (2010), 'The Reception and the Adaptation of Diana Coles' *The Clever Princess* in Japan', *Studies in Languages and Culture*, 25: 131–40.

Team Ghiblink (2005), 'A Second Interview with Cindy and Don Hewitt', *The Hayao Miyazaki Web*, May. Available online: http://www.nausicaa.net/miyazaki/interviews/hewitt_interview2.html (accessed 2 July 2017).

The Borrower Arrietty (*karigurashi no arietti*) (2010), Dir. Hiromasa Yonebayashi, Screenplay by Hayao Miyazaki and Keiko Niwa, [DVD], Japan: Studio Ghibli.

'The English Shore' (*igirisu kaigan*) (2020), *Hanamaki Journey* (*hanamaki no tabi*), Available online: https://www.kanko-hanamaki.ne.jp/spot/article.php (accessed 17 December 2021).

'*The Imaginary* – Winter 2023' (2023), *Studio Ponoc*. Available online: https://www.ponoc.jp/Rudger/en/index.html (accessed 11 April 2023).

The Secret World of Arrietty (2012), Dir. Hiromasa Yonebayashi, Screenplay Hayao Miyazaki and Keiko Niwa, English screenplay Karey Kirkpatrick, [DVD], USA: Disney.

'The Setting of *Āya and the Witch* is a Workshop Where "Fun" and "Dirty" Coexist' (*āya to majo no butai wa tanoshii to kitanai ga kyōzon suru sagyō heya*) (2020), *Animage Plus*, 26 December. Available online: https://animageplus.jp/articles/detail/34779/1/1/1 (accessed 20 October 2021).

Toboso, Yana (2012), *Black Butler* (*kuroshitsuji*), 15, Tōkyō: Square Enix.

Tonge, E. M. (1930), *Fanny Jane Butler: Pioneer Medical Missionary*, London: Church of England Zenana Missionary Society.

'Try and Guess How Much I Like You' (*donnani kimi ga suki da ka atete goran*) (2013), *Kin-iro Mosaic*, Season 1, Ep. 11, [TV programme] AT-X, 14 September.

Ueda, Nobumichi (2002), 'Isō Yamagata's *The Little Lord*: What is the Meaning of the Adaptation *Neikieji*?', *Translation and History* (*honyaku to rekishi*), 13. Available online: https://nob.internet.ne.jp/note/note_24.html (accessed 1 November 2021).

Uemura, Rei (2021), Private correspondence with Catherine Butler, 28 September.

Ueno, Ryō (1978), 'Alice in Īhatov – Kenji Miyazawa' (*īhatovu no arisu – miyazawa kenji*), extract from *The Peter Pan of Our Time* (*warera no jidai no pītā pan*), Tōkyō: Shōbunsha. Available online: http://www.hico.jp/ronnbunn/uenoryou/warera/warerano.htm (accessed 8 May 2022).

Urry, John and Jonas Larsen (2011), *The Tourist Gaze 3.0*, London: Sage.

Vaclavik, Kiera (2019), *Fashioning Alice: The Career of Lewis Carroll's Icon, 1860–1901*, London: Bloomsbury.

Venuti, Lawrence (1995), *The Translator's Invisibility: A History of Translation*, London: Routledge.

Venuti, Lawrence (1998). *The Scandals of Translation: Towards an Ethics of Difference*, London and New York: Routledge.

Voickaert, Didier and An van. Dienderen (2007), *Patrasche – a Dog of Flanders, Made in Japan*, [TV programme] Belgium: Elektrischer Schnellseher. Available online: https://vimeo.com/106272795 (accessed 4 December 2021).

Wakabayashi, Judy (2008), 'Foreign Bones, Japanese Flesh: Translations and the Emergence of Modern Children's Literature in Japan', *Japanese Language and Literature*, 42 (1): 227–55.

Watson, Nicola J. (2006), *The Literary Tourist: Readers and Places in Romantic and Victorian Britain*, Houndmills: Palgrave Macmillan.

Watson, Victor, Mihoko Tanaka, and Catherine Butler, eds (2021), *Lucy M. Boston: An Artist in Everything She Did*, Hemingford Grey, Cambs.: Oldknow Books.

Weatherly, Frederic Edward (1874), *Elsie's Expedition*, London: Frederick Warne.

Westall, Robert ([1982] 1984), *Break of Dark*, London: Penguin.

Westall, Robert (2006), *Blackham's Bomber* (*burakkamu no bukugekiki*), trans. Mizuhito Kanehara, Tōkyō: Iwanami Shoten.

Williams, Wendy S. (2020), '"Free-and-Easy", "Japaneasy": British Perceptions and the 1885 Japanese Village', *Brewminate*. Available online: https://brewminate.com/free -and-easy-japaneasy-british-perceptions-and-the-1885-japanese-village/ (accessed 27 June 2022).

Yamada, Kentarō (2004), 'On Problems of Translation in English Versions of Anime: A Case Study of *Spirited Away*' (*eigoban anime sakuhin ni miru honyaku no mondai: sen to chihiro no kamikakushi no baai*), *Bulletin of the Faculty of Global Information*, Siebold University of Nagasaki, 5 (December): 195–205.

Yamada, Kentarō (2005), 'On Problems of Translation in English Versions of Anime 2: A Case Study of *My Neighbour Totoro*' (*eigoban anime sakuhin ni miru honyaku no mondai 2: tonari no totoro no baai*), *Bulletin of the Faculty of Global Information, Siebold University of Nagasaki*, 6 (December): 273–84.

Yamamura, Takayoshi (2020), 'Travelling *Heidi*: International Contents Tourism Induced by Anime', in Takayoshi Yamamura and Phillip Seaton (eds), *Contents Tourism and Pop Culture Fandom: Transnational Tourist Experiences*, 62–81, Bristol: Channel View Publications.

Yamane, Tomoko (2003), *The Road Pioneered by Kenji Miyazawa's Sister Toshi: Towards 'Night on the Milky Way Train'* (*miyazawa kenji imōto toshi no hiraita michi: ginga tetsudō no yoru e mukatte*), Tōkyō: Asabunsha.

Yamazaki, Kore (2014), *The Ancient Magus' Bride*, Vol. 1, Tōkyō: MAG Garden.

Yamazaki, Kore (2015), *The Ancient Magus' Bride*, Vol. 3, Tōkyō: MAG Garden.

Yamazaki, Kore (2017a), *The Ancient Magus' Bride*, Vol. 7, Tōkyō: MAG Garden.

Yamazaki, Kore (2017b), *The Ancient Magus' Bride*, Vol. 8, Tōkyō: MAG Garden.

Yamazaki, Kore (2022), Interview with Catherine Butler, 29 June.

'Yellow Car Owners Join Rally in Support of "Ugly" Car' (2017), *BBC News*, 1 April. Available online: www.bbc.co.uk/news/uk-england-gloucestershire-39456449 (accessed 18 December 2021).

Yokoyama, Toshio (1987). *Japan in the Victorian Mind: A Study of Stereotyped Images of a Nation 1850–80*. Houndmills: Macmillan.

Yoshida, Shinichi, Shō Hara, Okiko Miyake, and Seigō Tanimoto, eds (2001), *Anglo-American Children's Literature Guide: Works and Theory* (*eibei jidō bungaku gaido — sakuhin to riron*), Tōkyō: Kenkyūsha.

Yoshino, Genzaburō ([1950] 2021), 'On the Occasion of Publication' (*hakkan ni sai shite*), in Akiko Wakana (ed.), *The History of Iwanami Shōnen Bunko: 1950-2020* (*iwanami shōnen bunko no ayumi*), 100, Tōkyō: Iwanami Shōnen Bunko.

Yoshizaki, Masaki (2021), *An Illustrated History of Japan and Britain, 1600–1868* (*zusetu nichieikankeishi*), Yokohama Archives of History Museum, Tōkyō: Harashobyō.

Yufuin Floral Village (n.d.). Available online: floral-village.com (accessed 17 December 2021).

Ziomek, Kirsten L. (2014), 'The 1903 Human Pavilion: Colonial Realities and Subaltern Subjectivities in Twentieth Century Japan', *The Journal of Asian Studies*, 73 (2): 493–516.

Index